P9-DEA-405

*f*P

ALSO BY STANLEY COREN

The Intelligence of Dogs

Sleep Thieves

The Left-Hander Syndrome

What Do Dogs Know? (with Janet Walker)

THE FREE PRESS

New York   London   Toronto   Sydney   Singapore

Why We Love the Dogs We Do

How to Find the Dog
That Matches Your Personality

Stanley Coren

THE FREE PRESS
A Division of Simon & Schuster Inc.
1230 Avenue of the Americas
New York, NY 10020

Copyright © 1998 by Stanley Coren
All rights reserved,
including the right of reproduction
in whole or in part in any form.

THE FREE PRESS and colophon are trademarks
of Simon & Schuster Inc.

Designed by Carla Bolte

Manufactured in the United States of America

10 9 8 7 6 5 4 3 2 1

Library of Congress Cataloging-in-Publication Data
Coren, Stanley.
    Why we love the dogs we do: finding the dog that matches your personality/Stanley Coren.
      p.   cm.
    Includes bibliographical references (p.   ) and index.
    ISBN 0–684–83901–6 (hc)
    1. Dogs. 2. Dogs—Selection. 3. Dog breeds. 4. Dog owners—Psychology.
    5. Human-animal relationships. I. Title.
    SF426.C685   1998
    636.7'081—dc21   97-50333
                                                                  CIP

For the material discussed in the section "Eugene and Blemie," the author has relied on *The Unknown O'Neill*, ed. Travis Bogard. Copyright © 1988 by Yale University.

Credits for use of illustrations are as follows:

Photographs of George Bush, Jean Harlow, Humphrey Bogart, Winston Churchill, John Steinbeck, Eugene O'Neill, Franklin Delano Roosevelt, John F. Kennedy, Richard M. Nixon, Queen Victoria, Queen Elizabeth II, Harry S Truman, Lyndon B. Johnson, and E. B. White, by permission of Corbis, 902 Broadway, New York, NY 10010. Photograph of Sigmund Freud, by permission of Mary Evans Picture Library, 59 Tranquil Vale, Blackheath, London SE3. Photograph of Dwight D. Eisenhower, courtesy of the Dwight D. Eisenhower Library. Photograph of Elizabeth Taylor with Richard Burton, by permission of Archive Photos, 530 West 25 St., New York, NY 10001. Photograph of Elvis Presley, by permission of Photofest, 22 West 23 St., New York, NY 10010.

This book is dedicated to my children

REBECCA *and* BENJAMIN

Contents

Preface

Approximately one out of every four families in North America owns a dog. When a dog and its human fit each other well, the resulting bond can make both lives richer and more satisfying. The love for a well-chosen dog can transcend life itself. For instance, the composer Richard Wagner, best known for his operas which make up the Ring Cycle, loved his Newfoundland dog Russ so much that he was buried beside him. In a similar vein, according to Harper's Index, an estimated one million dogs in the United States have been named as beneficiaries in their masters' wills. Now contrast this happy picture of satisfied dog owners with the fact that nearly half of all puppies purchased as pets do not successfully make it through the first year with the people who adopt them. These dogs are returned to their breeders, left at shelters, killed by their owners or by a veterinarian at their owner's request, or simply abandoned.

Why is it that some people form lasting and warm relationships with their dogs, while others get no joy at all from their pets? The answer lies in matching the person to the dog. The best matches happen when the personality of the person fits the behavioral characteristics of the dog. In this book we will explore why we love the dogs that we do, and also why some breeds of dogs turn out to be disasters for particular people. This book will show you how to select the breed of dog that best fits your personality, using a selection procedure based on the largest survey of human-canine relationships ever taken. This survey looked at the personalities of over six thousand people and determined the dogs that these people loved and hated. But there is a lot more than this to talk about. Along the way we will meet some interesting and famous dogs and people, and also encounter some fascinating stories about the human-canine bond.

As always I would like to thank my loving wife, Joan, for her invaluable assistance in the early drafts of this book.

Chapter One

Loving and Hating Dogs

I t was a hot day. The light wind off the Mediterranean Sea did little
to cool the men, who were on their hands and knees. They were
gently uncovering something buried in the sandy soil using small
trowels and brushes. They were archaeologists, and the site that they
were excavating was known as Ein Mallaha. It is located on the coast of
what is now Israel and is one of the remains of many small villages that
were built near the shore. The archaeologists call them Natufian com-
munities; they date back to around ten thousand years ago. This Old
Stone Age settlement was moderately sophisticated. There were about
fifty round huts, some with stone foundations. There were some agricultural tools, such as flint sickles and grindstones for wheat. There was
also evidence that animals, such as sheep, had been domesticated.

The location where the archaeologists worked was an ancient cemetery. The Natufians buried their dead with treasured personal ornaments and special tokens of the deceased. Thus these graves provide
valuable information about the people and the culture of this time.
This archaeological team had already uncovered some carved bone and
stone artwork and were hoping for more.

The body they were uncovering was that of an elderly man. He was
in a curled position, with knees up near his chin—the traditional burial

posture of the time. As they uncovered the upper part of the body they found that the man's head was resting on his left hand. Working to clear the area around the hand, they found that it had been gently placed on the chest of a four- or five-month-old puppy. A surprised scientist stood up and brushed one eye with the back of a sand-covered hand. "He must have really loved dogs," he said, "to have chosen to take one along on his journey to eternity."

A HISTORY OF COMPANIONSHIP

Even from the dawn of civilization, some five hundred generations ago, we have evidence of the powerful bond between some people and their dogs. If we had some kind of video camera that could go back in time, we could see for ourselves, for instance, that Rameses the Great had four dogs that he particularly loved. According to information carved into his tomb, one was a great hound named Pahates but called Kami by his master. This dog was so special that it was allowed to sleep with the Pharaoh. If our time-traveling camera does a fast-forward, we can find other historical and powerful figures sharing their beds with their dogs. Alexander the Great, resting from his battles, was known to sleep beside his great Mastiff, Peritas. Mary Queen of Scots spent her long hours of prison confinement with her small spaniels, and they comforted her through the night. In 1587, when she was beheaded, it was found that she had hidden one of the toy dogs under her voluminous robes. Afterwards, according to one eyewitness, it "would not depart from the dead corpse" and had to be carried away. It is reported that the person who ordered her execution, Elizabeth I, spent her own last night in life "counsolled only by her dogge"—a very similar toy spaniel. One of Elizabeth's direct successors eventually gave his name to that breed of spaniel. Charles II of England also slept with his Cavalier King Charles Spaniels and even had a ceiling mural in one of his bedrooms decorated with them.

Fast-forward again to the time of Czar Peter the Great of Russia. He slept with his Italian Greyhound, Lissette, and in one instance this relationship may have saved a life. A member of the court had been falsely accused of corruption. Peter's wife, Catherine, was apprised of the circumstances and attempted to intervene on the accused man's behalf. Czar Peter, not known for his calm demeanor, flew into a violent rage and forbade her ever to mention the case again in his presence. Distraught at the mounting evidence of the man's innocence, Catherine wrote a message to Peter, petitioning for clemency. She then signed it with Lissette's name, affixed her paw print, and tied the note to Lissette's silver collar. Later that evening when Peter was preparing for sleep he found the message. He sat on the edge of his bed gently petting Lissette's head and then, without further comment, called for his secretary and had a pardon drafted that night.

At about the same time that the Russian leader Peter was resting beside his Italian Greyhound, the Prussian leader Frederick the Great was also sharing his bed with a similar dog. Like the old man at Ein Mallaha, he loved his dogs so much that he wished to be buried near them. He had a special mausoleum constructed on the palace lawn, where it overlooked the graves of eleven of his dogs. Although political unrest nearly prevented his wishes from coming true, Frederick now rests inside that royal crypt next to the body of his last dog.

Stories such as these, which show how deeply individuals bond to their dogs, could be told of literally millions of people, ordinary and exalted alike. There are stories of kings and also of presidents: Lyndon Johnson, who filled the White House lawn with his pack of Beagles; Ulysses S. Grant, who appointed his Newfoundland dog to the post of White House steward; or George Bush, who told me that during his presidency he would often be joined in his morning shower by his Springer Spaniel, Millie (see plate 1). There are actors and entertainers who dote on their dogs, such as comedian Joan Rivers. Her Yorkshire Terrier, Spike, has been called "the world's laziest dog" because he doesn't have to walk anywhere on his own power. Rivers has hired a man to tote him around in a Louis Vuitton carrying case. She also gave Spike a catered Bark Mitzvah party with kosher food and decked him out in a yarmulke with his name embroidered on it. Then there are the serious scientists and their cherished dogs, such as Sigmund Freud, whose Chow Chow, Jo-Fi, attended many of his therapy sessions (plate 2). Freud said that the dog helped to calm and reassure his patients, especially young children. Later he claimed that he depended on Jo-Fi's judgment to tell him about his patients' mental states. The dog would lie down at various distances from the person being treated, depending on the degree of stress that the patient was under.

Add to these the hundreds of millions of ordinary people who dearly love their own family dogs. There's Aunt Martha, whose Christmas card includes a picture of the kids and their Golden Retriever, Honey, all sitting around Uncle Max, who is dressed like Santa Claus. There's also the videotape you received in the mail, presenting Cousin Fred playing the clarinet while his Border Collie, Babe, plaintively wails the vocal parts. All of this is clear evidence for how much we love, care for, and think about our dogs.

DOGS TO LOVE OR NOT

Stories like these make dogs sound like the silver lining on the storm clouds of life. After hearing such tales, it is hard to suppress the desire to go right out and get a dog to share its life with us. Unfortunately, human relationships with dogs are not always so sunny and warm. Some people have temperaments that permit little love for any dog. Other people seem to get along with some kinds of dogs and have strong negative feelings for others. The secret lies in matching the personality of the person to the behavioral characteristics of the dog. An incompatible pairing of a dog and a person can be a disaster.

Just a few paragraphs back, I described some famous kings and generals who were so fond of their dogs that they slept with them. Sleeping with a dog is actually quite common for people who are happy with their pet. One recent survey of Americans found that about half of all dog owners allow their dogs to sleep on the bed with them. The people most inclined to sleep with their dogs are single females between the ages of eighteen and thirty-four. Nearly three out of five women in this group allow their dog on the bed. Those most likely to boot the dog out of bed are married men over forty-five years of age. However, even in this group, just shy of 40 percent still sleep with their dogs.

Affection for canines can be problematic, though. In that same survey the researchers found that 13 percent of the couples that they studied included one partner who so objected to the dog being on the bed that the dispute strained the relationship with their human partner. Consider General George Armstrong Custer, the one who was wiped out at the Battle of Little Big Horn. Custer had frequent heated disputes with his wife, Libbie, over the presence of dogs on their bed. Eventually she threatened to sleep elsewhere if her husband insisted on sharing the bed with his dogs. The Custers finally compromised: when Custer was at home the dogs could sleep in their bedroom but not on their bed. In the field, however, Custer shared his mattress with his Greyhounds, Blucher and Byron, and his white Bulldog, Turk.

For some people, love or hate for dogs is quite breed-specific. Charles Darwin, whose Theory of Evolution is the cornerstone of biological thinking today, truly loved some dogs. His favorites were terriers. He often wrote about his West Highland White Terrier's adventures around his house and speculated on the dog's thinking processes. On the other hand, Darwin had no patience or love for large hounds. He was once given a Talbot Hound, one of the immediate predecessors of our present day Bloodhounds. He described it as "graceless, noisy and drooling," "witless and lacking in self-control," and "with no visible merit of consequence to civilized society." In the end, the terrier-loving Darwin had the hound taken from the house and shot.

Another case of dogs that fit and don't fit into a person's lifestyle comes from former president Ronald Reagan. Reagan has had many dogs during his life. Before his political career started he had a pair of Scottish Terriers. Later, as governor of California and then president of the United States, he received many dogs as gifts. There was a Golden Retriever named Victory, an Irish Setter named Peggy, a Siberian Husky named Taca, a Cavalier King Charles Spaniel named Rex, and a Belgian Sheepdog named Fuzzy. Of these Reagan's favorites were a pair of Scottish Terriers and the Cavalier King Charles Spaniel. However, there was also Lucky, a Bouvier des Flandres who was given to him during his early years at the White House. Poor Lucky just never fit in with Reagan's personality. Bouviers are large dogs that have been specialized to herd cattle. Although quite friendly, they can be dominant and demanding. Reagan had no patience for this rambunctious dog who continually attempted to herd him across the lawn by snapping at his heels and bumping at his side. On one occasion, Lucky even drew blood with a nip on the presidential hindquarters, a trick Bouviers use to make cattle move along at a swifter pace. Although she clearly exasperated Reagan, Lucky certainly was luckier than Darwin's hound. Instead of getting shot behind the barn, she was ultimately "retired" to Reagan's ranch in Santa Barbara, California, thus effectively removing her annoying presence from his daily life.

I was quite surprised to learn how many dog and human pairings do not work. A series of surveys in North America and Britain suggest that four out of every ten puppies do not last even one year with the people who adopt them. These dogs are returned to their breeders or placed in shelters, killed by their owners or taken to veterinarians for euthanasia, or simply abandoned. An additional 8 to 10 percent suffer the same fate in their second year. Even in apparently happy homes, some 9 percent of dog owners admit that at one time or another they have deliberately tried to lose their dogs. Most commonly, this kind of behavior is found among married women in the twenty-five to thirty-four-year-old range. Fortunately only about 2 percent of these dogs remain missing, since guilt usually drives people back to the scene of the abandonment to try to find their missing pet. The conclusion to be drawn from this is that there are many human–dog combinations that simply don't work.

You have probably been in homes where dogs are loved and in others where their lives are not so happy. It is easy to spot the behaviors that indicate whether the relationship between a person and a dog is working or failing. Let's look at the homes of two hypothetical dogs that we will call Lassie and Laddie.

Lassie has just wandered into the kitchen to investigate some food smells, and her owner pauses in her task of making dinner to speak to the dog. "Are you hungry, Lassie, or just hopeful? I'll bet you plan to just hang out around here in case I get sloppy and drop something. Is that your plan, girl? Well, stay close, Fur Face, and you might get lucky."

In that simple exchange we find all the elements of a relationship that is working. The dog's presence is noticed and responded to and, perhaps, she is spontaneously touched in a friendly manner. The dog has a name, and even a nickname. Nicknames, even if they are given spontaneously and forgotten a moment later (like "Fur Face" in this case), are important signs of affection. Research has shown that we may have dozens of such names that we use for a loved spouse or child. My daughter, Rebecca, had to put up with names like "Princess" or "Pumpkin," while my son, Benn, found himself called "Trooper" or "Young Hero" among the many names that came and went. Psychologists say that such alternate names are signs of affection—part of a sort of secret code between you and someone you care about.

Let's look at the less cordial situation in Laddie's house. It is the same scenario, with Laddie wandering into the kitchen because the smell of cooking food has wafted through the house. Laddie's owner ignores his entry as she moves around the room. The dog is standing in the middle of the floor, and eventually the owner brushes against him accidentally. She turns and looks at him. "Why are you always underfoot? Just go away and don't be a pest. Don't expect any extra food from me—you're too fat already. Scat!" She waves her hand in a dismissive gesture.

Her husband enters the room as this scene is unfolding, and the woman turns to him. "The dog is always in my way and I'm tripping over it. I don't understand why it can't learn to keep out of my way. Why don't you put it outside for a while so I can get something done?"

This little scene tells us volumes about the relationship between the person and the dog. To begin with, the dog's arrival is not seen as desirable, or as a chance to show a momentary flicker of affection. His presence is simply an interruption, which is responded to with annoyance. Notice that Laddie is an "it," without gender or identity. Laddie is not a family member, he is "the dog." In family conversations he has no name, neither a formal given name nor any pleasant nickname. Psychologists refer to this as *depersonalization*. It is the kind of behavior we engage in when we don't want to acknowledge someone as an individual, with his own identity and personal feelings. Thus an executioner might say, "Bring out the prisoner. It is time to carry out the sentence." He would not say, "Go get Freddie. It's time to kill him." The word "prisoner" is a label; it has no particular individuality, since there are many prisoners. "The dog" is a similar depersonalized label. Names, whether Freddie or Laddie, refer to individuals, each with an identity of their own and a right to consciousness, life, and maybe happiness. Notice that the labels "prisoner" or "dog" allow you to think of the individual as an "it." If something is nameless we do not consider its unique characteristics, such as its sex. The moment a personal name is used we must accompany it with personalized pronouns. Thus Freddie becomes a "him" while Lassie would be a "her."

Many people do not recognize the depersonalized nature of this kind of interaction where a dog is concerned. However, what would you think about a parent who turned to his or her spouse and said, "Go get the child. It's time to change its diaper and feed it"? With references like "the child" and "it" and never a mention of the baby's name, one might immediately suspect that we were dealing with a loveless relationship, and begin to wonder about the safety and well-being of the child.

THE CASE OF HARRISON'S HOUND

Even when a dog is loved by its master there is no guarantee that it will be loved by everyone in the household. Sometimes a person's fondness for a particular dog can blind them to the distaste that other family members may have for the animal. This can often lead to embarrassing or uncomfortable situations, and can certainly increase the stress on a relationship. Take the case of Rex Harrison, the British stage and screen actor.[1] Harrison is best known for his part as Professor Henry Higgins in the musical *My Fair Lady,* which won him both a Tony and an Oscar. He also appeared in many films such as *Major Barbara* and *Doctor Dolittle.* Harrison already had a Basset Hound named Homer when he married Elizabeth Rees Harris. Her son Damian remembered meeting Homer for the first time, and described him as "the most spoilt dog." At that time Homer had been around for years. Damian claimed that Homer "was the only person who had managed to stick it out with Rex—and Rex loved him." In Harrison's eyes, Homer could do no wrong. Each day, a brush would be brought in and the dog would lie at his feet while the actor would brush his ears. "Homer was like him— they knew they had soul mates in each other."

The problem was that, although Harrison loved Homer, his new wife, Elizabeth, emphatically did not. They simply did not get along, and Harrison appeared to be oblivious to the developing stress. Elizabeth later complained vehemently about the dog. "Homer was ghastly. He hated women. He would stand in front of the door just as you were ready to go out and trip you up." Each morning she and Harrison would have breakfast in bed with his tray on one side and hers on the other. "Homer would come right the way round and slobber all over my breakfast, leaving the spittle all over it, and then he would wag his tail to Rex, who would pat him and say what a good dog he was—and my breakfast was ruined every damn time."

Elizabeth seemed to feel that the dog was actually using his drooling as a weapon against her. "Homer loathed me. If we were going out, he would stand and wait until I was dressed and then do his slobbering bit; so I would have to run or jump or hide behind the curtain from him."

Elizabeth seemed to attribute all of the annoying behaviors that Homer displayed to premeditation and willful scheming, even when, to a casual observer, they seemed to be what you might expect from an old lazy dog. For instance, since Homer slept in the basement he would have to go down the steps to sleep in his quarters. Elizabeth claimed that when Harrison was away on tour or on location, Homer would refuse to go downstairs unless she took him in the elevator. "He would just sit there, and he weighed a ton so I couldn't move him. So I would have to get the lift and then he would go." Her interpretation was that he was doing this just to make her angry.

In the end, Elizabeth felt that Homer might have played a significant role in the disintegration of her relationship with Harrison, and may have contributed to their divorce. She often complained about how sexist Homer was and how he was trying to make her life miserable. When she did, Harrison would just smile and tell her that she was exaggerating. "Then he would lean down and pat Homer—like he was trying to reassure the damn dog rather than listening to me. It infuriated me." In the end, she reflected about how the atmosphere between them began to change and things began to go downhill. She would later recall this time, saying, "I couldn't help thinking about how he seemed to care more for that wretched dog than for me."

THE SENATOR AND THE POET

One out of every four households in North America contains a dog, and in some countries, such as England, Germany, and France, the numbers rise to one out of every two or three households. Despite these numbers, scientific investigation of the factors that go into our choice of dogs, and what constitutes a good match between a person and a dog, is virtually nonexistent. The reason is probably that research on topics like love or affection, even between humans, let alone between humans and dogs, is considered frivolous by many social scientists who want to appear to be concerned with more "serious" matters. It is considered reasonable to study conditions that lead to stress or aggression in a family, or even the underlying causes of divorce, but somehow it is not "scientific" to study factors that lead to comfort or love. For instance, a senator from Wisconsin, William Proxmire, once became almost apoplectic when he heard that the U.S. National Science Foundation had awarded an $84,000 grant to a psychologist to study love. He raged:

I object to this, not only because no one—not even the National Science Foundation—can argue that falling in love is a science; not only because I'm sure that even if they spend $84 million or $84 billion they wouldn't get an answer that anyone would believe. I'm also against it because I don't want the answer. . . . So, National Science Foundation—get out of the love racket. Leave that to Elizabeth Barrett Browning and Irving Berlin.[2]

If so much anger is aroused by an attempt to study the attraction between men and women, imagine what Senator Proxmire might have said if the research project had to do with how and why we develop affection for particular types of dogs. Or why we love certain dog breeds and do not get along with others. As a psychologist, however, I know that these questions can be answered scientifically, and that the answers are important to people. If you select a breed of dog that you can develop a warm companionship with, the quality of your life can improve greatly. Selecting the wrong breed of dog can increase the stress and misery in your life significantly, and often ends in the death or abandonment of the dog. For this reason, although I love the poems of Elizabeth Barrett Browning and the songs of Irving Berlin, I think that we should rely on science to answer the question of why we love certain breeds of dogs and why we are neutral to downright negative about some other breeds.

Although Elizabeth Barrett Browning may not have contributed directly to a scientific understanding of compatibility between certain breeds of dogs and particular people, she is, herself, an interesting case study of how deep affection can form between a person and a dog.[3] Elizabeth Barrett Browning is best known as a romantic poet. Among her most famous works is the collection *Sonnets from the Portuguese,* which she dedicated to her husband, the poet Robert Browning. These poems contain some of the best-known love lyrics ever written in English, with familiar lines like "How do I love thee? Let me count the ways." From adolescence on, Elizabeth's health was poor, probably because of a spinal injury which was originally thought to be incurable and kept her confined to her bed for much of the time. This confinement, however, gave her the opportunity to write, and she became well known in literary circles for several volumes of poems. Some of her poems, like "The Cry of the Children" and "Lady Geraldine's Courtship," were so well received that she was mentioned as a possible successor to William Wordsworth as poet laureate of England.

Robert Browning read some of Elizabeth's poems and began to write to her to praise her poetry. He himself was already on the way to becoming one of the best known of the Victorian poets, particularly for his dramatic monologues. A short time later the two poets met and fell in love. Their courtship was bitterly opposed by Elizabeth's father, who was a dominant and possessive man. The whole episode had the flavor of high melodrama, with the requisite tense climax and happy ending, as the two lovers eloped and then fled from England to live happily ever after in Italy. This romantic tale was eventually immortalized in a popular play, *The Barretts of Wimpole Street,* by Rudolf Besier.

As a young woman, Elizabeth was often depressed by her illness and confinement, and her friend Mary Russell Mitford thought that it might be diverting for her to have a dog. Elizabeth had a fondness for animals in general, although her tastes in dogs were quite specific. Her brothers owned dogs, which she did not like. According to Elizabeth, one of her brothers' dogs was "an odious bloodhound." Then there was a Mastiff who was "a cannibal who glories in battle and the taste of raw meat." Finally, her youngest brother had a terrier that she judged "the ugliest dog of all Christendom." She had, however, developed a fondness for Mary Mitford's Cocker Spaniel, Flush. Eventually Flush sired a litter, and Mitford gave Elizabeth one of his offspring, a little golden-colored male that she had named after his father, Flush.

The puppy had an instantaneous effect on Elizabeth's spirits. "Flush amuses me sometimes when I am inclined to be amused by nothing else," she told her brother George. Flush was soon spending most of the day and night in bed with Elizabeth, where "his ears were often the first thing to catch my tears."

Every one of Flush's whims was indulged. For a while he would not touch unbuttered bread, then he would eat only muffins, then his taste shifted to sweet sponge cakes and macaroons. As for meat, he would not eat mutton, but only beef or fowl, and then only if cut into tiny bits and fed to him. "If you were but to see him eat partridge from a silver fork," she wrote to Mitford. When Elizabeth drank a glass of milk, she would save half of it for Flush. She recognized that she was being overindulgent ("Voices to the north and south cry 'Flush is spoilt!'" she wrote), but as the dog's preferences changed with the seasons she continued to coddle him. "Of course, he has given up his ice creams for the season, and his favorite substitute seems to be coffee—coffee, understand, not poured into the saucer, but taken out of my little coffee cup . . . He sees that I drink out of the cup and not out of the saucer; and in spite of his nose, he will do the same. My dear pretty little Flushie!"

In Victorian England there were several rings of dognappers, who would abduct dogs of middle- or upper-class families and hold them for ransom. This trade was lucrative and relatively low in risk since English law was rather ambiguous about whether dogs were to be considered property. Flush was kidnapped no less than three times, each time being ransomed back for a higher sum. The third time the ransom demanded was more than Elizabeth's father was willing to pay, and far more than Elizabeth could get from her own resources. She was beside herself with anxiety and grief, not eating and barely sleeping, moaning to those around her, "Flush doesn't know that we can recover him, and he is in the extremest despair all this while, poor darling Flush, with his fretful fears, and petty whims, and his fancy of being near me. All this night he will howl and lament, I know perfectly—for I fear we shall not ransom him tonight."

Eventually the strain built to a climax, and Elizabeth decided that she would go to the thieves and negotiate Flush's release. Her father did not know of her plans, but her brothers were aghast, warning that she would be robbed and murdered. Nonetheless, one evening, five days after Flush had been stolen, Elizabeth got into a cab with her frightened but loyal maid, and they drove through what she later described as "obscure streets" to the rough neighborhood of Shoreditch. This was where the gang of *dog banditti* known as "The Fancy" had their headquarters, and she knew from the previous kidnappings that their leader was a man named Taylor. The cab driver stopped at a pub and asked the way, and when they arrived at the address he had been given, several men came out and invited Elizabeth to come in and wait for Taylor, who was not at home. Her maid was terrified and begged her mistress to do no such thing. She agreed, and sat in the cab. Fortunately, when the cab driver had gone to the pub seeking Taylor's whereabouts, he had explained why Elizabeth was there. Several people in the pub felt some pity for her and had tagged along behind the cab. Now as she and her maid sat there they were surrounded by what Elizabeth later described as a "gang of benevolent men and boys who 'lived but to oblige us.'"

After some time had passed, Mrs. Taylor—"an immense feminine bandit"—appeared and promised to inform her "dear husband," when he returned, that a lady had called and was waiting for her dog. Elizabeth told Mrs. Taylor the amount that she could afford as "a reward" for Flush's return, and she was assured that such a generous contribution would be acceptable. Elizabeth returned home to await Taylor's appearance to arrange the final exchange. In the end, Flush was returned and the ransom paid was the more affordable price that Elizabeth had negotiated during her adventure.

When not worrying about his safety, Elizabeth was concerned about Flush's education. She became quite convinced that the spaniel had almost human intelligence. "My Flush clearly understands articulate language, acting in a correct and knowledgeable manner when I say 'dinner,' 'cakes,' 'milk,' 'go downstairs,' 'go out,' or even when Crow [her housekeeper] tells him 'Go and kiss Miss Barrett.'" Since Flush had mastered language to such an extent, Elizabeth decided to teach him to read. When she announced this to her brothers they were beside themselves and laughed so hard that tears came to their eyes. They watched with amazement while she held up a card with the letter *A* printed on it and another with the letter *B* on it. Holding the cards on either side she instructed the dog "Kiss *A,* Flush—and now Kiss *B,*" waiting till the dog pressed its nose against the appropriate card. When he did he was rewarded with a bit of cake. Unfortunately, Flush's reading lessons did not go as well as the poet had hoped, and she later dismissed his failings with an apologetic "I am afraid that he has no very pronounced love for literature."

Her next attempts were to teach him numbers and arithmetic, with the aim of making Flush competent enough to play dominoes with her. "I have read of a gentleman and his dog doing so, and I felt jealous . . . I can't help it." The lessons were amusing to watch. Elizabeth would hold a piece of cake and slowly count to three. Flush's task was to take it on three and not sooner. The spaniel's inadequacy in mathematics was taken not as an intellectual limitation but rather as a matter of preference. "His soul has the sensitivities of an artist, hence he finds the mechanics of arithmetic both tedious and inconvenient."

When Elizabeth and Robert eloped and fled the family home, she brought with her only two bags of luggage and, of course, Flush. The newlyweds traveled to Italy to start their new life, and soon Robert was expected to be as solicitous toward Flush as his mistress was. He did take good care of Flush, for his wife's sake, but often complained that the dog was vociferous, arrogant, overbearing, and tyrannical with him. He also declared that Flush seemed to consider him "to be created for the special purpose of doing him service."

Elizabeth never lost her love for Flush. She also never lost her belief that he was intelligent enough to learn language if he so desired. From her new home in Italy she wrote to Mitford that Flush highly approved of his new home and of the various canine playmates in his new neighborhood. She informed her friend that Flush was now "going out every day and speaking Italian to the little dogs."

Although Elizabeth Barrett Browning may not have done research on the issue of human and dog compatibility, she is a perfect example of the reason that we ask the question "Why do we love certain dogs and dislike others?" Why did she have such disdain for her brothers'

Bloodhound, Mastiff, and terrier, and yet have such a deep affection for her spaniel, Flush? Despite Senator Proxmire's loud complaints, some of us are quite interested in the answer to a question like this—and science can provide us with an answer. In this book we will explore why we love the dogs that we do, and also why certain breeds of dogs turn out to be catastrophes for particular people. In the following pages I will try to show how you can select the breed of dog that best fits you, based on your personality. To do this we will use some scientific data from a study of over six thousand people and the dogs that improved or diminished the quality of their lives.

Chapter Two

Can You Love Dogs and Still Love People?

I t was midday, and I had just finished a quick lunch in order to take my Flat-Coated Retriever, Odin, out for a romp. On days when he accompanies me to my university office I try to arrange at least one brief exercise period outside on one of the grassy open areas nearby. This day I had brought along a plastic Frisbee for him to chase.

It has been claimed that the first Frisbees originally were just empty pie tins from the Frisbee Pie Company in Vermont. Supposedly some students from nearby Middlebury College started tossing them around and then later developed the toy. It was intended to be a toy for people, but everybody knows that these plastic disks are the ultimate dog exercising device. In fact, in 1989, in honor of the fiftieth anniversary of the "invention" of the Frisbee, Middlebury College unveiled a bronze statue of a dog jumping to catch one. I like them because they don't make noise, are easy to control, stay in the air a long time, and attract a dog's attention. Best of all, my dogs get a lot of exercise while I can just stand there and occasionally flick my wrist to launch one into the air.

As Odin dashed around after his toy, a woman stopped to watch. Without bothering to introduce herself, she commented, "I don't understand why people like you are willing to lavish so much love and affection on your dogs. You know that there are needy and abused children who could use some of that concern and attention."

Somewhat startled, I blurted, "You don't have a dog, do you?"

"Of course not! I don't have any desire to waste my time on any useless pets. I have important and meaningful things to do," she said. Then, with a dismissive snort, she turned her back on me and began striding away. Her dramatic exit was a bit marred by Odin, who danced around her with his orange Frisbee in his mouth and his tail in full vibration. Clearly he had hopes that he had found a new playmate. She waved him off with a "Get away from me, you stupid animal," and stormed away. Odin momentarily dropped his Frisbee and stared after her with his tail at half-mast.

In some respects this woman's comment reflects one of a pair of beliefs held by a significant number of people in the world. The first of these beliefs is that loving a dog somehow is evidence that we have little warmth left over for people. The second is that we really love dogs only when we have no other person to love and be loved by. Is it the case that we love our dogs because we cannot, or do not want to, have affectionate relationships with our fellow humans?

The data say that this is not true. There are a number of research reports which show that loving a dog is not at all in conflict with loving people. According to several very large-scale studies conducted by Dr. Reinhold Bergler, director of the Institute for Psychology in Bonn, Germany,[1] and Dr. Nienke Endenburg at the University of Utrecht in the Netherlands,[2] the evidence is that individuals who form emotional bonds with dogs and other animals also tend to be very sociable and caring in their everyday lives. This suggests that dog owners are exactly the people who are most likely to assist the needy and abused in society.

In some respects we knew this already. Most people are familiar with the story of Saint Bernard of Montjoux, an eleventh-century monk of the Augustinian rule. He was a man who saw little difference between caring for animals and caring for people. Bernard founded a monastery more than eight thousand feet up in the Swiss Alps, located on one of the principal roads that connected Switzerland to Italy. This road was used by merchants, by Swiss laborers seeking winter employment in Italy or returning home for the summer, and by people of the northern countries who were making the pilgrimage to Rome. This isolated hospice provided winter travelers with a refuge from wind, cold, blizzards, and avalanches. Saint Bernard and his fellow monks were dedicated to helping those who were lost, injured, or icebound. The dogs named for Saint Bernard assisted the monks in their searches for travelers who had strayed off the main road. The monks seldom left the hospice without dogs, because the mountain fogs can come on suddenly, making it impossible to see even one foot ahead. Without the dogs the monks would never find their way back to the hospice.

Together the monks and dogs have saved thousands of travelers. The greatest of the dogs, Barry, saved forty-four people, and set the pattern of work for most Saint Bernard rescue dogs. The dogs go out in teams of three, and when a lost traveler is found, two of the dogs lie down beside him to keep him warm, while the third returns to the monastery to get help. The dogs themselves decide which ones stay and which go on each rescue.

It is difficult to dispute the fact that Saint Bernard loved people, having dedicated his life to their rescue. Yet Saint Bernard's affection for dogs ran very deep. Tradition ascribes to him the words *Qui me amat, amat et canem meum,* which translates into the familiar expression "Love me, love my dog." I wonder what my critic would have said about that.

However, to better test the case, let's look at a couple of individuals who have demonstrated a great amount of love and caring for dogs and other animals. In these two cases affection and protective feelings for animals actually shaped their lives. If, somehow, loving animals is associated with not loving people, then these individuals should prove to be quite antisocial and uncaring when it comes to humans. Having expended all of their warmth on beasts, such people should have no love left for humans.

HUMANITY MARTIN

In the United Kingdom, the start of the animal welfare movement is usually credited to Richard Martin.[3] Martin was a big, laughing Irishman, with a quick temper that earned him the nickname "Hair-Trigger Dick." He liked to live well, and his tendency toward extravagant living often caused some real concerns among his creditors. Early in the nine-teenth century, Martin entered the British Parliament as the M.P. from Galway. It wasn't long after the start of his term of office that he pro-posed a bill in the House of Commons designed to make cruelty to an-imals punishable by law. His ideas were not appreciated by the other parliamentarians. They greeted his speeches with ridicule, interrupting him with catcalls, laughs, and whistles. When called upon to respond to his ideas, instead of addressing the issues that he was raising, they abused him personally. They mocked his Irish brogue, challenged his personal integrity, and even publicly questioned his sanity. Martin, however, was committed to animal welfare and would not give up. When his first bill was thrown out, he immediately brought in another. When that bill was amended to the point that it no longer accom-plished anything meaningful, he presented Parliament with another—and so it went.

Martin's campaign was not making much progress until a fairly dra-matic incident occurred. He was speaking—again—on the issue of cru-elty to animals when a member of the opposition began to taunt him. The politician laughed at Martin and scoffed, "You don't even know what cruelty really is!"

This time Martin did not try to control his temper. "I do so, sir. If you will step outside of this chamber I shall explain it to you."

The two men stepped out of the chambers and then left the Parlia-ment building. At the top of the stairs, the rotund politician paused and laughed again. "You were about to give me your explanation . . ."

Martin lifted his ornate walking stick, swung it twice, and knocked the opposition member to the ground. "That is a little of what is meant by cruelty, sir. Would you like a little bit more of it?"

"No," moaned the politician as he rose from the ground, "I have had more than enough."

"Well, sir," said Martin, "a poor dog or a donkey is not able to say that he has had enough or too much and therefore wants protection."

The opposition member stared at Martin. He swayed slightly and then placed a hand on Martin's shoulder to steady himself. "I under-stand now. It has been a painful act of learning, but because of it I will support your act."

The member of Parliament was as good as his word. With a show of support from the opposing party the bill was taken more seriously, and in 1822 the first animal welfare act was passed. It was limited in scope, but further versions would strengthen it over time. Two years later Martin founded the first humane society in Britain. It received support from King George IV, who gave him the nickname of "Humanity Martin." George's daughter, who would soon become Queen Victoria, became a patron of the humane society and allowed it to be called the Royal Society for Prevention of Cruelty to Animals.

It should be obvious that Martin had a deep affection for animals, but we must now ask if this was counterbalanced by a reduced concern for fellow humans as the cynics suggest. At the time when Martin began his tenure as a parliamentarian, he was a wealthy landowner in Ireland. His estate was enormous, extending from Galway to Clifden, and it included the forty-mile-long road that connected the two towns. He could have generated a huge amount of wealth from such extensive properties. However, he chose to use his land in such a compassionate manner that, in the end, it cost him much of his fortune. Then, as now, there were often outbursts of violent conflict in Ireland based upon religious differences. When sectarian persecution drove the Catholics out of the north, Martin stepped in to find them a place to live. He subdivided sections of his land into small farms, providing rent-free homes and a means of livelihood for nearly a thousand families. Later, on other sections of his estate, he built cottages to house homeless refugees from the Napoleonic wars. This was certainly not a man without feeling for human beings.

Perhaps the feelings that Martin had for people are best seen in situations where the humane treatment of animals seemed to be in conflict with sympathetic treatment of people. In these cases he often found a compassionate way to resolve the issue. A story is told about Martin becoming quite incensed when he saw a street vendor who had overloaded his donkey with fruit and vegetables for sale. The poor animal was staggering under the weight, but the owner kept trying to move the donkey along more quickly by yanking sharply on the lead tied to its head. Each yank simply made the overburdened beast more unsteady, and finally it sank to its knees, while its owner yelled and pleaded with it to get up and move. Temper at full boil, Martin called a nearby constable and had the donkey's owner immediately brought before a magistrate. Once in court, Martin's testimony graphically described the abuse to the animal that was the direct result of putting such an excessive load on it, pointing out that the vendor was compounding the suffering by his rough tugging and pulling at the donkey's reins. At the close of the hearing the judge agreed with Martin. According to the new laws covering animal welfare this man was clearly guilty. The magistrate then fined the man and warned him that more severe punishment would result if he was caught repeating the offense.

The poor fruit seller was dismayed. "Your Lordship," he moaned, "I am only a poor man. I didn't intend to do my animal harm. I depend on this creature's strength to help me earn a livelihood for my family. This fine that you have put upon me is a great deal of money—at least to someone who earns as little as I do. I don't know how I can possibly pay it and I am afraid of what will happen to my wife and children if I have to go to jail."

Before the judge had time to respond to this plea, Martin was on his feet. "M'Lord, I feel that I have made my point before this court. Because of your just and fitting ruling in this matter, I am sure that this beast will not be harmed again. I also do not believe that my actions should cause a working man of such limited means, or his family, undo suffering. Therefore, I, personally, will pay the fine imposed upon him by this court." Martin then walked over to the clerk, paid the fine, and strode briskly out of the courthouse—probably looking for another wrong to right. Obviously, Martin had the capacity to love both humans and animals.

THE RESCUE OF MARY ELLEN

Henry Bergh, who eventually founded the American Society for the Prevention of Cruelty to Animals, was much slower in demonstrating his passion and concern for dogs and other animals.[4] The son of a prosperous New York shipbuilder, Bergh spent the first fifty years of his life in genteel society, doing the things expected of a wealthy man with a "proper" education. As a young man he traveled through Europe, sight-

seeing and writing a little poetry now and than. On his return he pa-
tronized the theater and even had some modest success in writing plays.
Given this background it is not surprising that Bergh was extremely
fashion-conscious, wearing well-tailored suits and spats, and carrying a
walking stick with an ornate head. Bergh's wealth allowed him to spend
about half of each year in expensive and fashionable resorts in America
and Europe; the rest of his time was spent in his home, New York City.
His lifestyle put him at ease in most public situations and gave him the
opportunity to get to know many people in politics and the arts.

In 1863 a chain of events began that would change Bergh's life.
When Abraham Lincoln became president of the United States, he
named Bergh as the new secretary of the American legation to Russia in
Saint Petersburg. It was a purely political move, designed to please
some wealthy and well-placed people in New York. At this time Bergh
was simply known as an affluent dilettante who was intelligent, had
good social skills, knew something about the arts, and would make a
presentable representative of the United States at formal occasions.
Bergh was viewed as being only mildly political in his interests, although he had given support both to Lincoln's Republican Party and to
the antislavery movement in general; certainly he was not known to be
a crusader for animal welfare.

One day after Bergh had taken his post in Saint Petersburg, he was
walking down an avenue when he heard a cry of pain. He looked down
the street and saw a droshky, a low, four-wheeled open carriage with a
bench running down the center. Passengers sat on the bench with their
feet hanging over the side, resting on a bar near the ground. Droshkies
provided cheap transport in the city, but given their openness and the
bouncing of the cart on the rutted streets, it was not unheard-of for passengers to be unexpectedly jolted out of their seats and onto the road-
way. An unfortunate passenger who happened to fall near a wheel could
suffer major injuries. The cries that he heard that morning led Bergh to
the conclusion that a woman or a child had fallen from the droshky and
had been badly hurt.

Bergh rushed forward to see if he could be of any assistance, but as
he rounded the front of the vehicle he was surprised to see that the
sounds were actually coming from a horse who was being viciously

beaten by its angry driver. "Even though I could see that it was only a horse being cruelly whipped, I still heard the cries as if they were the suffering of a tortured human. This burned like a brand in my soul and when the driver ceased his punishing, I gazed at that dumb brute, whose skin was covered with cuts from the whip. As I looked at his dark brown face I could see the tracks of tears that had been running down his cheeks. These were the same tears that would signal anguish in a tormented and injured child."

It was an image that was to live with him for the rest of his life. He would later admit, "I was never specially interested in animals—though I always had a natural feeling of tenderness for creatures that suffer. What struck me most forcibly, was that mankind derived immense benefits from these creatures and gave them in return, not the least protection." Bergh must have thought long and hard about this event and its implications. He certainly came home from Russia a changed man—now fully committed as a crusader for the cause of animal welfare. To promote that cause he would use all of those skills that had served him as a dramatist, and all of his social and political contacts, to bring about laws, regulations, and special programs to improve the lot of animals. He founded the American Society for the Prevention of Cruelty to Animals, which became a focus for lobbying efforts; and in a short time Bergh and his supporters had exerted so much pressure that New York enacted strong and meaningful animal welfare laws that would serve as a model for legislation in other states across the U.S.

It is interesting to note that after founding the ASPCA, Henry Bergh often received the same kind of censure that was used by my critic and has been aimed at dog lovers in general. Bergh was frequently criticized by newspaper writers who claimed that he favored animals over humans. One editor of a sporting magazine wrote, "He wanders the landscape looking for abuses levied against dogs and cats, cows and cab horses. In his zeal he will stop a crowded omnibus if he feels that the horse drawing it is overworked. What ill-advised virtue is this when myriad children are being beaten and starved. The young and weak of our own humanity are forced into heavy labor and suffering. Better that Mr. Bergh should tend to our own first, than waste his efforts on four footed beasts created by God to serve man's needs and pleasures."

Was Bergh really unfeeling toward people because too much of his affection and concern was reserved for animals? Let's consider the evidence. In the major cities of the time, such as Bergh's New York, many children had to beg, steal, and scavenge to survive. Some were forced into sweatshop jobs, where they were set to heavy tasks for long hours and received only pitifully low wages. Others were forced to live and to sleep—and sometimes to die—on the dirty streets. Bergh had certainly helped bring about some laws to protect animals from abuse. However, there was little legal precedent for protecting children, and this was true until early 1874. It was then that an extreme case of child abuse brought Henry Bergh into the picture.

The situation began with one Mrs. Etta Wheeler, a church worker trying to provide assistance for people in the New York tenements. One church member was very distressed about the cruel treatment of a child named Mary Ellen, and mentioned it to Mrs. Wheeler in the hope that she might be able to intervene.

Mary Ellen had been indentured as a house servant by the wife of a mason. The process of indenture is not familiar to many people today, but it has a long history. Basically it was a form of contract labor where a person borrowed money and then agreed to pay off the debt by working for a specified length of time. The lot of some indentured servants was often worse than that of slaves before the U.S. Civil War. There was an economic logic for this, since slaveowners thought of their slaves as an investment whose resale and long-term value would drop if they were maltreated. On the other hand, the short-term indentured servants could be abused almost to death because their "masters" had only a temporary interest in them, and they would be leaving at the end of their term. In poor families, indenture often meant selling children into virtual slavery. A parent would borrow the money and indenture the child to work off the debt, usually for a period of seven years or longer. This is what had happened to Mary Ellen.

Even by the standards for indentured servants of the time, Mary Ellen was being abused. The child was beaten daily with a cowhide strap, and her screams were overheard by dozens of neighbors in the densely populated tenement. Over a period of several months, Mrs. Wheeler had tried to rescue little Mary Ellen. When she approached the residence, however, she was verbally abused and had the door slammed in her face. Mrs. Wheeler then sought direct legal intervention. She went to the police and described what was going on. The police, however, did nothing except to point out that indenture contracts were written so that the holder had all the legal control over the child that parents normally had. In effect the law viewed contract holders as adoptive parents of the child during the term of the work contract, and there was no law that prevented parents, whether adoptive or natural, from physically disciplining their children. Any attempts to take Mary Ellen away from her abusers would be viewed by the law as violating the relationship between a parent and a child, an action that was virtually unheard-of at that time. When she turned to various church organizations for help, they told her that if the family that Mary Ellen was indentured to would not respond to humanitarian appeals, then they, like the police, could do nothing.

Mrs. Wheeler was frustrated and was becoming depressed and anxious about not being able to help this unfortunate child. Finally, her niece asked, "If no one else will help this abused child, why not go to Mr. Bergh? He is the man who has looked after the welfare of animals, and I have been taught that we humans are nothing but higher animals." Desperate for some form of aid for the child, Mrs. Wheeler acted at once. Within an hour of this conversation, she arrived at the headquarters of the ASPCA. Pleading that she needed Bergh's help, she managed to get an immediate interview with him. Sitting in his well-appointed office, she once again told the story of Mary Ellen.

"If the police say that there are no legal grounds to intervene, Mrs. Wheeler, what would you have me do?" Bergh asked in a concerned tone.

"Mr. Bergh," she replied, "the grounds on which you protect the dumb animals of creation is based upon their absolute helplessness in the face of human cruelty. Tell me, is there anything more helpless than a defenseless child? If you can't interfere on other grounds, possibly you may find some way of reaching this child on the grounds that it is an unfortunate little animal of the human race."

Bergh stood up and announced, "I shall do this for Mary Ellen and perhaps it will help others in the same circumstances."

For the rest of this story we must turn to Jacob A. Riis, a newspaper reporter and photographer who later became in influential social reformer.[5] In 1874, Riis had held the position of a newspaper police reporter for less than a year. He was assigned to cover New York City's Lower East Side. Someone had alerted him that Henry Bergh was going to appear in court that day, not with a case affecting a dog or other animal, but in a case involving a child. Given Bergh's high profile Riis suspected that there might be a story there, so he hurried down to the court. This is how he described the scene some years later:

I was in a courtroom full of men with pale, stern looks. I saw a child brought in, carried in a horse blanket, at the sight of which men wept aloud. I saw it laid at the feet of the judge, who turned his face away, and in the stillness of that courtroom I heard the voice of Henry Bergh.

"The child is an animal," he said. "If there is no justice for it as a human being, it shall at least have the rights of the cur in the street. It shall not be abused."

And as I looked I knew I was where the first chapter of the children's rights was written, under warrant of that made for the dog. For from that dingy courtroom, whence a wicked woman went to jail, came forth the New York Society for the Prevention of Cruelty to Children, with all it has meant to the world's life.

Riis was correct. The formal beginnings of the child welfare movement occurred as people filed somberly from that courtroom at the end of the case. As they went out, Mrs. Wheeler stopped to thank Bergh. She looked at him with eyes still red from crying and asked, "Could there not be a society for the prevention of cruelty to children, which would do for abused children what has been so well done for animals?"

Bergh took her hand and said, "Mrs. Wheeler, you need not ask. When first I saw Mary Ellen I had already decided that there shall be one."

When the new child welfare society was formed, Bergh wanted it to be separate from the ASPCA. However, in more than three hundred societies in North America, the child welfare and animal welfare movements were linked together under one banner. The organizers of these societies felt that it was possible for most people to follow the lead of

Henry Bergh. They reasoned that the human heart is large enough to contain a reservoir of affection for animals as well as for children and other people in need. As the cases of Richard Martin and Henry Bergh clearly show, a devotion or even a life-consuming passion for animals does not exhaust an individual's store of love and warmth—there is plenty left over for human beings as well. One may wonder whether the converse of this statement might also be true. Perhaps those who show no love for dogs and other animals do not have the capacity to truly love people either.

Chapter Three

The Image Dogs Create

There are many reasons why we come to have dogs in our lives. Sometimes we *need* a dog to perform a particular job, such as retrieving birds when we are out hunting, herding sheep, guarding our home or business, or even simply being a companion. In some instances, our choices of breed are limited by the dog's instinctive patterns of intelligence and its physical capacities. It takes little effort to teach a Collie or an Australian Cattle Dog to round up and drive herds of sheep, cattle, or even geese. A Doberman Pinscher or an Airedale Terrier, however, can never be taught this task, since they are dogs whose natural instincts are more in accord with chasing and scattering the flock, while the tiny Lhasa Apso or Shih Tzu, even if they had herding instincts, simply lack the size and speed to do the job.

When it comes to other functions, however, like being a watchdog, the choice is much broader. A watchdog's job is to sound the alarm when someone approaches the house. While Rottweilers, Boxers, and German Shepherd Dogs may first spring to mind, this job can effectively be done by a Dachshund, a Yorkshire Terrier, and even a Chihuahua. The reason is that even a small dog can make noise. The sound of any dog's bark will alert the household and presumably send a potential burglar off to look for a quieter target. The Scottish author and poet Sir Walter Scott, best known to many people for his books *Ivan-hoe* and *Rob Roy*, once received some advice on the matter of watchdogs from a very credible source. Scott began his career as a lawyer, working in his father's law office, and his debut at the bar involved a successful defense of a burglar. The grateful client, who was in fact guilty not only of this particular crime but of several others, gave Scott the following bit of wisdom: "Always keep a small dog that barks, rather than a large dog, which you think may serve as a more formidable guard, but may spend most of its time sleeping. Size doesn't matter, just the sound." Scott took his advice and always kept terriers, which are vigilant little dogs, always ready to give voice at any sound or at anyone's approach.

Broad choices among breeds are also possible for many other functions. Suppose you are a duck hunter and are looking for a dog to retrieve your game. For this task most people will think only of the classic retrievers: the Labrador Retriever, Flat-Coated Retriever, Chesapeake Bay Retriever, and so forth. While these dogs do this work very well and require only a minimum of training, game birds can also be retrieved by Pointers, setters of all sorts, most of the big and small spaniels, and even Poodles. Poodles as retrievers may be a surprise to most people; however, Poodles actually started as a sporting breed. They were bred from retriever stock, namely the European Water Dog, which is now extinct but served as the starting point for the Portuguese Water Dog, the Irish Water Spaniel, and the American Water Spaniel as well. If both a Poodle and a Labrador Retriever can do the job, what factors might induce one person to choose the Lab and another to choose the Poodle?

THE PROPER APPEARANCE FOR THE JOB

Why certain dogs are chosen and others are not depends as much on human nature as on the nature of the dog. The fact is that sometimes our selection of a breed of dog is intimately associated with an image that we would like to convey to other people. The importance of the image that a dog projects about its owner should not be underestimated. It can sometimes cause people to pass over a breed of dog that they are emotionally attracted to, simply because they feel that they "wouldn't look right" with a particular kind, or size, of dog. Sometimes issues about the image that the dog presents even intrude into situations where one might expect that ability to do the job would be far more important than the dog's appearance. This became apparent to me a couple of years ago in California.

I had been invited to Van Nuys, California, to speak to the California Narcotic Canine Association, a group that provides education and support for law enforcement officials who use dogs to sniff out narcotics. I found myself surrounded by several hundred police officers who worked with what they affectionately called "dope dogs." This is a group of intelligent and dedicated law officers who really care about their jobs and their dogs; they had come to attend workshops that could improve their skills and also would help them to understand and care for their dogs better.

Everyone knows that the dog's sense of smell is superior to that of humans, but you may not be aware of just how good the dog's scenting ability is. An average dog has around 220 million scent receptors in its nose, as compared with only 5 million in the average human. To put it another way, if we could lay out flat the nasal membranes of a typical dog they would cover up to seven square meters (more than the outside surface area of an average dog) while our own nasal membranes would cover only about half a square meter (less than the size of a page from a tabloid newspaper). With this advantage dogs can often identify smells so faint that even our most sensitive scientific instruments cannot recognize them.

The idea of narcotics-detecting dogs was conceived late in the 1960s. Since then dogs have been trained to detect marijuana, heroin, cocaine, explosives, and agricultural matter, such as fruits or vegetables, which may be banned from import into certain countries. Today most large police forces have dope dogs, and they are often found at border crossings and at international airports where contraband substances typically enter the country.

Several narcotics-search dogs have achieved a reasonable amount of fame in their own right. There was the team of Rocky and Barco, two Belgian Malinois dogs that became honorary sergeant majors in the Narcotics Division of the State of Texas. In 1987 alone, Rocky and

Barco provided evidence that resulted in over 250 arrests and the seizure of narcotics that had a street value of over $300 million. The Mexican drug smugglers who were most affected by these activities were so angered that they put a $70,000 price on the head of each of these dogs. Yet the bounty for Rocky and Barco is dwarfed by the $1 million offered by Colombian heroin dealers for anyone who would kill Winston, a Labrador Retriever working for the British government who had cost them nearly $1 billion in lost drug shipments.

Some of these dope dogs actually receive star treatment, and K-9 Collector Cards are distributed by city and county police departments to honor them. In 1993, for instance, the U.S. Customs Service created the All-Star Drug Detecting Dog card series. These glossy cards look much like the ones for baseball, basketball, or hockey stars, except each shows a color picture of a particular dope dog. The flip side lists the dog's name, breed, age, weight, and tag number. Instead of a batting average or scoring totals these cards include the "total seizure value to date" and a brief description of some of the dog's most significant exploits. Cliff, a German Shepherd working for the Kansas police, had so many accomplishments that the state put out a whole series of K-9 cards dedicated to Cliff alone, with each card showing him working at a different project.

My task at that California meeting was to talk about the selection of dogs for drug detection work. In reality it is a very easy task, if all that you are interested in is the dog's ability to smell. Basically any breed can do this kind of work, since all dogs have exquisitely sensitive scenting abilities. It is probably best to stay away from dogs with very short faces and pushed-in noses, like English Bulldogs or Pekingese, mainly because they are subject to a variety of respiratory problems, and it is very difficult to smell much of anything if you have a runny nose. Sex makes a bit of a difference, since a series of scientific studies have suggested that male dogs are somewhat better scent trackers. This sex difference may be due to the fact that males tend to use their noses more each day as they engage in territorial and sexually related behaviors, rather than being a pure difference in scenting ability.

Of course, a good dope dog needs more than just the ability to pick up a scent. It has to be willing to work with people, capable of learning reasonably quickly, and so forth. There is also a lot of evidence that training can significantly improve scenting accuracy in dogs. However, even when these considerations are taken into account, that still leaves dozens of breeds of dogs—big, medium-sized, small, and even tiny—that can do the job.

I spent a good deal of time talking with officers who used narcotics detection dogs that week. One thing that became quite clear was that all of them were very sensitive about the particular breed of dog that they had working beside them. Virtually all of the dope dogs were large breeds, including Malinois, German Shepherds, Labrador Retrievers, Doberman Pinschers, and some Rottweilers. Such big dogs are necessary for patrol work and the apprehension of criminals, since it is often important for the dog to be large enough to knock a criminal down, and they should look fierce enough to hold a suspect at bay. During my presentations, however, I pointed out that for the specific task of narcotics detection large dogs weren't any better than many smaller dogs. When I said this some of the audience members began to chuckle. One person in the audience pointed at another officer. "Hey, he even tries to work with a Springer Spaniel."

The target of this wisecrack cringed and said, "Ease off, he does his work fine."

Another shouted, "Come on, you don't mean that something like a Miniature Poodle can do the job."

"Yes, I do," I replied.

"Yeah, well I'd rather go back on traffic duty than be seen on the street with some ball of fluff at the end of a string!"

The bantering in the room made it quite clear that most of the officers agreed. It was not just a matter of whether the dog could do the job of detecting the narcotics, but its appearance was important. It made a statement about the person at the other end of the leash, and for someone in law enforcement, the statement made by a small, delicate dog was entirely wrong.

Interestingly, several of the police officers revealed that the dogs chosen for their image at work were very different from the dogs chosen for companionship or as family dogs. One officer had championship Lhasa Apsos at home, while another had Shih Tzus. These wee, fluffy dogs did not fit the image at all. One made sure to tell me that the little dogs at home were his wife's idea and that they were his wife's dogs. The other admitted that he was fond of his little dogs. He confided:

I didn't tell anybody that we had toy dogs for a long time. I was afraid that they would just razz me to death over it. But the fact is, I actually like those little guys. It's not like they're working dogs, but then they don't really have to be. When the word finally got out (you can't keep secrets from other cops, you know), I took a lot of ribbing, but since I was out on the street with a regular police dog, the guys eventually let it drop. Just between you and me, when they do visit my house my buddies end up treating my dogs just like real dogs—I mean like big dogs—like they pet them and all that and don't act like they are embarrassed to be around them or anything.

It was obvious that there was still some ambivalence here, but at least the officer had a "proper police dog" on the street when he was working, so his image remained intact.

There was an interesting follow-up to this particular meeting. Early this year I met a man who works for the U.S. Drug Enforcement Agency (DEA). He told me that the DEA had started using small dogs, like Miniature Poodles, at airports.

You can see a big dog all the way across the terminal, and a lot of people go out of their way just to avoid getting near something that looks like it might be a drug detection dog. On the other hand, they either ignore the little dogs or sometimes even go into a "nice doggie" routine, and play with them. They don't even suspect anything is wrong until they're busted with the drugs still in their possession.

I remembered my experience with the California Narcotic Canine Association and asked him about the image problem associated with having a small dog.

Well, some guys didn't feel very good about the idea of being seen out there with that kind of "poof" dog. The way that we got their cooperation was by pointing out that this was an undercover operation and the dog was really undercover as well—like a disguised dope dog, you know—in a costume, sort of. Once we put it like that, they felt a lot better. Undercover work is flashy and macho regardless of what you have to wear or do.

DOGS OF THE RICH AND FAMOUS

The issue of image is also extremely important to people who are in the media and on public view. For some of these celebrities, the dog that they are seen with becomes a statement telling the world who they are. Take the case of Gerald McClellan, the former World Boxing Commission middleweight title holder. McClellan filled his house with Pit Bulls. "When I train I think about my dogs. When I fight I think about my dogs," he said. He then went on to tell about his fight with Julian Jackson for the middleweight world championship. It was a hard, pounding fight which had the crowd roaring. Suddenly, the whole crowd gasped as McClellan collapsed to his knees, the result of an obvious low blow from Jackson.

"Man he hurt me. I looked up and thought, I have to get up—my dogs would get up. I can't quit—my dogs don't quit." McClellan did get up, and he flew at Jackson with such an aggressive surge that he scored a technical knockout that very same round and walked out of the ring with the title.

Perhaps it was the Pit Bulls that McClellan identified with that kept him going in his last fight, in London, against Nigel Benn. Once more the battle was for the WBC title and once again McClellan didn't quit. This fight ended with him on one knee, as the referee ended his term as champion with a count of ten. What no one knew at that moment was that McClellan had fought on beyond the limits of safety. His brain was bleeding and a blood clot was forming. He reached his corner and collapsed. McClellan's next fight would be in a hospital, drawing inspiration from his dogs to help him battle for his very life.

McClellan's tendency to meld his self-image with the image of his dogs was obvious in an interview that he once had with Tom Junod for *Sports Illustrated.* At that time McClellan had four Pit Bulls. However, the count often changed because his males would occasionally fight among themselves, and now and then one was killed. Junod asked McClellan if he had ever considered neutering his dogs. There was a noticeable pause before the boxer replied, and when he did it was in a voice strained by some internal sense of outrage as though he had personally been attacked or insulted.

"Neuter? You mean . . . cut their *balls* off? Why would I cut their balls off? I wouldn't let nobody cut *my* balls off, and my dogs are my best friends—why would I let someone cut their balls off?" McClellan's voice was an octave higher than normal and his face was streaked with rage as he tried to provide some reason for his response. "They fight sometimes—so what? Two men can't live in the same house. Two men can't be boss. So they fight. I mean, I love my brother, but we fight all the time. Neuter my dogs? No. No. No way!"

Big men, especially professional athletes whose toughness and physicality are part of their image, tend to choose big, tough dogs which then become part of the picture that they present to the world. For example, Curt Schilling, a pitcher for the Philadelphia Phillies, surrounds himself with a squadron of Rottweilers. In our era Rottweilers, more than almost any other breed, are seen as the big, dominant, mean dog.

Of course these personalities can't have their dogs with them at all times. Some, however, have found a way to keep their dog's image always in view. That is the case with another professional baseball player, Greg Vaughn, an outfielder with the Milwaukee Brewers, and also with Bryant Young, a defensive tackle with the San Francisco '49ers. Both of these men display prominent tattoos of Rottweilers.

In addition to Rottweilers and Pit Bulls, the dogs that are chosen to reinforce the image of professional sports stars include Doberman Pinschers, Akitas, Mastiffs, and Great Danes. Evander Holyfield, heavyweight boxing champion of the world, owns a five-hundred-acre farm with an elaborate set of kennels and a platoon of Akitas. Once he had had a German Shepherd named Ego, but Ego just "didn't have enough fire in him or something" for the image that Holyfield wanted to project, so he now surrounds himself with the larger, stronger, and more aggressive Akitas. The fact that Akitas are often quite aggressive toward other dogs, including those of their own breed, often leads to fights among his pets. Holyfield doesn't view these bursts of hostility as a problem but rather as expressions of his dogs' indomitability. "They are tough dogs so they got to act tough sometimes to prove it."

Holyfield's most famous rival was probably Mike Tyson.[1] In 1986 Tyson was the youngest man ever to win the heavyweight boxing championship of the world. Six years later he was jailed for rape, and upon his release he attempted a comeback. In 1997, Tyson again faced Holy-field for the world championship in a bout held in Las Vegas. The result was a disaster, with Tyson virtually going berserk in the ring and biting off a piece of Holyfield's ear. With blood flying everywhere, the fight was stopped. Shortly thereafter, Tyson's boxing license was suspended. Tyson claimed that he had been provoked into biting Holyfield by what he viewed as a deliberate head butt in a previous round. It would have damaged his image to let that incident go unpunished.

The breed of dog that Tyson chose for his tough-guy image was the Bullmastiff. These are 130-pound dogs, sometimes known as "Keeper's Night Dogs," since they were originally used by gamekeepers to guard hunting preserves from poachers. In some respects this is the perfect dog for a professional boxer, since the Bullmastiff was originally bred to be quick enough to catch a fleeing person yet still be large enough to knock a man down. Tyson was quite a fan of the actor Sylvester Stallone, and in the first two of the *Rocky* films, Stallone appeared with a handsome red Bullmastiff named Butkus, which happened to be his own personal pet dog. To Tyson, this meant that he also needed a Bullmastiff to complete his image as a world champion boxer.

Tyson had his advisors look into the breed, and they told him that one of the best kennels for Bullmastiffs was Allstar, run by Mimi Einstein. She was contacted and eventually sold him a puppy who, by a quirk of fate, was named Allstar's Mel Gibson after another actor that Tyson admired. Despite this apparently good omen, things did not work out so well. Tyson himself was not interested in actually caring for the dog, since it seems to have been chosen for image, not companionship or function. Instead, he hired a couple whose job it was to take care of the dog, among other things. Einstein, who is a conscientious breeder, gave this couple extensive instructions on the dog's care. In addition she made it a habit to telephone the Tyson estate now and then to check on how the dog was doing.

After several months had passed, Einstein got a worrisome phone call from the couple who were caring for Tyson's dog. They had been fired, and they told Einstein that they were worried that the dog would not be adequately cared for. Apparently, the dog's main function was to be seen with Tyson now and then, and the boxer had demonstrated little concern or affection for the animal, viewing it much as one would view a fashion accessory. The slim fifty-year-old breeder immediately jumped into her car and went to Tyson's New Jersey home. She bustled into his living room, where he was surrounded by a crowd of bodyguards, staff, and various associates. "Where's the dog?" she demanded. There were puzzled looks, but someone gestured toward a door. Einstein opened the door and found a depressed and unattended dog, tied on a short tether in Tyson's kitchen. Ignoring the fact that she was now effectively kidnapping a dog that belonged to the heavyweight boxing champion of the world, she snapped a leash on the animal, led it to the car, and then returned it to the safety of her kennel.

Tyson and his associates later contacted Einstein and made a series of threats which frightened her enough that she had a security system installed. She agreed to return the dog, but only if Tyson met a series of conditions about the animal's care—conditions that were not much different from those required of prospective pet owners by many animal shelters. Faced with having to treat the dog as a family pet rather than as an image-building decoration, Tyson soon lost interest and the phone calls to the kennel stopped.

For some boxers, even a 130-pound Bullmastiff is not large enough to create the impression that they want. Mark Breland, former welterweight champion of the world, had a Doberman Pinscher. Breland would mentally prepare himself for his fights by staring at his reflection in the mirror. "After a while I could see myself start to look like my dog. When my nose was looking long and sharp and my ears got kinda points at the top, then I knew I was ready to fight." Despite the love and respect that he had for his Doberman, it was just not substantial enough for the image of a world champion boxer. So Breland now keeps two Mastiffs, named Diamond and Static, each weighing around two hundred pounds.

Then there is Wilt Chamberlain, the seven-foot, one-inch basketball player who scored 31,419 points in his career and is the only player to have ever scored one hundred points in a single game. Chamberlain had two Great Danes. As he explained, "I'm a big man and I like big dogs." Unfortunately, they may have been too big. Chamberlain was living in an older and elegant apartment building on Central Park West in New York City. As he later noted, "The dogs kept growing until only one of us could get into the elevator. It caused enough hassles so they finally kicked me out of my apartment."

Choosing a dog as an image builder involves a very different mindset than choosing a dog as a helper or companion. At one dog show I struck up a conversation with the owner of a major kennel northwest of Philadelphia.

We sell lots of dogs to athletes of all kinds and to some movie stars. I breed Dobies [Doberman Pinschers] and Rotties [Rottweilers] and my brother breeds Akitas. Word of mouth has gone out that we have good dogs, and some of these guys have come a couple of thousand miles just to get a dog from us. One football player came down to pick up a dog just last weekend—all the way from Chicago. He had just signed a professional contract with some team and now had the money to have a dog. When he called me he wanted to know how big my Rotties were—not how good, just how big.

One of the things that surprised me when I first started selling dogs to those guys was that they usually didn't want just one dog. It was always "I need two dogs that look good together" or something like that. My brother once had a football player come in to look at a litter of Akitas that he had. There were six puppies in all, four males and two females. He insisted on seeing the sire and when he saw how large and strong he was, that guy really seemed impressed. He asked, "Will the puppies grow up to be just as big as their daddy?" My brother told him that he expected that the males would grow up to look very similar to their father but the females would be a bit smaller, more like their mother. Then he just pulled out his checkbook and said, "That's OK then, I'll take the four boys." We're talking about good dogs from a good line, so we're also talking about thousands of dollars for those four dogs!

As this breeder noted, typically dogs that are selected to confirm an image are chosen in groups. If one big dog says that you are powerful and masculine, then clearly two, or four, will make that point even more evident. For instance, Evander Holyfield has seven Akitas, and Chris Green, a pro football player with the Miami Dolphins, has two. Kenny Norman, a professional basketball player with the Atlanta Hawks, has four Rottweilers, and so forth.

Selecting sets of dogs to convey an image is not limited to men who play professional sports. Adrian Paul, the handsome and macho actor who stars in the television series *Highlander,* owns five Rottweilers. William Shatner, best known as Captain Kirk of *Star Trek,* has at various times owned Doberman Pinschers and Great Danes—sometimes up to a half dozen at a time. From an earlier era, the handsome actor Rudolph Valentino, known for films such as *The Sheik* and *Blood and Sand,* tried to emphasize his masculine image with four Irish Wolfhounds. These are the tallest of all dogs, and the American Kennel Club standard specifies that they should be a *minimum* of thirty-two inches at the shoulder with a weight of 120 pounds. Even women who are image-conscious may have a set of dogs who reinforce the world's picture of them. Elvira, the campy horror movie star and television host, has two matched Rottweilers.

Although dogs may serve to reinforce an image, having a number of dogs in the house is not really conducive to establishing a strong personal relationship with each of them. As the number of dogs in a household increases, of necessity, the amount of time that can be spent with any one of them decreases. A dog that is a pet or a companion is entitled to an investment of your time. A dog that is merely part of your wardrobe may need care and maintenance, like a delicate item of clothing, but it does not require a personal commitment of continuous time and attention.

The real measure of a dog's worth, or at least of a dog's psychological importance to its master, is the amount of time that its owner has invested in that dog. The issue is time, not money. The effort that an owner puts into making the dog a companion, and training it to do what he or she wants a dog to do, creates a bond that makes separation from the dog very painful. I often see breed champion dogs, who have won numerous ribbons for their beauty and grace, who are sold off with little thought and with only a quick glance backward by their former owners. If, on the other hand, you would like to see an interesting human reaction, make an offer to buy a dog from someone who has personally trained it to win an advanced obedience degree. The owner will respond with incredulous laughter or shock. Such dogs are just not for sale.

Dogs chosen to reinforce the image of the owner are seldom trained by that owner. Instead, a trainer is viewed much like an auto mechanic who may be hired to finely tune and maintain a sports car that one wants to drive occasionally because it looks so good and trendy. A professional trainer or handler may be called in to make a dog easier to control, but when the owner gives commands later on, the dog may or may not respond reliably. As Evander Holyfield commented on Ing, one of his Akitas, who had just completed a course with a professional trainer, "He did real good. He listens to his trainer real good. He just don't listen to me. I still can't get him to do nothin.'"

Sometimes the way the dogs are trained becomes just another aspect of their use to create an image. The tough macho image is strengthened by having the animal professionally trained as a guard or attack dog. Chris Green, the Miami Dolphin football player, describes his Akitas as "silent but deadly." Basketball player Kenny Norman has four attack-trained Rottweilers, but he also owns a Cocker Spaniel and notes (with some embarrassment), "Well, she's pretty tough too!"

DOGS AS A FASHION STATEMENT

One of the more interesting cases of dogs being chosen to present a particular impression to the world was given to me by a lovely fashion model from Montreal. While we were waiting to be interviewed on a television show, we chatted a while.

Because of your book [The Intelligence of Dogs] *some people teased me a lot because I own Afghan Hounds and you said they were not very smart. The truth is that I really didn't pick them for their brains. They are smart enough to be good pets, which is all that matters. I really picked them for their looks. They are very beautiful and walk most elegantly. I think that they show off a woman with my build very nicely. I have four Afghans. One of them is black, one is that kind of honey brown, and two are white (except for their faces that are a little gray). I picked those colors because they match most of my wardrobe. I always wear some white, even if it is in my accessories, and like to dress mostly in blacks and browns. That means that if I have one of the colored dogs and one white one with me I am perfectly coordinated with my dogs. The reason that I have two white dogs is for when I have to wear colors. Two white Afghan Hounds will highlight any outfit.*

I'm not the first person who uses dogs as part of their wardrobe. . . . When I was starting out in this business someone told me a story about that beautiful blond actress Jean Harlow—from the 1930s and '40s, I think. You know she did that film Dinner at Eight *and some others where she always played the beautiful sexy woman. Anyway, there was this publicity photograph of her with one or two Old English Sheepdogs [plate 3]. Somebody asked her why she liked this kind of dog and Harlow said, "I like any dog that makes me look good when it stands next to me." I remembered that. That is why I have Afghan Hounds—they make me look good when they stand next to me.*

The model chose her dogs as an accessory to her clothing, but another beautiful woman chose a dog to go with her image *without* clothes. Rose Louise Hovick, better known as Gypsy Rose Lee, was a witty and sophisticated entertainer whose life story was turned into the musical play *Gypsy* and later became a motion picture with that same name. She was one of the first burlesque artists to turn a striptease into something with some grace and style that might legitimately be called "exotic dancing." In her appearances on Broadway and in the Ziegfeld Follies she delighted in beginning her act in a spectacular costume and ending with only a few strategically placed feathers or furs. The dog breed that she chose is known today as the Chinese Crested dog. It has gone by many names during its history, including the Chinese Sailor Dog and the Chinese Edible Dog. Both of these names reflected the fact that these dogs were often taken on board Chinese merchant ships, where they were used to hunt and kill rats on board. When all of the rats were gone, the dog was eaten as a special delicacy by the ship's officers.

When it was first introduced to Western countries, the breed had another name—the Chinese Naked Dog. This is because one of the varieties of this breed is virtually hairless, with only a tuft of hair on its head, a bit of a ruffed collar fringe, and a few silky tassels on knees, ankles, and tail. The rest of the dog's body is a broad expanse of bare pink skin, occasionally broken by silvery gray polka dots. "The dog is dressed just like me at the climax of my act," Lee quipped. She loved posing for photographs with these dogs, and there is a story that a certain state governor even went out and got a Chinese Crested just so that he could have his picture taken with Gypsy Rose Lee.

While the image-conscious person might look at the dog as part of their costume, it is often necessary to worry about the dog's image as well. If you are trying to appear tough and dominant, you will need to adorn your dog with the proper accoutrements—a heavy chain collar, or a leather collar with studs or even spikes. In addition, the dog must have the right name. Herschel Walker, who became the all-time leading yardage gainer in professional football in 1995, has a Rottweiler named Al Capone. Some other dogs owned by professional athletes include Slugger, Rocky, Hawk, Ghost, Jagger, Trooper, Rocket, and Shaka Zulu. Names like Fluffy, Honey, or Fifi just won't work.

A dog chosen for its looks and for the impression it gives about its owner is not a dog chosen for companionship. It is, in some ways, merely a tool or an object with a particular function. As with a guard dog that protects a home or business, there is no need to become fond of the dog in any way—it is just working to earn its keep. So the presence of a guard dog tells you virtually nothing about the person who owns that dog. The guard dog's owner could be warm or cold, dominant or submissive, introverted or extroverted—it doesn't matter since the dog is not a friend, just an employee. In the same way, dogs chosen to present a particular image say little about the personality of the individual (except that they have a personality that seems to require them to maintain a public image).

How common is it for people to select particular dogs as part of their desire to manipulate the impression that others have of them? It may well be more common than we would like to admit. Perhaps one of the more extreme examples of this comes from New York City. I was attending a dog show there and struck up a conversation with a Rottweiler breeder.

I thought that as a psychologist you would like to know that over the past couple of years I have sold eight dogs to a man who lives in the barrio [the Hispanic section of New York City]. He told me that he ran a service that he called "Rent a Rottie." The idea was that he would rent out Rottweilers to young men who wanted to look tough. This way they could have one or two big, mean-looking dogs, with impressive heavy metal collars, walking beside them. These young men could then strut around the neighborhood looking really macho and strong, impressing the girls and the other guys. The dogs were all trained well enough to walk on a loose lead and to look mean. That was all that they had to do. He told me that his clients will usually rent a couple of dogs for a weekend, or for "special occasions." When his clients are finished they just return the dogs. He must be making good money at it, because every six months or so he buys another dog or two for his business.

Chapter Four

Do You Look Like Your Dog?

There is a certain body of information that is known as "folk psychology." Most of the beliefs of folk psychology are stored in pithy sayings such as "Birds of a feather flock together," "Variety is the spice of life," or "Like father, like son." These sayings are always used by your Aunt Sylvia or your Uncle Milton to convey their views of the world and to explain various behaviors of people. Psychologists of the research variety, rather than of the folk variety, are quite suspicious of most of the information in folk psychology because it seems to cover every possible outcome. Thus the folk psychologist assures you that "absence makes the heart grow fonder" when your true love is found pining away while you're on an extended business trip, but would have used "out of sight, out of mind" if your true love had run off with a redhead while you were away. One of the most interesting aspects of folk psychology is that it is so robust and long-lasting, no matter how often it turns out to be wrong or irrelevant.

Folk psychology has a lot to say about dog behavior ("Barking dogs don't bite") and even more about the relationships between dogs and humans ("A dog is a man's best friend"). One of the most persistent of these beliefs is that "people select dogs that look like themselves," or the more incredible statement that "people eventually come to look like their dogs."

LOOK-ALIKE PEOPLE AND DOGS

The television talk show host Oprah Winfrey found out how widespread this belief is when she was putting together a special show about dogs and people. She asked people if they thought they looked like their dogs. People who thought that there was a resemblance between themselves and their dog were asked to send a picture of the master and dog together to illustrate the similarity. Oprah's staff was astounded to find that they had triggered a flood of hundreds of photographs. Not only did these dog owners believe that they looked like their dogs, but many of them claimed to be quite proud to look like their canine friends.

I had been asked to be on the show to illustrate some things about dog intelligence and dog communication. As I waited for the taping of the show to begin, I found myself surrounded by eight or nine dog and person duets, all selected because of their apparent similarity. For example, there was Joe, a large, heavy, round-faced, jowly man, and his Bulldog, Buffalo. Joe informed Oprah that he had always liked Bulldogs and didn't mind looking like one. "When I'm out with Buffalo people always look at us and ask who is walking who," he said.

In some instances the apparent similarity between the person and the dog was due to coloration. For instance, a blond woman named Jennifer had brought along Chelsea, a Golden Retriever whose fur matched Jennifer's hair color exactly. The illusion of similarity was enhanced by the fact that Jennifer also wore a sable-colored suit. Then there was Colleen, whose long brown curly hair framed the sides of her face very much the way the long curly brown ears of her Springer Spaniel, Becket, framed his face.

As they stood in the hallway, waiting to be called into the studio, my curiosity got the better of me. I asked the people closest to me, "Tell me, did you consciously select a dog or dog breed because you thought that it looked like you, or did you discover the resemblance later?"

A man named Art looked fondly down at his lumbering Basset Hound, A.J., and said, "I suppose I wanted a dog that walked like I do, kinda slow and unconcerned." A woman named Irene, with a round, smiling, flat face, hugged Kelty, her Pug, and said, "Well, I just thought that Pugs looked so sweet and friendly that I had to have one." Sandy, whose square face was only vaguely similar to that of her Boston Terrier, Golden Nugget, protested that she didn't look at all like her dog, "unless I'm dressed like this." Her hand swept in front of her indicating her black and white outfit, which was well coordinated with the black and white markings on her dog.

THE SIMILARITY FACTOR

Actually, there are some scientific data which could be used to predict that people might prefer dogs with some visual similarity to themselves. These data have to do with how we develop fondness or become attracted to anything, whether it is another person or even a lifeless object. We could write a new proverb to summarize the research findings: "Likeness begets liking." This means that the more similar others are to ourselves, the more likely it is that we will become fond of them.

When we talk about liking someone on the basis of their similarity to us, the notion of similarity can include much more than physical attributes. Psychologist Theodore Newcomb demonstrated how important psychological similarity—similarity of personality, beliefs, and attitudes—is in determining whom we become attracted to. To do this he used an incredibly elaborate research study which involved actually setting apart an entire student dormitory at the University of Michigan for a school term.[1] The students living in this residence had their boarding fees reduced as compensation for participating in the study. In return, when they first moved in they had to complete a series of questionnaires about themselves, and then, at the end of the semester, they filled out a new set of questionnaires which measured their attitudes toward the other people in the dormitory. Newcomb found that similarities in lifestyles and beliefs could predict who would form friendships with whom. For example, strong friendships were formed among a group of liberal arts students who were interested in literature and art and who were politically liberal. Another set of close friendships formed between several students who were politically conservative, interested in technology, and had served in the military before returning to the university, and so forth. People tended to sort themselves into groups whose members were similar to themselves.

Other studies have shown that people often find that those with similar personalities are more acceptable to them. It is an odd fact that, although one might feel that the best thing that could happen to a habitually depressed individual would be to pair up with an optimistic and happy person, this seldom happens. Cheerful people prefer other happy people, while depressed people seem to enjoy each other's company, perhaps confirming another piece of folk psychology: "Misery loves company."

Did you ever wonder what the secret is behind the success of computerized dating services? It is nothing more than a matter of matching on the basis of similarity. These services use extensive questionnaires to find out some basic information about their clients, including their religion, their family's social status and income, their political beliefs, their taste in music, entertainment, and sports, and so forth. Then they match people on the basis of as many dimensions as possible. The closer the match, the more likely that people will develop an attraction for one another. The interesting thing is that this matching process includes appearance as well as attitudes and personal history. How tall a person is, how much they weigh, hair color, and skin tones influence liking. While most people like individuals who are physically attractive, the most successful matches involve pairing people of about the same degree of attractiveness. Thus the beautiful people are happiest with other beautiful people, average-looking people with average-looking partners—making it highly unlikely that in real life the ugly, misshapen Quasimodo of *The Hunchback of Notre Dame* would end up living happily ever after with the beautiful gypsy Esmeralda.

Dogs have no religious or political beliefs to match, but they do have personalities and attitudes. Consider Humphrey Bogart, who was known for the strong, rugged, impenetrable roles that he played in classic motion pictures like *The Maltese Falcon, Casablanca, Key Largo,* and *The Treasure of the Sierra Madre.* Director Howard Hawks once commented that "Bogey thinks that he has to live up to the reputation of all of those tough guys he plays." Hard-drinking and rowdy in his personal life, Bogart not surprisingly owned dogs with tough and self-sufficient characters, such as Boxers and Scottish Terriers (plate 4).

Another film star who has occasionally been described as tough and independent is Whoopi Goldberg, who has appeared in well-received films such as *The Color Purple* and *Ghost*. In one interview she described her own personality as being close to that of the character that she played in *Sister Act*—brash, self-assured, and in control—"but without the nun's habit," she was quick to point out. Perhaps it is a personality match that explains why she has chosen a tough and dominant Rhodesian Ridgeback as her companion.

A reasonable contrast with Whoopi Goldberg is actress Jamie Lee Curtis. She has been the star of films in a variety of genres, from horror in *Halloween*, to action in *True Lies*, to romance and comedy in *Forever Young* and *A Fish Called Wanda*. She is described as being bouncy, bright, energetic, playful, loyal to her family, and caring. These are virtually the same adjectives that one would find in any breed description of Golden Retrievers, which are the dogs that she surrounds herself with at home. It is tempting to argue that her affection for this breed may be based on similarity of temperament, although, as we will see later, this kind of matching is far from the whole story.

THE FAMILIARITY EFFECT

You might feel that it would take quite a leap to get from selecting a dog whose temperament matches the person's, to selecting a dog that would actually look like the person. Yet there is a way to get there using a subtle yet simple psychological mechanism called *familiarity*. The folk psychology adage "Familiarity breeds contempt" is quite wrong. Rather we should be saying "Familiarity breeds contentment."

To see how familiarity works, let's consider a study by psychologists Richard Moreland and Scott Beach.[2] These investigators began by selecting four young women who looked like average college students. These women were to serve as their confederates in the research. One of these women had an easy job; she simply posed for a photograph. The other three also were photographed, but, in addition, they had to attend a college class for a designated number of sessions. One woman was required to be at five class sessions, another attended ten, and the third attended fifteen sessions. The sessions that the women attended were randomly spaced through the semester. The class used for this study was held in a large lecture hall, seating two hundred students. Each time one of the women attended, she would enter early so that she could sit on the first row where she might be casually seen by other students. The women never asked questions and never spoke with the students around them. All that they did was sit and take notes like everybody else.

At the end of the term, members of the class were brought together one last time. They were shown the photographs of the four women and asked if they recognized them. Virtually none of the class members did, since their attendance had been so unobtrusive. Next, the students were asked to look at the pictures again and then to rate these women on a number of traits, estimating just how attractive each woman was, how intelligent, how warm, how popular, and how honest. Finally they were asked how much they thought they might like each woman, and whether they might like to spend time with her. The results showed that the best predictor of just how much students liked each woman was simply how familiar they were with each of them. The more often a woman attended the class, the more attractive and desirable she was seen to be. In other words, simply being around where they can be seen frequently causes people to be liked better.

The interesting thing about this effect is that it works for everything, for objects as well as people. For example, consider the Turkish words *biwongi* and *afworbu*. Do they mean anything better or worse than the Turkish words *kadirga* or *nansoma?* Well, if you do not know how to speak Turkish, there should be no reason to find any of them any more pleasant than the others. However, in a study conducted at the University of Michigan, psychologist Robert Zajonc showed students such words different numbers of times.[3] Some words were presented frequently, some not so often. Later students were asked to simply rate these words, and to decide whether they thought that each word meant something good or bad. Words that were seen more frequently were rated as better, luckier, and nicer. The same effect works for faces, patterns, or Chinese characters: the more frequently you see them, the better you like them. This phenomenon has been named the "mere exposure effect," since merely being exposed to something will increase our liking for it.

The mere exposure effect explains how certain public eyesores eventually became loved and cherished community symbols. Consider the following example. As part of an international exposition at the end of the nineteenth century a project was funded to prove how far science had advanced. A great structure was to be erected in the center of the city. It would be twice as high as the dome of Saint Peter's Church in Rome and twice as high as the Great Pyramid of Giza, yet it would be built in a matter of months. The result was an open latticework tower, made of 6,300 metric tons (about 7,000 tons) of iron, that was 300 meters (984 feet) high.

While people were amazed that such a structure could be built so quickly, they were not particularly impressed by its aesthetic qualities. There was much criticism about the "pile of ignoble iron that has been heaped in the center of a beautiful city of marble and stone." People mused openly about when this "useless metal skeleton" would be cleared from the city's skyline. Now one must understand that this iron tower is not art, nor does it have any intrinsic beauty. It commemorates no great event, nor glorifies any religion or political movement. You cannot visit this tower as a museum—simply because there is nothing to see inside it. Yet today this empty monument is visited by twice as many people as visit the famous Louvre Museum.

If you have not yet recognized what I am talking about, it is the Eiffel Tower in Paris. Why has this bare, functionless tower become so famous? The answer is simply because it is there and is visible in glimpses from virtually every place in the city. Nearly every panoramic photograph of the city contains a view of the tower, so millions of people around the world are exposed to it many times in their lifetime. This is the perfect set-up for the mere exposure effect to make it likable. Simply because we see it all the time, we start to feel that it is beautiful and think of it affectionately even though it appeared quite ugly to those who first saw it.

This same effect has occurred many times in other places with other things. In 1969, the people of Grand Rapids, Michigan, received a new giant sculpture that was to be placed in the center of town. It was a huge free-form metallic construction created by the artist Alexander Calder. While a few people thought that it was impressive, a greater number commented in the media and in letters that it was "a waste of money," "an embarrassment," and even "an abomination." However, this sculpture was highly visible, and someone passing through the downtown area could hardly avoid momentary views of it. This would add up to hundreds of glances at it over each year. As we could have easily predicted based upon its increasing familiarity, affection for this artwork grew. If you now visit Grand Rapids you will find that, much like the Eiffel Tower, this sculpture is an object of great civic pride. It appears prominently on city posters, advertising, and tourist literature, and even on local bank checks.

DO YOU LOOK LIKE YOUR DOG?

Believe it or not, we have now progressed to the point where we are getting close to the interesting part of this scientific story—namely, your face. We all are quite familiar with our own face. We see it every morning when we get up and trundle off to the bathroom. In the mirror, as we shave or put on makeup or comb our hair—there is our face, staring back at us. We are confronted with this particular pattern thousands of times each year as we pass by various reflecting surfaces. Therefore, as in the case of everything else that we have seen many times, we should be rather fond of it. This fondness was demonstrated in a clever way by psychologists Theodore Mita, Marshal Dermer, and Jeffrey Knight,[4] who photographed students at the University of Wisconsin at Milwaukee. The students received a pair of pictures of themselves and were asked which of the two they preferred. One of these pictures was just a typical photograph, printed quite normally. The second was a photograph that was printed as a mirror image, with left and right sides reversed. Virtually all of the students preferred the mirror image photo, which makes sense, because we most often see our own faces in a mirror which performs exactly this kind of reversal. When the same pairs of photos were shown to close friends, however, they chose the normal photograph as being the better-looking one. Again this makes sense, since friends are used to seeing us naturally, without the reversed image provided by a mirror.

Since we have seen our own face so often, we have probably developed an affection for that pattern, and it is also likely that we will transfer some of that sentiment to anything that is similar enough to remind us of our face. Some psychologists have argued that that explains why children who look very much like one of their parents tend to be favored and treated more lovingly by that parent. It might also explain why people end up with dogs that look something like themselves. If the general features of one breed of dog's face look something like the general features of our own face, then, all other things being equal, that breed should arouse a bit more of a warm and loving response on our part.

Little scientific work has been done on this issue, so in order to gather some data I conducted an experiment involving 104 women students at the University of British Columbia. First, the students were shown slides containing portraits of four different dog breeds. Each portrait was simply the head of a dog looking toward the camera. The four breeds included an English Springer Spaniel, a Beagle, a Siberian Husky, and a Basenji. For each dog, the women simply rated how much they liked the look of the dog, how friendly they thought it was, how loyal they thought it might be, and how intelligent it appeared to be.

Afterwards I asked some questions about the women and their lifestyles. As part of this, they were asked to look at a series of schematic sketches of hairstyles and to indicate which was their own most typical style. I was not interested in details of their coiffure, but only in certain general characteristics. Specifically I divided these hair styles into two groups. The first group contained longer styles that covered the ears, while the second group showed shorter hair or longer hair that was pulled back, so that the woman's ears were visible. The results were rather interesting. In general, women with longer hair tended to prefer the Springer Spaniel and the Beagle, rating these breeds as more likable, friendly, loyal, and intelligent. Women with shorter hair and visible ears tended to rate the Siberian Husky and the Basenji more highly on these same dimensions.

These results may well have to do with familiarity effects on liking.

Longer hair has a framing effect around a woman's face, much like the framing effect caused by the longer, lopped ears of the spaniel or Beagle. Shorter hair gives more visible, unframed lines to the sides of the woman's face and allows her to see her own ears. Both the Siberian Husky and the Basenji lack the drooped ears that frame the face like long hair, and both have clearly visible pricked ears. We are not talking about a universal preference—some women with short hair preferred the long-eared dogs and vice-versa—but the size of this effect is large enough to be statistically reliable. Taking this result at face value (no pun intended), the data might suggest that we have some preference for dogs whose appearance is somewhat reminiscent of our own, confirming the folk psychological belief that we look like our dogs to some degree.

Still, one must be careful and conservative in supporting the claim that we look like our dogs. Some cases that are offered as evidence for this theory are flawed. Like folk music, folk psychology is often a bit out of tune. The most common example that people give me in support of the look-alike theory is Winston Churchill. He was, of course, the British prime minister who helped to guide England through the dark days of World War II. I can't count the number of times people have told me that "he looked just like his pet Bulldog." The fact that Winston Churchill in his mature years looked like a Bulldog is indisputable. The round full face, the flattened features, the jowly cheeks, the large wide mouth, the skin folds around the eyes all look much like those of the English Bulldog. The problem is that Churchill did not own a Bulldog. The British often consider the Bulldog as the symbol of their country, and Churchill was a leading political figure in Britain. This is what probably led to the erroneous conclusion in the public mind that the great man who looked like a Bulldog, and whose country was represented by a Bulldog, also owned a pet Bulldog!

Occasionally, someone will correct the above statement with a quick "Oh, Churchill didn't have a Bulldog, he had a Pug." As far as looks are concerned, I suppose that Churchill certainly looked more like a Pug than like an Afghan Hound. I personally think that Churchill is better as a Bulldog than a Pug, but a Pug would have a certain passing resemblance to his countenance. At his country home at Chartwell one could find Churchill surrounded by several dogs. Three of them belonged to his children. It was his daughter Mary who owned the Pug. The reason why some people have the impression that the Pug belonged to Churchill (aside from the look-alike factor) is that Churchill once wrote a poem about the dog. It came about when the Pug was ill and Churchill decided to write a playful little rhyme to cheer up his daughter:

> Oh, what is the matter with poor Puggy-wug?
> Pet him and kiss him and give him a hug.
> Run and fetch him a suitable drug.
> Wrap him up tenderly all in a rug.
> That is the way to cure Puggy-wug.

Churchill's own dog certainly had not been selected on the basis of visual similarities. If you could have looked at Churchill's bedroom, curled up around his feet on the bed you would have found a Poodle named Rufus (plate 5). With his narrow pointed muzzle, clean unwrinkled face, and close-set eyes, this dog did not look even faintly like his master. Yet this was a truly loved companion. Rufus was with Churchill on many of his trips, and even hobnobbed with Franklin D. Roosevelt's dog Fala on several occasions. Once, the two dogs played together below decks on the U.S. battleship *Augusta,* while their masters discussed major policy matters that would determine the course of World War II.

Churchill would often talk to Rufus in much the same playful manner and tone that he used when talking to his children. He would sit the dog on his lap and begin a discourse with something like "Listen to me, dear. You might learn something, and then later you may offer your personal comments and insights." It was never clear whether the comments that followed were intended only for the dog, or were actually aimed at human listeners who might be nearby.

Sometimes it was quite obvious that the dog was the sole focus of his conversation. For instance, one evening Churchill was at his usual home, Chequers. The film *Oliver Twist* was being shown, and, as usual, Rufus was seated on his master's lap. The film had just reached the point where the evil Bill Sikes is about to drown his dog (the only living thing that had remained loyal to him). As this heart-rending scene began to unfold, Churchill reached over and covered Rufus's eyes. "Don't look now, dear. I'll tell you about it afterwards," he was heard to whisper to the dog.

One might suggest that a Poodle was not actually Churchill's choice for a favorite dog, but rather some accidental match that just worked out somehow. This, however, is not true. Rufus was Churchill's own choice, and when the original Rufus died, the great man replaced him with another who looked virtually identical to the first one. "He is named Rufus II—but the II is silent," Churchill explained.

Obviously, folk psychologists should look at cases other than Winston Churchill if they want to prove that people choose dogs that look like themselves. While there may be some inclination for us to favor dogs whose appearance is vaguely similar to our own, this is just a tendency, not a compelling force.

Chapter Five

A Personality Primer

How do we actually choose our dogs? Unfortunately, we often do so by paging our way through glossy books with beautiful pictures of perfect dogs. In these books all of the dogs, regardless of breed, are described as being "intelligent, loyal, and a good family dog." In the end we pick some breed that looks handsome, or that we have seen in the movies or on TV, or one that has been recommended by a friend. Then, most people who are trying to pick carefully will probably go to a breeder who has a new litter of puppies. The moment people stand in front of a box or kennel filled with puppies, it's all over. Everybody loves a puppy—every puppy. Psychologists have shown that this is partly due to the way that our brains are wired. We have an automatic response to those faces, with their short noses and large eyes and maybe even their smell. These are the same characteristics that human babies have, and it makes good sense for the survival of the species. We sense these characteristics and we want to care for and nurture the individual who has them, hence we love, nurture, and protect babies—and puppies. In the end we go home with our new pet, who may be a marvellous choice, or may be a disaster.

A person should never choose a dog simply because the puppies are cute and lovable. Back in the first chapter I mentioned that approximately half of the dogs purchased as puppies end up returned, abandoned, or destroyed by the end of the second year of their lives. All of these dogs, however, started out as darling and endearing puppies. Their fate, however, depends on more than their charming appearance which produces a "love reflex" in us, and it involves more than the joy one gets from interacting with a playful puppy. How much you will love the adult dog is all a matter of "fit." A good fit involves choosing a breed of dog that is appropriate for the personality of its owner.

PERSONALITY TYPES

First let me make clear what I mean by "personality." In everyday conversation, we use the word in phrases like "She's got personality" or "He is very bright but he doesn't have much personality." In these instances we are using "personality" to mean a set of desirable characteristics, such as a sense of humor, friendliness, good social skills, some evidence of warmth and caring, and so forth. This is not the way psychologists use the word, since, if we accepted that definition, we would have to say that Jack the Ripper or Attila the Hun had no personality at all!

There is another way that we sometimes use the word "personality" in our everyday conversation. When someone says, "Tell me about Peter's personality," you might respond by saying something like "He's the aggressive type. He sort of pushes people around and tries to dominate them," or, "He's really one of those warm and friendly kinds of people. He'll always help you when you are in trouble." Notice that this involves categorizing people into separate groups on the basis of their behavior. Psychologists refer to this as classifying people into personality *types,* a word that we often use in everyday language when we call someone an "aggressive type" or an "ambitious type" or a "loving type" of person. Since personality is an essential element in our discussion of the compatibility between a person and a particular breed of dog, it is worthwhile to take a moment to look at its scientific basis.

There is a long history of psychological classification of people into personality types. We can trace this kind of thinking all the way back to Hippocrates, the Greek physician who lived around 400 B.C. and who is usually credited with being the "Father of Medicine." His name is most frequently associated with the Hippocratic Oath, which in various modified forms is still often required to be taken by medical students at their graduation. Hippocrates also developed what may be the oldest formal theory of personality.

According to Hippocrates, people could be classified into four personality types, which were supposed to depend on the concentrations of four types of bodily fluids, called *humors*. The four humors were blood, black bile, yellow bile, and phlegm. The *sanguine* personality, with an excess of blood, was cheerful and easygoing. The *melancholic* personality type had an excess of black bile and was depressed and moody. The *choleric* type, with an excess of yellow bile, was aggressive and excitable, while the *phlegmatic* type, with an excess of phlegm, was calm and unresponsive.

Hippocrates' theory, with its view that body chemistry determines personality, has survived in some form for more than 2,500 years, and the words describing these types are now part of the language. Thus to be sanguine about something means to be comfortable, happy, and optimistic. The word "melancholy" is used to mean sadness and depression, as in the old torch song "Melancholy Baby." Today we tend to use the word "phlegmatic" for a person who doesn't say much. The slang phrase "hot under the collar," describing someone who is angry, comes from the phrase "hot and under the choler," meaning that a person was acting the way a choleric personality would.

No scientist today believes that personality is really determined by these four humors. These primitive interpretations of body chemistry have been superseded by our more detailed understanding of physiology. The personality theorist who is looking for physical factors that might cause particular behavior patterns is most likely to study hormones and neurotransmitters, or to look for chemicals produced within the brain, such as endorphins. However, the classification of personality into these four types is still occasionally written about seriously. Hans J. Eysenck, a German-born British psychologist, is well known as a personality theorist who has focused on the biological basis of behavior. In recent years he has reconsidered Hippocrates' four personality types in light of what we know about human behavior today. He reached the conclusion that division of people into sanguine, melancholic, choleric, and phlegmatic types still has some usefulness as a descriptive way of classifying people according to their behaviors, even if the underlying biological mechanisms that that early physician proposed are all wrong.

Many other schemes have been used to classify people according to types. Once a category is established, everybody who fits into that category is said to have the same personality type. Some of the personality types that have been proposed include authoritarian, submissive, introverted, extroverted, stable, neurotic, self-actualized, moral, Machiavellian, masculine, feminine, and many, many more.

PERSONALITY TRAITS

When you actually try to classify people on the basis of personality types, you immediately run into difficulties. The main problem is that most people are complex and simply don't fit into a single type. Consider, for example, the fictional character of the Godfather, played by Marlon Brando in the films *The Godfather* and *Godfather, Part II*. What personality type is this character? Well, using Hippocrates' system we would be hard pressed to classify him. In some scenes he is clearly aggressive, willing to have people killed on his behalf, touchy, sensitive, and easily insulted. Taken together these characteristics might identify him as a choleric personality type. In other scenes he is extremely quiet, a listener rather than a talker, and he is controlled and restrained in situations where others are excited. Taken together these characteristics might define him as being a phlegmatic type. In still other scenes he is extremely loving and caring toward his children, his grandchildren, and his wife. In the opening wedding scenes in *The Godfather*, he demonstrates a confident, optimistic demeanor that could classify him as sanguine. So what is the true personality type of this character? Because of problems like this, many modern psychologists have decided that trying to pigeonhole people into discrete groupings or types simply doesn't work.

Personality theory is not the first case where psychologists have had to abandon simply categorizing people into fixed classes. The same thing happened when psychologists tried to deal with intelligence. Initially the desire was to classify everybody into one of three types: normal intelligence, brilliant, and stupid. It became obvious that this didn't work either because so many people are brilliant in some areas and almost witless in others. Consider a person whose name has become virtually synonymous with genius—the Nobel Prize–winning physicist Albert Einstein. Discoverer of the law of relativity and the photoelectric effect, he was not only a brilliant physicist but also had a high degree of verbal intelligence, as his many philosophical writings show. He was also a talented cello player. He was not, however, without areas of mental incompetence. His intellectual downfall was simple arithmetic. His addition and subtraction skills were so bad that his personal checkbook was always completely out of agreement with the records of the bank. Along similar lines I can tell you stories about a brilliant research chemist who can't follow a simple recipe to successfully bake a cake, or a renowned clinical psychologist who can't figure out the first steps toward housebreaking his dog. In all of these individuals, the tendency to act intelligently and the tendency to act stupidly are found in the same person. Whether we are dealing with a genius or a dolt seems to depend on the situation, the problem that has to be solved, and the specific abilities required.

Instead of simply putting people into categories labeled "intelligent" or "stupid," contemporary intelligence tests measure a broad range of specific abilities. Thus a modern intelligence test might give separate scores for a number of different mental capacities, typically including vocabulary, mathematical ability, problem solving, reading ability, creative thinking, memory, general knowledge, and many others. As in the cases I mentioned before, it is possible for people to have a mixture of scores, going from very high on some skills to rather low on others. Looking at a set of such scores, it is no longer really possible to classify a person as the "smart type" or the "dumb type."

Many psychologists who study personality adopted an approach similar to that used by scientists who study intelligence. They began to measure a set of specific aspects of personality. We can't call these aspects "abilities," since they are behavioral tendencies rather than skills. Instead these are called *personality traits* or sometimes *personality factors.*

Some of the most popular personality tests today are designed to measure five specific traits, including how neurotic a person is, how introverted versus extroverted, how conscientious, and how agreeable they are. The fifth trait is called openness, and it includes how much you like new experiences versus a predictable routine. The reason that these five traits were selected is that they give a broad, stable picture of a person's personality. In fact, these particular trait measurements are so widely used that they have earned the title of the "big five." The problem with the big five measures of personality is that the tests involved are usually quite long, commonly well over 100 items, and sometimes as many as 350. In addition the scoring is quite complicated and often has to be done by computer.

Sometimes psychologists need only selected measures of personality traits which focus on particular aspects of the person's behaviors or behavior tendencies that are important in specific situations. For this reason, shorter tests have been designed to measure a few specific aspects of personality. Some of these measure *temperament traits,* which are personality factors that influence the person's emotional state and are therefore important to understanding how a person might deal with stress or conflict. These include measures of how nervous, anxious, impulsive, or excitable a person is. Other tests measure *character traits,* which include how honest, moral, and scrupulous the individual is.

Mental orientation traits, which have to do with the way people think and what they think about, are often measured when individuals are trying to select a job or profession. There is a firm belief among psychologists that your personality plays an important role in your choice of a career. For this reason personality tests are often used to help guide people in their choice of a vocation (and also to tell employers if a job applicant is the best person to fill their needs). One successful vocational choice test measures two mental orientation traits, namely the person's preference for dealing with people versus things, and whether the individual prefers to work with data and facts or with ideas and theories.

THE INTERPERSONAL PERSONALITY TRAITS

When you are trying to select a dog that will make you happy, your most important characteristics are the *interpersonal traits,* which have to do with how you get along in the social world, respond to people, use love or power, try to manipulate the behaviors of others, and so forth. These traits are so important because dogs are brought into a family not as objects to be looked at, or machines to be manipulated, but rather as companions, partners, friends, or even as added family members.

The fact that we treat dogs as part of our social life (like friends, associates, or companions) is perhaps best shown by the fact that we talk to dogs. Not only do we talk to them, but we talk to them in very specific ways. Consider the results of an informal study that I conducted when I was giving a workshop on human and dog relationships for a group of around 150 dog owners. I asked the audience, "How many of you talk to your dogs? Before you answer this, you should know that I don't mean the kind of talking that we do when we tell the dogs what to do (such as when we want them to sit or come) but rather the kind of talking that we might do to another adult or a child." When they responded with a show of hands, it appeared to me that every single person in that room was admitting that they spoke to their dogs. When I went on to ask them to give examples, virtually all of them said that they usually greet their dogs when they come home and say good-bye when they leave. Another common form of "conversation" involves complimenting the dogs—telling them that they are pretty or handsome. Many people admitted to telling the dogs how they felt about their behaviors, such as calling the dog silly, bad, or clever. Most also admitted that they often ask questions about matters of interest to their canine companions, such as "Do you want to go for a walk?" or "Do you want a snack?" In addition, the vast majority of the audience said that they occasionally asked questions that the dog really could not be expected to answer (or even care much about), such as "Do you think it's going to rain today, or should I go to work without my umbrella?" or something like "Do you think I should dress up for this party or can I get away with casual clothes?"

Psychologists Kathy Hirsh-Pasek and Rebecca Treiman were actually able to show that there is a special form of language that we use when we are talking to dogs.[1] We all know that our language changes under different circumstances. In formal situations, such as when we are talking to authorities or to an audience, we use more reserved and ceremonial language than we do when we are talking with family and friends. Written language is more information-packed and more complex than spoken language. This is why, when you read a written piece aloud, it often sounds stiff, complicated, and convoluted—not at all like conversational language. There is also a special kind of language that we use when we talk to children. It is simplified language, often done in a singsong rhythm, sometimes in higher voice tones, with lots of repetitions. Psychologists have called this special language form *motherese,* since it is heard most commonly when mothers are talking to their infants and young children. It is not confined to mothers, however, since virtually everyone, whether male or female, parent or not, tends to lapse into it when talking to a very young child. Hirsh-Pasek and Treiman found that the way we talk to dogs is very similar to motherese, and they dubbed this form of language *doggerel.*

The doggerel that we speak to our canine companions is quite different from the speech that we use around other adults. For example, the average length of an utterance to an adult is ten or eleven words, while for dogs it is around four words. We speak a lot more in imperatives or commands to our dogs, such as "Come over here" or "Get off the chair." We also ask twice as many questions of our dogs as we do of humans, even though, as I noted earlier, we really don't seem to expect any answers. These are usually trivial conversational questions, like "How do you feel today, Lassie?" We also use a lot more tag questions when we speak to dogs. A tag question is an observation that turns into a question at the very end, such as "You're thirsty, aren't you?" When we talk to our dogs we mostly talk about the present. In fact, around 90 percent of doggerel is in the present tense, which is half again as much as our normal speech to adult humans. When we talk to our dogs we are also twenty times more likely to repeat, partially repeat, or rephrase and repeat things than we would with humans. An example of rephrasing and repeating would be "You are a good dog. What a good dog."

A major difference between doggerel and motherese is in terms of something that we call *deixis,* which refers to sentences that point out specific bits of information: "This is a chair" or "That bowl is blue." Sentences of this sort are usually viewed as some attempt at instructing other individuals. Motherese contains many more statements of this sort than does normal speech to adults. Doggerel, on the other hand, contains only half as many such statements as does conversation with adult humans. Apparently, most of our speech to dogs is of a more social nature, and whether the dogs learn anything from it is of little concern to us.

A major difference between doggerel and other speech is the tendency to occasionally mimic the sounds that our dogs make. For example, one evening when I was speaking to my son, Benjamin, on the phone, I could hear his Miniature Poodle, Brandy, in the background. Brandy gave a sharp bark and then made a sound like an elongated "arowel." My son paused in our conversation to talk to the dog. "'Arowel' yourself, Brandy. I'm on the phone right now. I'll get to you afterwards." His "arowel" perfectly mimicked the sound that the dog made. Mothers seldom imitate their child's random speech sounds, and to imitate the speech sounds or tones of another adult would probably be considered mocking or insulting. For some reason, imitating dog sounds is just another device we use to keep our conversations with our canine companions going.

The overall sound of doggerel is quite different from the sound of our speech when we talk to mature humans. We use a higher tone, and we emphasize our intonations and emotional phrasings. We use a lot of diminutives, such as when we refer to a walk as a "walkie" or a ball as a "ballie" or the dog as "cutie." We also distort words and phrases to make them less formal as when we use terms like "wanna" or "gotcha." So if you hear a woman ask in a sing-song voice, "Do ya wanna go for a walkie?" you can probably safely infer that she is talking to her dog; there is a small chance that she is talking to a very young child, but virtually no chance that she is talking to her husband or an adult friend.

The existence of doggerel suggests that we interact with dogs socially in the same way that we interact with other people, or at least with children. However, we have numerous social interactions with our dogs in addition to simply talking to them. We attempt to mold the behaviors of our dogs, much the way that we try to shape the behavior of our children (and of course our spouses or partners). We play with our dogs, socialize with them, and often treat them much as if they were actually four-legged people in fur coats. For all of these reasons, it is the interpersonal aspects of our personalities that prove to be the most important in determining what kind of relationship we have with our dogs.

However, before we look at how specific personality patterns of people determine their reactions to specific breeds of dogs, we first have to take a little side trip to look at the behaviors of dogs.

Chapter Six

A New
Dog Classification Method

While the actual number of dog breeds in the world is not really known, more than four hundred breeds are officially acknowledged by various kennel clubs around the world. A purebred dog of a certain type is one which will breed true to a certain set of characteristics. In the United States, England, and Canada, there must be a recorded genealogy that goes back for at least three generations within the same recognizable breed before a dog can be called "purebred." Many national dog registries are old enough that the genealogies go back hundreds of generations; *The Foxhound Kennel Stud Book,* for example, was first published in England in 1844. The number of dogs in the various breed registries is often quite large, and in fact, the American Kennel Club (AKC) has enrolled over 38 million dogs since it began in 1884.

Many of today's dog breeds have a common ancestry and have become distinct simply because breeders began a process of selection based on specific physical characteristics. For example, Cairn Terriers and West Highland White Terriers started out as the same breed. In fact, puppies in the same litters were often sorted out, with the white ones called West Highland Whites and the other colors called Cairns. It was found that if you separated out the white terriers and bred them together you always got white offspring, which allowed separation of the breeds. Today the standards for these two breeds indicate that the West Highlands can only be white, while the Cairns can be "any color except white." Structurally and behaviorally the two breeds remain virtually identical, so if your personality is suitable for a West Highland White Terrier, then (color preferences aside) you will also be happy with a Cairn Terrier.

There are many similar instances in other breeds. The Belgian Shepherds consist of three breeds, the Groenendael (or Belgian Sheepdog), which is black; the Belgian Malinois, which is short-haired; and the Belgian Tervuren, which is long-haired with a black-tipped, reddish mahogany or fawn-colored coat. Except for these coat differences the dogs are virtually identical. Hence if you like any one of the Belgian Shepherds you should like the other two breeds. Just how trivial breed differences can be is, to my mind at least, best shown by the Norwich Terrier and the Norfolk Terrier. Both are splendid little terriers whose only difference is that the Norwich has pointed ears, while the Norfolk has drop ears. For years, both types could be shown under the general heading of Norwich Terrier. In 1964 in Britain and in 1979 in the United States, the kennel clubs decided to divide them into two breeds based on ear shape. There is no other difference between these breeds. Obviously, if your personality matches the temperament of the Norwich Terrier, you will equally love the Norfolk Terrier, unless you have an overpowering need for a particular ear shape (which may also reflect upon your personality).

TRADITIONAL BREED GROUPS

From the time of the Renaissance, people interested in dogs found that it was convenient to classify the various breeds into broad groupings, according to their functions. Early authorities used fairly large categories, such as "beast dog" (for hunting dogs), "coach dog" (which included guard dogs), and "vermin dog" (containing mostly the terriers). In England one of the earliest classification schemes reflected the popular prejudice against immigrants by including a separate category called "foreign dog." With the founding of the Kennel Club of England in 1873, a more formal breed classification scheme was introduced and, with minor modifications, the American and Canadian kennel clubs used the British system as the starting point for their own.

Remember that the grouping of dog breeds is based on their functions. Thus it is not surprising that the first group is called *sporting dogs* in the U.S. but it is more accurately called *gun dogs* by the British. These are the dogs that are supposed to assist a hunter. In this group are found the dog breeds that seek out game, including some that indicate the presence of their quarry by pointing at it, and some that flush or spring the game so that the hunter can shoot it. This group also includes dogs specifically designed to reduce the labor and discomfort associated with hunting by retrieving game both on land and from the water. The list of sporting dogs includes some of the most recognizable breeds of dogs, such as the spaniels, pointers, retrievers, and setters as well as some multipurpose dogs such as the Weimaraner and the Vizsla.

The second group of dog breeds is the *hounds,* which are also hunting dogs, but of a much more independent variety. Some of these are supposed to track their quarry by the faint odor they leave as they move over the landscape, hence these are called "scent hounds." Others have keen eyesight and tremendous speed. Their task is to visually locate their quarry in the distance and run it down, hence they are called "sight hounds." The hunter is needed only if the game finds refuge in a den, burrow, or tree. In all other cases, the hounds are supposed to be able to dispatch their target when they catch it, without any human intervention. This is a very diverse group, which includes the fastest runners in dogdom, such as the Greyhound, Afghan Hound, and Saluki. It also includes dogs that are still slow even at full speed, such as the Dachshund and the Basset Hound. In addition, this group contains dogs that were specially bred to hunt particular kinds of game, including the Irish Wolfhound, Scottish Deerhound, Otterhound, Norwegian Elkhound, Foxhounds, and Coonhounds. As you can see, all of these names contain the name of the quarry in their own breed label. Included in this group is the Dachshund, since *dach* is the German word for badger, which was the game that these little dogs, with their powerful jaws, were supposed to hunt.

The *terrier* group includes a broad range of big and small dogs.

These dogs were designed to keep farms and farm buildings free of vermin, such as rats or foxes. The word "terrier" comes from the Latin root *terra,* meaning earth or ground, which provides a hint about the techniques these dogs frequently use—digging underground, or wiggling their way into burrows or dens to find their targets. For this purpose many were deliberately kept small. Some were also bred to have rough, hard, or wiry coats, which would serve as protection against abrasion from rocks and rough ground, and could additionally provide a kind of armor against the teeth of their quarry. Some of these small, short-legged terriers were carried in a basket on horseback during hunts. They were put to work only when the game animal had been driven into its den. Some other, larger terriers with long straight legs were designed to run with horses and hounds on the hunt. They could also pursue fast-moving vermin over open ground. The names of terriers often reflect the geographical location where they were first bred, such as the Australian Terrier, Airedale Terrier, Scottish Terrier, Irish Terrier, Manchester Terrier, Welsh Terrier, Kerry Blue Terrier, or West Highland White Terrier. Some others carry names of individuals that were supposedly important in their development, such as the Jack Russell Terrier, or the Dandie Dinmont Terrier.

The *working dog* group is a set of dogs with various practical functions, such as guarding or protecting property or people, pulling or hauling loads of materials, or doing search and rescue work. All of these tasks require strong, muscular dogs, which range in size from medium to large. Among the working dogs are popular guard dogs such as the Doberman Pinscher and Rottweiler. Dogs designed for pulling sleds or carts or for general rescue work include the Alaskan Malamute, Siberian Husky, Bernese Mountain Dog, Great Pyrenees, Saint Bernard, and Newfoundland.

The American Kennel Club also has a separate *herding dog* group, although in Britain these dogs are considered part of the working dog group. Many herding dogs are indispensable in their ability to keep herds of sheep and cattle together, and to move them under the direction of a human shepherd. The livestock generally move in response to the barking of the dog, who may also circle the animals and nip at their heels. Some dogs simply stare at members of the flock in order to freeze them in position or to move them in a given direction. Other dogs in this group serve mostly as guards, warding off wolves or coyotes that might threaten their charges. The herding group includes the various varieties of Collies, Corgis, and Belgian Shepherds, plus the familiar Old English Sheepdog and the German Shepherd, and more exotic dogs such as the Puli and the Briard, among others.

In the *toy* dog group we find a collection of dogs that were bred specifically to provide companionship. These were supposed to be small, lightweight, portable, and agreeable animals, the sort of pet that aristocratic ladies could carry with them. Some of these dogs, such as the Pekingese and the Japanese Chin, were originally owned by royalty. No one outside the royal families was allowed to own these breeds, and any attempt to take one of these dogs out of their country of origin was punishable by death. These dogs were often prized more for their looks than for any other characteristic. Thus the Pekingese was supposed to look like the Chinese Celestial Lion, and each year a contest was held to determine the dog that best approximated this ideal. Other toy dogs were designed simply to be smaller versions of familiar large dogs. Thus the Cavalier King Charles Spaniel and the Papillon were miniature spaniels, the Italian Greyhound is a miniature version of the larger Greyhound, and the Toy Poodle is a scaled-down version of the Standard Poodle. Other dogs found in this group include tiny terriers like the Yorkshire Terrier and the Toy Manchester Terrier, plus some dogs with extremely fancy coats, like the Shih Tzu or Pomeranian, or no coat at all, like the Chinese Crested.

For the American Kennel club, the *non-sporting* group is a potpourri of dogs, made up of those breeds that simply don't seem to fit into any of the other groups. In Britain, there is no comparable catchall classification; most of the non-sporting breeds are recognized, but they are distributed over the other groups. Certainly an argument could be made that some of these breeds truly belong in other groups. For example, a case could be made for placing the Dalmatian and Schipperke in the working group since both once served as watchdogs—the Dalmatian for carriages and the Schipperke for barges. The Poodle could be put in the sporting group, since it started out as a retriever and even today does well in field trials for retrievers. Similarly, the Bichon Frise could happily be placed in the toy group as a small, fluffy, and pleasant companion dog. Others would be much more difficult to place, such as the Chow Chow, which was originally bred to serve as a food item, the wrinkled Chinese Shar-Pei, the Tibetan Spaniel (which is not a true spaniel), or the Tibetan Terrier (which is not a true terrier).

Even if we accept these groupings of breeds as being sensible for some uses, they are not really practical for our purposes. To match a dog with a person's personality, we need a way to group the various breeds of dogs on the basis of their behavioral characteristics and their temperament. The only one of the existing breed groups which comes close to being consistent in terms of temperament is the terrier group. Most terriers are independent, tough dogs, with a predisposition to bark when they get excited (and they get excited very easily). Within the other breed groups there is a wide variety of behavior styles and temperaments. For instance, the hound group includes the friendly and sociable Beagles and Basset Hounds and also the sharp, tough-minded Rhodesian Ridgebacks and Basenjis. The toy group includes the solitary and independent Manchester Terrier and the sociable "love-sponge" that is the Cavalier King Charles Spaniel. The sporting group includes the stable and unflappable Clumber Spaniel and also the playfully hyperactive Irish Setter. The herding group includes the submissive and sometimes skittish Shetland Sheepdog and the dominant and self-confident German Shepherd. If we want to match people to groups of dogs, we will have to do better than the kennel clubs in classifying the dog breeds.

THE DOG TRAITS THAT MATTER

My first task, then, was to determine the various characteristics of dogs that had the most influence on people's satisfaction and lifestyles. I started to make a list, beginning with the dog's activity level, its intelligence, its friendliness, and so forth. It quickly became clear to me that my list might be very idiosyncratic, and reflect the fact that I live in a city and keep my dogs mostly as companions. The job that my dogs have, if they can be said to have one, is to compete in obedience competitions and to demonstrate for my classes what dogs can actually learn. To get a good general picture of the characteristics of dogs that are important, I needed some other viewpoints. I therefore contacted eleven dog experts: two veterinarians, two dog obedience instructors, two dog obedience judges, two conformation or show dog judges, one field dog trial judge, a tracking trial judge, and a dog behavior analyst. All of these people knew a lot about dogs, so I asked them to simply make a list of all of the characteristics that they thought might be important in determining how happy a person would be with any breed of dog.

Next I took the eleven lists that my group of experts had generated, plus my own, and sat down and sorted through them. These lists included just about every imaginable dimension of dog behavior. My experts did not just indicate that activity level was important, but distinguished between indoor activity, outdoor activity, and general restlessness. Sociability and dominance were not single dimensions in the eyes of these experts, but had to be subdivided into how friendly or dominant a dog was to a variety of different individuals. There were separate listings for their sociability around adults, with children, within the family, with strange adults and unfamiliar children. The experts even included sociability around familiar dogs, unfamiliar dogs, and other animals. The list of behavior dimensions also covered items like the amount of grooming that the dog needs and whether it sheds or not.

I was eventually able to simmer these items down to what I felt were the twenty-two most critical dimensions of dog behavior. To be on the final list a characteristic had to appear on the lists of more than half of my experts, and it had to be a dimension that other dog experts would be able to actually evaluate for any dog. Next I contacted a large number of different dog specialists, including veterinarians, dog trainers of several sorts (basic obedience, competition training, agility and other dog sport trainers, protection dog trainers, etc.), dog judges of all kinds (obedience, conformation, field trials, search and rescue, tracking, terrier trials), several writers of dog books, and some canine psychologists and behavior analysts. I gave each of them a list of dog breeds and asked them to rate each of the breeds that they felt that they really knew well, on each of the twenty-two dimensions. Since I knew that this would involve a major commitment of time, I gave each expert a list of forty breeds. Each expert had a different list, so that all of the major breeds would eventually be covered. The experts could add any breeds that they knew particularly well and wanted to include, or drop any breeds that they didn't know well enough to rate. When I sat down and did this task myself, it took me over three hours to make my own ratings of forty breeds. Because of this I was really worried that not many experts would actually take the time to complete this chore. It was thus a pleasant surprise to find that ninety-six busy professionals took the time to return a set of ratings to me.

When I looked at the data I found that I had 133 breeds of dogs that at least twenty of the experts had rated on the twenty-two behavior dimensions. Now I had to use this information to create a new dog classification scheme, based on the way that dogs behave, rather than what they look like or what jobs we give them to do. This involved some pretty high-powered statistical techniques that are probably of interest only to psychologists, dog behaviorists, and other scientists. I've tucked that information into a technical note at the end of the book for those people who do want the details. For the nonscientist I can say that the ultimate aim of nearly a month of statistical analysis was to identify clusters or groups of dogs, all of which had certain shared characteristics. These are the characteristics which appear to be important to people and play a role in breed selection. I resorted to a computer analysis and statistical procedures, rather than my own personal judgment, in order to be as objective as possible. In the end I found myself looking at a new classification system for dogs. Not the traditional sporting, hound, terrier, working, herding, non-sporting, and toy classifications of the American Kennel Club, but a seven-category system based on how the breeds relate to people.

THE NEW BREED GROUPINGS

I have tried to give each of the seven final breed groups a descriptive name based on the behavioral characteristics that the computer analysis indicated were most distinctive about the groups. If my dog experts are correct in their ratings and if the computer analysis has done what it is supposed to do, then these dog groupings are different from any previous classification system. Because the statistical analysis has classified dogs on the basis of behavioral similarities, this should mean that if you like any one breed of dog in a particular group, then you will probably like most of the other dogs in that group. Obviously some dogs in each group will be a closer match to the ideal dog for any individual. However, since the dogs in each group share a set of important characteristics, you should find yourself liking (or disliking) all of the dogs in a group to a similar extent.

Let's now look at the individual dog groups.

GROUP 1. FRIENDLY DOGS

(includes affectionate and genial dogs)

Bearded Collie	Flat-Coated Retriever
Bichon Frise	Golden Retriever
Border Terrier	Keeshond
Brittany	Labrador Retriever
Cavalier King Charles Spaniel	Nova Scotia Duck Tolling
Cocker Spaniel	Retriever
Collie	Old English Sheepdog
Curly-Coated Retriever	Portuguese Water Dog
English Cocker Spaniel	Soft Coated Wheaten Terrier
English Setter	Vizsla
English Springer Spaniel	Welsh Springer Spaniel
Field Spaniel	

Friendliness and approachability are the defining characteristics of this group. All of these dogs like people and tend to seek people out. Their friendly nature makes them good companions but only fair watchdogs, at best. While most of these dogs have medium-range activity level, there is a lot of variability on this dimension. The Bichon Frise and the Cavalier King Charles Spaniels are only moderately active dogs, while the Springer Spaniels and Flat-Coated Retrievers are quite active. The dogs in this group tend not to be particularly dominant or protective, which means that they are often useless as guard dogs. Some of these breeds may sound the alarm when someone comes around, but they are often inconsistent in this job. If a burglar actually entered your home, these are dogs who would not attempt to interfere with his activities and would probably show him where you hide your jewelry—just to be hospitable. While all of these dogs benefit from a good romp and vigorous exercise, they are also quite suitable for city living where they may have to be indoors most of the time.

GROUP 2. PROTECTIVE DOGS

(includes territorial and dominant dogs)

Akita	Gordon Setter
American Staffordshire Terrier	Komondor
Boxer	Kuvasz
Briard	Puli
Bullmastiff	Rhodesian Ridgeback
Bull Terrier	Rottweiler
Chesapeake Bay Retriever	Schnauzer (Standard)
Chow Chow	Staffordshire Bull Terrier
German Wirehaired Pointer	Weimaraner
Giant Schnauzer	

In some ways, this group is exactly the opposite of the Friendly group above. Any dog in this group would make a pretty good watchdog, and the larger ones make good guard dogs. These breeds tend to establish a territory, usually their home, and act quite protective about it. They are not unpleasant or unfriendly dogs at all times, but are average in their sociability with people that they know. Some, especially the Akita, Chow Chow, Rottweiler, and Komondor, can be quite suspicious of strangers, and all act initially in a standoffish or suspicious manner with unfamiliar people. If they are brought up in a friendly setting and are given the opportunity to interact with many new people, their sociability toward strangers can be increased quite a bit. Some, like the Boxers and the Schnauzers, can actually be turned around so that they seek new company. All of these dogs are muscular and quite strong, which can make them a bit of a handful when you are trying to train them. On the other hand, if you are strong enough to control them, most learn at a reasonable rate and can become quite dependable and obedient dogs.

GROUP 3. INDEPENDENT DOGS

(includes personable and strong-willed dogs)

Afghan Hound   Greyhound
Airedale Terrier   Harrier
Alaskan Malamute   Irish Setter
American Foxhound   Irish Water Spaniel
American Water Spaniel   Norwegian Elkhound
Black and Tan Coonhound   Otterhound
Borzoi   Pointer
Chinese Shar-Pei   Saluki
Dalmatian   Samoyed
English Foxhound   Siberian Husky
German Shorthaired Pointer

The dogs in this group are generally quite accepting when it comes to interacting with people, although they don't seek out human companionship the same way that the Friendly (Group 1) dogs do. The animals in this group may also be a bit pushy or dominant around other dogs. These are dogs with their own minds, who will often appear to be more interested in their own plans than in those of their human masters. This independent and headstrong nature often makes them difficult to train. Their behavior is spontaneous and also quite variable, which means that sometimes they may go to great extremes to please you, while at other times they may act as if you don't exist. All of these dogs are quite active and are happiest outdoors; some may not thrive in the city, especially if they must be indoors most of the time. Most dogs in this group, especially the Airedale, Greyhound, and Irish Setter, have a strong sense of playfulness.

GROUP 4. SELF-ASSURED DOGS

(includes spontaneous and sometimes audacious dogs)

Affenpinscher   Brussels Griffon
Australian Terrier   Cairn Terrier
Basenji   Irish Terrier

Jack Russell Terrier

Lakeland Terrier

Manchester Terrier

Miniature Pinscher

Miniature Schnauzer

Norfolk Terrier

Norwich Terrier

Schipperke

Scottish Terrier

Shih Tzu

Silky Terrier

Smooth Fox Terrier

Welsh Terrier

West Highland White Terrier

Wire Fox Terrier

Wirehaired Pointing Griffon

Yorkshire Terrier

This group comes the closest to a typical kennel club category, since most of the animals in it are terriers, toy terriers, or descended from terriers, with the exception of the Basenji, Schipperke, and Wirehaired Pointing Griffon. These dogs are mostly compact in size, and none is truly large. Despite the fact that they are not massive, these dogs are quite sure of themselves. Of many it can be said that "there's a lot of dog in that little package." They make good watchdogs since they will readily sound the alarm when someone approaches their home. They are fairly active dogs but they are quite adaptable, suitable for both outdoor living where they have lots of room to run, and also for city living where they are indoors most of the time. They are quite spontaneous and often audacious in their behaviors, and this often makes these dogs amusing to watch. This same spontaneity and impulsiveness can sometimes make the dogs in this group difficult to train. Once you have their attention, however, they prove to be good problem solvers and willing workers.

GROUP 5. CONSISTENT DOGS

(includes self-contained and home-loving dogs)

Bedlington Terrier

Boston Terrier

Chihuahua

Dachshund

Dandie Dinmont Terrier

English Toy Spaniel (King Charles)

French Bulldog

Italian Greyhound

Japanese Chin

Lhasa Apso

Maltese

Pekingese

Pomeranian	Skye Terrier
Pug	Tibetan Terrier
Sealyham Terrier	Whippet

For the most part, this group of dogs includes breeds that are perfectly happy living in the city and put up with indoor living quite well. The central personality characteristic of these dogs is their predictability. Whether the dog is timid or pushy, placid or jumpy, its behavior from day to day will be virtually the same regardless of the time or the situation. These are small, self-contained dogs, who will allow you to be affectionate, but can live quite happily with very little caressing and are often content to rest quietly across the room from you. They like being at home, and, perhaps more than other breeds, thrive in a consistent family and social environment. Although these are accepting dogs that like people (particularly their own family), they will stand up for themselves if pushed too far. All of these breeds are on the small side, and many have been quite successful in the dog show ring because of their handsome and often unique looks.

GROUP 6. STEADY DOGS

(includes solid, good-natured, and tolerant dogs)

Basset Hound	Great Dane
Beagle	Great Pyrenees
Bernese Mountain Dog	Irish Wolfhound
Bloodhound	Mastiff
Bouvier des Flandres	Newfoundland
Bulldog	Saint Bernard
Clumber Spaniel	Scottish Deerhound

Although the dogs in this group vary quite a bit in size, from the relatively small Beagle through the medium-sized Bulldog and up to the giant Irish Wolfhound, all have a number of features in common. All tend to be quiet indoors, except for the Beagles who may occasionally "sing" with little howling sounds as they wander around. All of these breeds will settle in easily and not make a fuss if confined for long periods. On the other hand, the dogs in this group are perfectly happy if required to live outdoors most of the time. They are agreeable around people, and like human company. Solidly built, with no evidence of fragility about them, most of these dogs will tolerate more roughhousing than other breeds tend to permit, and many will even put up with rough physical handling that appears to come almost to the point of abuse. They have some of the same kind of predictability that we saw in the Consistent dogs (Group 5), meaning that their day-to-day behaviors are quite constant. These dogs are a little on the impenetrable side and tend to drift off in their thinking, making them a bit difficult to train, simply because their attention wanders. Once they have learned something, however, they do retain it well.

GROUP 7. CLEVER DOGS

(includes observant and trainable dogs)

Australian Cattle Dog	German Shepherd
Australian Shepherd	Maremma Sheepdog
Belgian Malinois	Papillon
Belgian Sheepdog	Pembroke Welsh Corgi
Belgian Tervuren	Poodle (Toy, Miniature, and
Border Collie	Standard)
Cardigan Welsh Corgi	Shetland Sheepdog
Doberman Pinscher	

These intelligent dogs have a work ethic and willingness to learn that make them the easiest breeds to train for most tasks. They are always scanning their environment for new happenings, and because of this, their behavior sometimes appears to be a spontaneous reaction to the world around them. This same feature often leads to clever and unique solutions to problems and sometimes to humorous situations. The downside is that these same watchful tendencies can occasionally distract them from the task that they were set to do. Their general vigilance also makes them good watchdogs. With perhaps the exception of the Border Collie (which has a very high activity level for urban lifestyles), these dogs are adaptable and can live reasonably well under city or indoor conditions. However, most of these dogs will also benefit from regular vigorous exercise. These are the dogs that are most often successful when complex activities have to be learned. They are people-oriented, which means that getting their attention is not usually any problem. Their competence and comprehension combined with their dedication to their masters often make them good workmates as well as good companions.

Let me remind you that these new breed groupings are based on the behavioral tendencies of the dogs, their lifestyles, and their temperaments. If you like the character and personality of one of the breeds in a group, then it is a reasonable bet that you will also like the other breeds in that group. The converse is also true. If one breed in a category has proved to be a disaster for you, then you are probably better off staying away from all of the dogs in that group.

Now that we have our dogs grouped according to the most important behavioral dimensions, our next step is to look at human personality to see which aspects are most important in predicting the dog breeds that we will love—or hate. Before we do that, it might be useful if we first get some information about your own personality. To do this, you will first have to take a little test.

Chapter Seven

Measuring Your Personality

S ince I will be talking about how a person's personality affects his
or her satisfaction with various dogs, I presume that you will
first want to know something about your own personality so
that you can find out which dog breeds are best for *you*. For that reason,
I have provided a means to measure certain aspects of your personality.
Specifically, we will measure those personality traits that affect how you
interact with people and presumably with dogs as well.

Before you go any further into this book you should spend a few minutes taking the personality test that appears below. It will provide you
with your own set of scores on the four personality traits that I will be
talking about during much of the rest of the book. When you fill out this
personality measure be careful—all of us have a tendency to want to appear "perfect." Answer the items as truthfully as you can, even if an answer is not quite as flattering as you might like. After all, you are trying to
select a dog—not to impress the world.

The test is quite simple. It consists of a set of words that are used to describe people's personal characteristics, along with the definitions of those
words. For each of these words I want you to decide how accurately the
word describes you. Select one of the answers from the scale below, and
then write the number corresponding to that answer in the space provided beside each word.

Rating Scale

1. Extremely inaccurate
2. Very inaccurate
3. Moderately inaccurate
4. Slightly inaccurate

5. Slightly accurate
6. Moderately accurate
7. Very accurate
8. Extremely accurate

For instance, suppose one of the words below is HELPFUL. If you think that this is an *extremely accurate* description of you, you would simply write the number 8 on the line to the left of the word HELPFUL. If you think that this word is a *moderately accurate* description of you, then you would write in the number 6. If HELPFUL is only a *slightly inaccurate* description of you, write the number 4 next to it, and so forth. Don't spend too long thinking about each individual word. Generally speaking, your first impressions of your personality are the most accurate.

Now, how accurately do these words describe you? Fill in the number that corresponds to your answer.

__3__ **Shy:** you lack self-confidence and tend to be uncomfortable around other people.

__7__ **Undemanding:** you don't demand or expect much from other people.

_____ **Gentle-hearted:** you are warm or kind to other people.

_____ **Outgoing:** you enjoy meeting other people.

_____ **Assertive:** you tend to be aggressive and outspoken with other people.

_____ **Cunning:** you are crafty, skillful at manipulating others, and a bit devious.

_____ **Unsympathetic:** you are not easily swayed or emotionally moved by other people's problems.

_____ **Introverted:** you feel more comfortable by yourself and are less interested in having other people around.

_____ **Unaggressive:** you tend to be mild-mannered and not forceful around others.

_____ **Not Deceptive:** you are not tricky or misleading, and tend to be straightforward when dealing with others.

_____ **Kind:** you are thoughtful, caring, and accommodating to other people.

_____ **Friendly:** you like to be with others and are open and warm around them.

_____ **Dominant:** you tend to lead others and like to command and take charge in a group.

_____ **Tricky:** you can be deceiving, or able to fool others, to get what you want.

_____ **Hard-Hearted:** you are unconcerned about other people and don't care much about their feelings.

_____ **Unsociable:** you don't enjoy meeting people or being in the company of others.

Once you have entered all of your answers, we next have to compute your scores. The score sheets will walk you through the simple arithmetic involved (each calculation takes only about a minute). We will be measuring four separate aspects of your personality: extroversion, dominance, trust, and warmth. Exactly what each of these individual personality traits means, and what your scores say about your behavior as a person, will become clearer in the next chapters. First, however, you need to find your own personal scores.

Start by computing your **extroversion** score. Using the score sheet marked "Extroversion," begin by entering the number that you put beside FRIENDLY on the score sheet and then the number you put beside OUTGOING. Add these two numbers plus an additional 20 points to get Total 1. Now enter the numbers corresponding to your ratings for IN-TROVERTED and UNSOCIABLE and add them together to get Total 2. Next, subtract Total 2 from Total 1 to get your final extroversion score. As an example: If your scores were **Friendly** = 7, **Outgoing** = 6, **Intro-**

EXTROVERSION

1. Add the following two scores
   and then add 20.

   ____ **Friendly**

   + ____ **Outgoing**

   + 20

   = ____ Total 1

2. Add the following two scores.

   ____ **Introverted**

   + ____ **Unsociable**

   = ____ Total 2

3. Next subtract Total 2 from Total 1.

   ____ Total 1

   − ____ Total 2

   = ____ Your **Extroversion** Score

4. Check the text to find the interpretation of your score.

   ✓ **High**

   ____ **Medium**

   ____ **Low**

---

verted = 5, **Unsociable** = 4, then Total 1 is 7+6+20=33 and Total 2 is 5+4=9. Subtracting Total 2 from Total 1 gives you 33−9=24. If these were your actual answers, this would mean that your extroversion score was 24.

The interpretation of your extroversion score is as follows. If you are a woman, a score of 28 or more is highly extroverted, a score of 20 or less is low on extroversion, while scores of 21 through 27 are medium range. If you are a man, a score of 28 or more is high, a score of 19 or less is low, while scores of 20 through 27 are medium. Make a check mark on the score sheet in the place provided to indicate whether you are high, medium, or low on this scale. Later on I will tell you what this means in terms of your personality and the kinds of dogs that you might be most comfortable with.

DOMINANCE

1. Add the following two scores   2. Add the following two scores.
   and then add 20.

   ____ **Dominant**   ____ **Shy**

   + ____ **Assertive**   + ____ **Unaggressive**

   + 20

   = ____ Total 1   = ____ Total 2

3. Next subtract Total 2 from Total 1.

   ____ Total 1

   − ____ Total 2

   = ____ Your **Dominance** Score

4. Check the text to find the interpretation of your score.

   ____ **High**

   ____ **Medium**

   ____ **Low**

Next we will compute your **dominance** score. Use the score sheet marked "Dominance" and follow the instructions. It works just like the **extroversion** scoring, except, of course, the words scored are different. To interpret your dominance score, if you are a woman, a score of 23 or more is high, a score of 16 or less is low, while scores of 17 through 22 are medium. If you are a man, a score of 24 or more is high, a score of 18 or less is low, while scores between 19 and 23 are medium. Check whether you are high, medium, or low on the dominance scale.

Next we will compute your **trust** score. If you are a woman, a score of 26 or more is high on trust, 18 or less is low, while scores of 19 through 25 are medium. If you are a man, a score of 25 or more is high, 18 or less is low, while scores of 19 through 24 are medium.

TRUST

1. Add the following two scores and then add 20.

    ____ **Undemanding**

    + ____ **Not Deceptive**

    + 20

    = ____ Total 1

2. Add the following two scores.

    ____ **Cunning**

    + ____ **Tricky**

    = ____ Total 2

3. Next subtract Total 2 from Total 1.

    ____ Total 1

    − ____ Total 2

    = ____ Your **Trust** Score

4. Check the text to find the interpretation of your score.

    ____ **High**

    ____ **Medium**

    ____ **Low**

Finally, you have to compute your **warmth** score. If you are a woman, a score of 30 or more represents high warmth, a score of 23 or less means low warmth, while scores of 24 through 29 are medium. If you are a man, a score of 28 or more is high, a score of 20 or less is low, while scores between 21 and 28 are medium.

GATHERING DATA ON PEOPLE AND DOGS

The personality test that you have just taken is a simplified version of a test called the *Interpersonal Adjective Scales,*[1] which is usually referred to by its initials, IAS. This test was based on one designed by psychologist Jerry Wiggins of the University of British Columbia. Dr. Wiggins's long career included designing parts of one of the personality tests most fre-

WARMTH

1. Add the following two scores and then add 20.

_____ **Kind**

+ _____ **Gentle-Hearted**

+ 20

= _____ Total 1

2. Add the following two scores.

_____ **Hard-Hearted**

+ _____ **Unsympathetic**

= _____ Total 2

3. Next subtract total 2 from Total 1.

_____ Total 1

− _____ Total 2

= _____ Your **Warmth** Score

4. Check the text to find the interpretation of your score.

_____ **High**

_____ **Medium**

_____ **Low**

quently used by therapists and researchers to find out if a person has psychological problems. That test is called the MMPI, which stands for the *Minnesota Multiphasic Personality Inventory.* After years of studying people with problem personalities, he became interested in understanding how normal people's personalities affect the way they interact with others. It took him nearly twenty years of research to develop the IAS and to explore the psychological implications of what it measures.

In its full form, the IAS is four times longer than the test that I give here, and it requires a computer program (or a huge amount of hand calculation) to produce a vector score that describes an individual's personality in a complex mathematical space. If you don't need the scientific power provided by the full IAS, the length of the test can be reduced and the scoring can be simplified, as I have done here. I won't bother you with the technical details of how this was done, except to mention that this shortened test is based on two separate scientific studies which selected the items for the test. For scientists or those who want a fuller explanation, all of this is described in the Technical Notes at the end of the book. The important conclusion is that this short version gives scores that are very similar to scores from the full IAS test and are adequate for general use. I have also renamed the personality dimensions with labels that make more sense to an average person. The technical labels that are used in the original test, such as PA or FG, are useful for scientific communication, but not for everyday discussions.

One of the nice features of the IAS personality test is that it can be used to analyze the personalities of well-known people or historical figures who are not available for testing. A personality profile can be obtained by having historians or other experts who know the person well fill out the IAS the way that they believe most accurately reflects the individual's personality. Later on in this book, when I talk about the personalities of some famous or historically important people, I use this technique for a couple of examples. Specifically, in each instance I arranged for four appropriate experts (historians, political scientists, professors of literature, art, music, film, and theater, or whatever specialty was suitable for the person I wanted to evaluate) to complete the IAS for that person. After scoring each test, I combined the ratings from the experts to produce the personality profile of that individual. Most of the experts reported that they had no difficulty doing this, and the reliability of these ratings is shown by the fact that there was an extremely high degree of agreement among these authorities in their scores.

Once we have a way to measure personality, we next have to see whether a person's personality can predict the kind of dogs he or she will prefer. To determine the relationship between an individual's personality and the dogs that they love and hate, I had to conduct a large survey and analyze the data. It may be interesting to look at the process involved in such a study. First I gave this personality test to 6,149 people from all walks of life, with an age range from sixteen to ninety-four. All of these were presently or had once been dog owners, and finding them involved a bit of scrounging. I set up a booth at various dog shows and pet fairs, collected information at a large open house that was held at my university, surveyed students from dog obedience classes, and also collected data from the audiences who attended many public talks that I have given. Friends and associates who were members of various unions and church groups circulated questionnaires at their meetings, and my brother Dennis, who was a high school teacher, even distributed survey forms to people that he knew in the educational system. In addition to the dog owner data, which is the most crucial, I also gathered information from 1,223 cat owners and 1,564 people who had never lived with either a cat or a dog.

All of these people were given a survey form which contained the basic questionnaire that you have just taken (without the score sheets). In addition, they were asked a number of questions about any dogs (or cats) that they had lived with. These questions concerned such things as the dog's breed, how well they got along with the dog, how much they liked the dog, and so forth. Perhaps the most important question that this large group of people was asked was whether they would choose to live with that particular dog breed again, if given a choice. On the basis of this data each dog breed was given a score that reflected how well it fit into the individual's life.

In the end, all these data were statistically analyzed to give us a picture of the personality characteristics that were compatible with the different breeds of dogs. However, even with the very large number of people that I tested, we had only a few examples of some of the rarer breeds. For this reason, rather than doing the analysis for individual breeds of dogs, we looked at the personality traits that best fit each of the seven new breed categories that I described in the previous chapter. In this way we ended up with at least five hundred personality scores for each of the dog breed groups. This is enough to make our predictions very stable and solid. Statistical analyses confirmed that if you like one of the dog breeds in any particular breed group, you are also very likely to like most of the other dogs in that group. The specific methods that were used to analyze the data are described more fully in the Technical Notes at the end of this book.

A final point to keep in mind is that we will be looking at four separate personality traits and describing which dog breeds fit with various values on each. Because personality is a complex thing, different aspects of your personality may work best with different breeds of dogs. How you get to a final "best fit" dog breed is discussed in Chapter 15, "Putting It All Together." For the time being, however, there is a simple rule of thumb to keep in mind. If the same group of dog breeds is suggested by two or more of your personality scores, then there is a good chance that dogs from that group will fit with your temperament. If a group of dog breeds fits three of your personality traits, then you should look quite seriously at this group the next time you choose a dog because it is a very strong match. If you happen to be lucky enough to find a dog group that fits all four of your personality dimensions, then you very likely have the potential for a "cosmic companionship."

<< *Chapter Eight* >>

Dogs for Extroverted and Introverted People

The first personality dimension that helps to predict which dog breeds will fit in with your personality is *extroversion.* If you score high on this personality trait then I will refer to you as being "extroverted" as opposed to people who are low on this trait, whom I will call "introverted." First of all, let's look at the typical behaviors of extroverted and introverted people, so you will recognize them in people that you know.

The person who has high scores on the extroversion trait is inclined to be very outgoing in social situations. If you are such an extrovert then you are likely to be described by other people as being cheerful, friendly, and sociable. High-scoring extroverts are people-oriented individuals who prefer hobbies that allow them to interact with other people, and enjoy social clubs or any "crowd scene" where they have a lot of opportunities to mingle. They are gregarious, and often end up in jobs that involve lots of public contact, such as publicity director, drama coach, retail salesperson, sales manager, sports promoter, television producer, actor, journalist, or traveling salesperson. If you feel comfortable volunteering to be a master of ceremonies for some social activity, you are probably high on the extroversion scale.

Extroverts are good at dealing with people. If they are trying to get

< 91 >

you to agree with them, or to do them a favor, their favorite tactic is to appeal to your reasonableness. They will tell you why you should agree, or point out how you might benefit by doing what they want. This makes them popular because, even if you don't finally agree, it is pleasant to have others treat us as reasonable people and not resort to threats or intimidation.

It is easy to find the extroverts in any setting—just look for the largest crowd of people. The highly extroverted people may be wearing flashy or extremely trendy clothing. They will be telling jokes, perhaps talking louder than the people around them. At a party they will probably talk with almost everybody in the room. They may be the first ones on the dance floor, and may dance much of the night. They never shy away from group activities. When they engage in games they are most likely to be cooperative with other people, trying to organize people into teams, rather than being strongly competitive in the "I'm number one" sense.

Contrast the highly extroverted pattern to that of the introverted person, the individual who is low on the extroversion dimension. If you are one of these introverted people, you will tend to avoid many social interactions, not because you are hostile or unfriendly, but simply because being surrounded by a noisy crowd doesn't make you feel very comfortable or happy. For this reason people who are low on the extroversion trait will use certain strategies to limit their social contacts. They may refuse invitations, and will seldom take the extra time and effort to make a lot of friends or to interact with people. Part of this is simply due to the fact that introverts may sometimes feel anxious and embarrassed when there are other people around, and may be uncomfortable getting conversations started with strangers, or expressing personal feelings in a social setting. For this reason other people may describe introverts as being aloof, distant, or even unsociable.

Introverts are happiest in job settings where they do not have to interact with other people, and are relatively isolated from any social pressures, real or implied. Perhaps this is why we find so many people who are low in extroversion in occupations where much of the work can be done alone or needs only minimal interaction with other people. The jobs of writer, poet, composer, cartoonist, historian, geologist, meteorologist, horticulturist, tree doctor, gardener, and independent research scientist often appeal to people with low extroversion scores. Introverted people are not particularly good in positions where they need to get other people to agree with them, or to do certain things. Interacting with other people only when they must, introverts simply have not worked out a consistent set of strategies to manipulate the opinions of other people.

Introverts are often not as visible as extroverts merely because they tend to keep to themselves. If you are low on the extroversion scale you probably prefer staying at home, perhaps spending your free time simply listening to music, or practicing a musical instrument by yourself. You might find that your greatest pleasures involve reading, watching television, or wandering quietly along the beach at sunset. You might prefer to eat lunch by yourself, in a quiet corner of a cafeteria, rather than chat with friends or associates. If introverts must go to a party, they tend to be quiet, often entering a room full of people without talking to anyone. Introverts prefer to be with the people that they already know in such situations, rather than meeting new people. Thus if an introvert comes to a party with a date, they will tend to stay quite close to that person during the evening, and probably the only people that they will meet and interact with are the people whom their date introduces them to. Given a chance, they might slip off into the kitchen, if there are no people there, or maybe find a quiet corner where they can sit and observe the other people.

If your extroversion score is in the medium range, then you are like the majority of people. This means that you sometimes show patterns of behavior that are similar to that of the highly extroverted person, and sometimes show more introverted patterns. A medium score on extroversion means that a lot of your behaviors will be more dependent on the situation than on your internal predispositions. When your friends want to go out and carouse around town, you may go along; on the other hand, when you find yourself at home alone you may not be distressed at all, since you have an opportunity for quiet individual activities, like reading, watching TV, or playing a computer game.

Your degree of extroversion does affect the dogs that you are apt to choose. Highly extroverted people tend to select breeds that are quite different from those selected by people who are low in extroversion. In addition, analysis of the data shows that the dog groups that will work out well for you depend on your sex as well as your extroversion score. A general summary of the best dog groups for men and women is shown in Table 1. A full listing of the dogs in each group is found in the Breed Groups appendix at the back of the book. It might be useful to put a bookmark there so you can refer to it easily.

Simply presenting a table is a pretty sterile way of showing how dogs and people fit together based upon their degree of extroversion. So let me tell you the stories of a couple of well-known people and their relationships with their dogs.

JOHN AND CHARLEY

Let's consider the case of the Nobel Prize–winning novelist John Steinbeck,[1] who wrote such classics as *The Grapes of Wrath, East of Eden,* and *Of Mice and Men* and even took a turn at writing movie scripts such as *Viva Zapata!* and *The Red Pony.* He had a well-documented relationship with his dog and he was certainly an extrovert.

Steinbeck was born in Salinas, California. He attended Stanford University rather intermittently, and there he showed many of the personality traits that would characterize his whole life. Easily making

TABLE 1

Dog groups that are most preferred by men and women with differing levels of extroversion.

Extroversion Score	Dog Groups For	
	Women	Men
High	Independent Protective	Consistent Clever
Medium	Consistent Clever	Friendly Self-Assured
Low	Steady Self-Assured	Independent Steady

friends, he had a few deep and meaningful friendships, as well as many acquaintances that he interacted with frequently in relaxed and informal relationships. Steinbeck especially liked being around people who had interests that were similar to his. He became active in the English Club at Stanford, and rented a tiny room in a sort of shack that was located off campus, in the backyard of a private home. Because of his easy extroverted nature, the shack became the focus of activity for classmates who were aspiring writers. They would gather there in the evenings to drink beer, exchange gossip, and discuss their private lives and their hopes for the future. Steinbeck named his place the Den of Pegasus after the mythological flying horse. He used to explain this name by referring to the legend that associated Pegasus with the invention of writing, and also indicated that Pegasus symbolized his own soaring ambitions. He would add with a laugh, "If a horse can fly, anything is possible."

Steinbeck did not do well at Stanford. He was often in trouble for his pranks and practical jokes. He also tended to miss classes and failed to turn in assignments because he was busy writing or socializing. Many years later his wife, Elaine, explained, "Everything that John does takes longer than he expected. That's because simply saying hello to somebody can end up as an hour-long conversation. Meanwhile, if he stops for a quick cup of coffee it can result in a discussion that takes an entire afternoon. I think that John believes that talking is more vital for life than breathing."

Some of the contemporary press stories about Steinbeck imply that he was actually introverted and a loner, because he seldom was willing to give interviews. This reluctance had nothing to do with his sociability, but rather was the result of the overwhelming volume and emotional nature of the criticism leveled at him by journalists and reviewers. Many of his books were popular, but many were also controversial. For instance, *The Grapes of Wrath* is about the migration of a dispossessed family from the Oklahoma Dust Bowl to California. It is filled with social commentary and protest in its description of the Joad family's exploitation by a ruthless system of agricultural economics. This book and some of his others threw him into the center of a social and political storm. People living in cities in Oklahoma, as well as people in California's agricultural areas, felt that Steinbeck had maligned them. Attempts were made to ban his books from libraries and his life was even threatened. He found himself fighting for some modicum of privacy in the face of an avalanche of requests to speak and political movements to support. He even found himself labeled an oppressor of the poor because he was "exploiting their sad stories for profit, rather than donating the profits from his books to needy individuals or organizations."

After a while it became almost a game, where public figures and the press would try to find isolated items in his writing to serve as a focus of criticism. Thus prominent people from Monterey, California, blasted him for introducing them to the world with these lines from *Cannery Row:* "Its inhabitants are, as the man once said, 'whores, pimps, gamblers, and sons of bitches' by which he meant everybody." Californians never forgave Steinbeck for that phrase, even though it was followed by a line describing these very same inhabitants as "saints and angels and martyrs and holy men." Steinbeck once complained, "There's getting to be a fictitious so-and-so out there in the public eye. He's a straw man and he bears my name. I don't like him—that straw man. He's not me—he's the Steinbeck the public has created out of its own imagination and thinks ought to be me."

Although often not responsive to the press, Steinbeck continued to immerse himself in social activities. He was politically active as well, with strong views on social welfare and the Vietnam War, and his educational and artistic activities included a cultural exchange visit to the Soviet Union with playwright Edward Albee. He loved the social give and take, once noting, "I spent the evening two nights ago with 1,500 students in Stockholm. I didn't address them: we just argued, they all shouted at each other—they were stimulating, intelligent and exciting."

Although often described as having a "dark vision" of life because he wrote about the poor and oppressed, his real theme was the quiet dignity he saw in society's more deprived members. Although his characters are often trapped in an unfair world, they remain sympathetic and heroic even in defeat. He could also write playful and amusing literature as well; Rodgers and Hammerstein used his book *Sweet Thursday* as the basis for their musical *Pipe Dream.* He could also write with love and tenderness, as in his screenplay for *The Red Pony* where a boy's love for his horse provides him with an emotional escape from his bickering family.

Steinbeck had a number of dogs during his life. In the early days there were English Setters and then there was an all-white Bull Terrier named Angel. He also owned an Airedale Terrier about whom he had very mixed feelings. It seems that whenever his Airedale would go past the domain of a particular dog that Steinbeck described as a "shepherd-setter-coyote mix," a fight would break out. "Every week my dog fought this grisly creature and every week, he got licked." This went on for several months and then, one day, Steinbeck's Airedale got lucky. He caught the tough mongrel by surprise and really gave him a thrashing. In a sad tone Steinbeck notes what happened next. The beaten dog then "hung his head in the loser's corner," and at this moment the Airedale abandoned all chivalry. To the author's dismay, while the losing dog lay on its back in submission, Steinbeck's dog suddenly returned to him and savagely attacked his private parts. By the time the Airedale was pulled away from his victim, the latter "was finished as a father." Steinbeck ends his story by commenting that "there can be dogs without honor, even as with us." His feelings were so negative toward this Airedale that all through this story he never even once mentioned the dog's name.

The dog that Steinbeck had the warmest affection for, however, was appropriately drawn from one of the groups that is best for an extroverted individual, namely the Clever group. His dog was a black Standard Poodle named Charley (plate 6). According to Steinbeck, "He was born in Bercy on the outskirts of Paris and trained in France, and while he knows a little Poodle-English, he responds quickly only to commands in French. Otherwise he has to translate, and that slows him down."

When he was fifty-eight years of age, Steinbeck decided that he wanted to "rediscover" America. To do this he set out on a twelve-thousand-mile trip, which took him through thirty-seven states and Canada. He made his tour in a camper truck, accompanied only by his dog, and the result was the warm and gentle book *Travels with Charley.*

Steinbeck took Charley along to provide companionship but also as a way to initiate social contact. Steinbeck notes,

A dog, particularly an exotic like Charley, is a bond between strangers. Many conversations en route began with "What degree of a dog is that?" [Especially when camping, Charley was an important means of starting conversations.] *In establishing contact with strange people, Charley is my ambassador. I release him, and he drifts toward the objective, or rather to whatever the objective may be preparing for dinner. I retrieve him so that he will not be a nuisance to my neighbors*—et voilà! *A child can do the same thing, but a dog is better.*

While *Travels with Charley* is mostly read as an entertaining travelogue and social commentary, the book provides us with an interesting picture of a man interacting and communicating with his dog. Obviously Charley did not speak. In fact his only "word" was the sound "Ftt" which he would make in Steinbeck's ear. Steinbeck explains, "He is the only dog I ever knew who could pronounce the consonant F. This is because his front teeth are crooked, a tragedy which keeps him out of dog shows: because his upper front teeth slightly engage his lower lip Charley can pronounce F. The word 'Ftt' usually means he would like to salute a bush or a tree."

Most of the time Charley communicates with his tail, and Steinbeck reads much into his tail movements. The author asks him, "Should we stay the night, Charley?" and Charley wags his tail much as a professor might wag a pencil—once to the left, once to the right, and then back to center. Later on Steinbeck asks another question and observes the dog's response. "Two complete wags. At least he didn't leave the question open."

At other times Steinbeck does what many of us do with the dogs that we love, namely he talks to him. Much of the book could actually have been published under the title *Conversations with Charley.* Steinbeck talks to Charley about day-to-day matters, such as when to stop and camp, when and what to eat, when to move on to a new place, and so forth. He also talks to Charley about his feelings, and sometimes the conversations become quite deep and philosophical, such as when

Steinbeck has a long talk with Charley about the nature of prejudice and racial discrimination.

I have already mentioned doggerel, the simplified language that we use when we talk with our dogs, but without describing the contents of our conversations. Conversations with dogs can take one of three different forms. The simplest is just a monologue where the human being does all of the talking in a continuous stream while the dog provides just a friendly presence. The second form is a dialogue where there is some give and take but only one speaker. In this kind of conversation we look at the dog now and then, pausing at places where the dog might be expected to make a comment, and then continue on, as if the animal's silence had conveyed some meaning. Listening to this form of conversation is like monitoring one side of a phone conversation.

There is a third form of human and dog conversation which is familiar to many dog lovers but may seem quite odd to an outsider: when we not only talk to the dog but also provide the answers, essentially saying what we think the dog might say in response to our comments. We have all seen a simplified form of this behavior when parents talk to babies. A mother might, for example, give the child a toy, saying something like "Would you like this teddy bear?," and then when the baby smiles or reaches add (often in another voice), "Oh yes, Mommy. I like that bear." Human-canine conversations of this sort sound much like the clichéd Hollywood movie sequence where the schizophrenic carries on an argument among his various multiple personalities—each with a distinctive voice and each with its own character. Thus one day on Steinbeck's cross-country journey, when he found Charley simply staring blankly off into space, the author provided both parts of this conversation:

> *"What's the matter Charley, aren't you well?"*
> *His tail slowly waved his replies. "Oh, yes. Quite well, I guess."*
> *"Why didn't you come when I whistled?"*
> *"I didn't hear you whistle."*
> *"What are you staring at?"*
> *"I don't know. Nothing I guess."*

"Well, don't you want your dinner?"

"I'm really not hungry. But I'll go through the motions."

Later on, Steinbeck noticed that Charley seemed a little depressed and decided to cheer him up by baking him a birthday cake. It wasn't Charley's birthday—in fact Steinbeck couldn't remember, or perhaps never knew, what Charley's exact birthday was—but he thought that a festive cake might brighten his mood. That resulted in the following exchange as the author prepared the ingredients.

Charley watched the operation with some interest. His silly tail made delicate conversation. "Anybody saw you make a birthday cake for a dog that he don't even know when's his birthday would think you were nuts."

"If you can't manage any better grammar with your tail, maybe it's a good thing you can't talk."

We all talk to our dogs, and sometimes provide their answers. However, only someone with a Nobel Prize in literature, like Steinbeck, would bother to criticize the grammar of the conversation that he himself put into the dog's mouth.

EUGENE AND BLEMIE

An interesting contrast to John Steinbeck is the playwright Eugene O'Neill,[2] who actually was the first American writer to win the Nobel Prize for literature. It is astonishing to note that in addition to the Nobel Prize, O'Neill won four Pulitzer prizes in drama for his plays *Beyond the Horizon, Anna Christie, Strange Interlude,* and *Long Day's Journey into Night.* Some scholars claim that after William Shakespeare and George Bernard Shaw, O'Neill is the world's most widely translated and produced dramatist.

Given his life history, one might have expected O'Neill to be the ultimate extrovert. He was born into the theater. His father, James O'Neill, was a successful touring actor who made his reputation in a stage adaptation of *The Count of Monte Cristo.* His mother, Ella, accompanied her husband in his travels across the country. She gave birth to Eugene in a hotel room, and O'Neill spent his early childhood in hotels, on trains, and backstage in the many theaters that his father worked in. His education was in boarding schools, followed by a year at Princeton University. He then took off for six years to gain what he called some "real life experience." Instead of a happy and educational period, O'Neill entered a period of time which very nearly ended his life. He found employment as a sailor but became a very heavy drinker, and for a while survived as a derelict on the waterfronts of Buenos Aires, Liverpool, and New York City. In a fit of depression he even attempted suicide.

O'Neill had "theater in his blood" and a life of interacting casually with many people in his early travels with his family. This means that someone who believes that environment determines personality would probably conclude that O'Neill would not only be strongly extroverted, but would feel lost without a constant flow of people around him. When he had a lot of alcohol in him, he was, in fact, quite outgoing and extroverted. When he was sober, however, he showed that his actual personality was extremely introverted.

There were early hints of how introverted O'Neill was that were picked up by his associates. For instance, he had a short stint as a reporter on the *New London Telegraph*. Some years later Robert A. Woodworth wrote an article about him entitled "The World's Worst Reporter." In it he recalled that O'Neill would sit in a corner of the city room smoking and daydreaming while the other members of the small staff of reporters "ran their legs off."

O'Neill first recognized his tendencies toward introversion and isolation when he ended up in a sanatorium in Connecticut for treatment of tuberculosis. He would later refer to this experience as his rebirth. An extended period of bed rest in a private room was followed by a move to a small cottage on the sanatorium grounds which was shared with a couple of other patients nearing recovery. He later told friends, "I sleep out on the porch every night mainly because I have come to appreciate the comfort of solitude."

It was during this time that O'Neill started to write plays. He found that in his writing he could escape from the noise, forced social interactions, and intrusions of a hostile world. The writing provided an acceptable reason not to interact with others. He later explained this to a young author, saying, "As long as you have a job on hand that absorbs all your mental energy you haven't much worry to spare over other things."

O'Neill's early plays were not very sophisticated, but a theater critic who saw promise in them persuaded O'Neill's father to send him to Harvard to study with George Pierce Baker in his famous playwriting course. O'Neill spent a year there, learning his craft. He then left, and immediately began writing one-act plays. These early efforts were successfully produced by the Playwrights' Theater in Provincetown, Massachusetts. Only five years after leaving Harvard, he saw his first full-length play (and his first Pulitzer Prize winner), *Beyond the Horizon,* produced on Broadway.

Whenever it was possible, O'Neill would follow a solitary and repetitive routine. His wife, Carlotta, reported that when he was writing O'Neill scarcely saw anyone except her. It was her job to preserve his isolation from servants, visitors, or anyone else. She later recalled, "Orders were that nobody was to go near him—not even if the house was on fire. He was never to be disturbed."

His routine was to get up at 7:30, have a quick light breakfast, and then shut himself into his study until 1:00 P.M. He would then emerge for lunch, during which he would go through the mail that Carlotta had sorted for him into folders marked "From agent or publishers," "Personal notes from friends etc.," "Requests," "From unknown playwrights," and so forth. Carlotta said, "I would have to sit there perfectly dumb. I didn't even want to make a sound with the chair that might disturb him." He might then return to his work, take a nap, or swim. Later in the day he and his wife would walk around the grounds. Most commonly he spent his evenings in front of the fireplace with his dog at his feet. Carlotta noted that after the isolation of the early part of the day, O'Neill could be very charming, sociable, and humorous; however, she qualified this by pointing out that "sometimes he wouldn't talk all day long."

O'Neill had a favorite dog, which was from one of the two groups best for strongly introverted males, namely, the Independent group of dogs. The dog was acquired during a stay in France. He often complained that the French took advantage of foreigners by charging them high prices and delivering less than the expected quality. The one item that he acquired there, and never showed any regrets about price, nor questioned the value, was a beautiful Dalmatian named Silverdeen Emblem. O'Neill called him "Blemie" (plate 7).

O'Neill had had two previous marriages before marrying Carlotta. There were three children by those marriages, and in O'Neill's eyes the children were evidence of his failure as a husband and father. His oldest son, Eugene O'Neill Jr., committed suicide at the age of forty, while his younger son, Shane, drifted aimlessly into a life of alcohol, narcotics, and emotional instability. O'Neill cut himself off from his daughter, Oona, when she was only eighteen. He was infuriated and upset when, against his wishes, Oona married the movie actor Charlie Chaplin, who was O'Neill's age.

O'Neill and Carlotta had no children, but he would often refer to Blemie as his only "successful child." Carlotta worried about how attached O'Neill had become to Blemie. This was proved to her by his tendency to pamper the dog—like when O'Neill purchased a four-poster bed for Blemie's personal use at night. However, she admitted that, after all, Blemie had been "the most pleasant and amusing child" that she and Eugene had had, and certainly was also "the most grateful."

O'Neill would take every opportunity to extol Blemie's virtues in letters and conversations. He often said that Blemie was everything that a dog should be, a comfort to his master in time of sorrow and a reason for added happiness in times of joy. O'Neill would get quite lyrical about Blemie. "No dog is as well bred or as well mannered or as distinguished and handsome." He would usually also declare that no dog would ever look as distinguished as Blemie did in the designer collar, leash, raincoat, and overcoat that were specially made for him at Hermes in Paris.

The motion picture actress Lillian Gish said that "Blemie acted as host at Le Plessis [O'Neill's home]. He would receive you at the door, go with you on a walk, follow the servant who brought in your breakfast tray. When a guest left, Blemie would throw himself on the floor with a sigh of relief, as though saying, 'Thank heavens they're gone.' He behaved exactly as though he were worn out with having performed the duties of a good host." Carlotta pointed out that Blemie also seemed to understand O'Neill's introverted nature and his need for quiet. "Like the servants, he went around on tiptoe when Gene was working," she said.

Blemie went with O'Neill on virtually all of his travels, and would come to the theater whenever he was working with the cast and director on the production of one of his plays. Because of Blemie's constant presence at rehearsals, actors sometimes assumed that it was permissible for them to bring their dogs in also. While *Mourning Becomes Electra* was being put into production, Alice Brady, who played the role of Lavinia, started bringing her dog, Sammy, to rehearsals. One day Sammy got into a fight with Blemie. O'Neill had to separate them since Sammy was only a tiny dog and was clearly getting the worst of the affair. O'Neill picked up Sammy, carried him into Brady's dressing room, and said, "Sammy met my dog outside. Sammy sniffed and said 'My mother's appearing in your father's rotten play,' and my dog naturally leaped on him. Sammy should know better." Just before the play opened O'Neill sent Brady's dog some flowers, in Blemie's name. The note said that he (Blemie) hoped that all was forgiven and that Sammy's mother would do a good job in his father's play.

Just as we saw in the case of Steinbeck, O'Neill often put words into his dog's mouth, although it was usually in the form of a comment to someone else. For instance, O'Neill was ill on the day that he received greetings from a friend, congratulating him on his fiftieth birthday. He replied with a note in which he wrote, "Blemie remarked to the cat: 'The Old Man doesn't look a day over 183.' And he was right. I didn't feel a bit older than that, either."

In October 1940, Blemie was obviously growing old and infirm and it was obvious that he would not be around much longer. O'Neill's feelings for Blemie ran quite deep, but he also knew that Carlotta was worried about how his dog's inevitable loss would affect him. Partly to assure her that he understood what was happening and was preparing for it, and partly to console himself, he wrote "The Last Will and Testament of Silverdeen Emblem O'Neill." It was a warm expression of his feelings for the dog, and perhaps the expression of a philosophy that could well serve as the epitaph for any loved dog.

I Silverdeen Emblem O'Neill (familiarly known as Blemie), because the burden of my years and infirmities is heavy upon me, and I realise the end of my life is near, do hereby bury my last will and testament in the mind of my master. He will not know it is there until after I am dead. Then, remembering me in his loneliness, he will suddenly know of this testament, and I ask him to inscribe it as a memorial to me.

I have little in the way of material things to leave. Dogs are wiser than men. They do not set great store upon things. They do not waste their days hoarding property. They do not ruin their sleep worrying about how to keep the objects they have. There is nothing of value I have to bequeath except my love and my faith. These I leave to all those who have loved me, to my master and mistress, who I know will mourn me most . . . Perhaps it is vain of me to boast when I am so near death, which returns all beasts and vanities to dust, but I have always been an extremely lovable dog.

I ask my Master and Mistress to remember me always, but not to grieve for me too long. In my life I have tried to be a comfort to them in time of sorrow, and a reason for added joy in their happiness. It is painful for me to think that even in death I should cause them pain. Let them remember that while no dog has ever had a happier life (and this I owe to their love and care for me), now that I have grown blind and deaf and lame, and even my sense of smell fails me so that a rabbit could be right under my nose and I might not know, my pride has sunk to a sick, bewildered humiliation. I feel life is taunting me with having overlingered my welcome. It is time I said good-by, before I become too sick a burden on myself and on those who love me. It will be a sorrow to leave them, but not a sorrow to die . . . What may come after death, who knows? I would like to believe with those of my fellow Dalmatians who are devout Mohammedans, that there is a Paradise, where one is always young and full-bladdered; where all the day one dillies and dallies with an amorous multitude of houris [the beautiful virgins in the Koran's vision of heaven], all beautifully spotted . . .

I am afraid this is too much for even such a dog as I am to expect. But peace, at least, is certain. Peace and long rest for weary old heart and head and limbs, and eternal sleep in the earth I have loved so well. Perhaps, after all, this is best. One last request I earnestly make. I have heard my mistress say, "When Blemie dies we must never have another dog. I love him so much I could never love another one." Now I would ask her, for love of me, to have another. It would be a poor tribute to my memory never to have a dog again. What I would like is that, having once had me in the family, now she cannot live without a dog . . . To him I bequeath my collar and leash and my overcoat and raincoat, made to order in 1929 at Hermès in Paris. He can never wear them with the distinction I did, walking around the Place Vendôme, or later along Park Avenue, all eyes fixed on me in admiration, but again I am sure he will do his utmost not to appear a mere gauche provincial dog . . . One last word of farewell, dear master and mistress. Whenever you visit my grave, say to yourselves with regret but also happiness in your hearts at the remembrance of my long happy life with you: "Here lies one who loved us and whom we loved." No matter how deep my sleep I shall hear you, and not all the power of death can keep my spirit from wagging a grateful tail.

Clearly, both introverts and extroverts can love their dogs; it is just that they love different dogs.

Chapter Nine

Dogs for Dominant and Not-So-Dominant People

The second personality trait that predicts which dog breeds you will get along with is *dominance*. People who are high on this dimension we will refer to as being "dominant" while people who are low we will call "non-dominant."

People who score high on dominance are generally described as being forceful, assertive, persistent, firm, self-assured, and self-confident. Highly dominant people are usually very ambitious and achievement-oriented. Taking charge of most situations, they are quick to make decisions and expect to win most of the arguments that they get into. These are the people who play games in a competitive manner—out to win as much as they can for themselves. In a committee they like to be in charge, and if they are not, they will often challenge the leader whenever the opportunity arises.

Dominant people like to talk to other people and like to persuade them or influence their actions. Much like extroverts, their favorite tactic to bring people over to their side is to use appeals to reason, but their arguments are more forceful. In addition to providing reasons in favor of their own position, they may aggressively demand that the other person provide reasons for not agreeing. If they don't win the argument (which is rare), then they are apt to explain away failure by saying that their idea was "ahead of its time" or "beyond his understanding." It is easy to find dominant people in a discussion group, often accompanying their arguments with active gestures; they usually want to stand up to talk to the group and they are the first to grab hold of the microphone in public settings.

This pattern of active, ambitious, and forceful behaviors probably explains why so many individuals in supervisory positions tend to be high on the dominance trait. We find many dominant people among business executives, hotel managers, restaurant managers, political campaign managers, advertising executives, school superintendents, business teachers, experts in forensic or criminal matters, police and law enforcement officials, welfare directors, and so forth.

At their best, highly dominant individuals are good directors and efficient administrators, especially if they have the power to enforce decisions. Highly dominant people can act with great conscience and heroism at times of difficulty. They are usually the people who, when happening upon a bad highway accident, will start directing traffic around the scene and making sure that someone has been sent for help. It is the dominant person who organizes a sandbagging operation during a flood, or is the first to gather a rescue team to find a lost child or help earthquake victims. At their worst, dominant individuals will use power simply because they have it. They will have other people run errands for them rather than doing the work themselves, they will interrupt conversations to make their points, they will try to decide which movie or restaurant a group will go to, they will tell other people what to wear and how to style their hair. Even worse, they will steal your TV remote control so they can determine which programs everyone in the room has to watch.

People who are low in dominance are sometimes called timid, bashful, shy, and unaggressive. These non-dominant people are simply not as "pushy" as those who are high in dominance. When given the opportunity, non-dominant people will avoid any sort of leadership role. They do not want to be in any situation where they have to be assertive or authoritative or where they must make decisions. This means that they are often happiest in situations that are structured and where the rules are clear and can be applied in a straightforward and nonconfrontational way. Thus people who are low on the dominance trait are often found among bank tellers, payroll clerks, general office workers, file clerks, court stenographers, retail workers, and gas station attendants. Non-dominant people with high levels of technical expertise are happiest as computer equipment operators or repair personnel, people who maintain machinery, electronic and radio equipment operators, and so forth.

Such individuals are often seen as being fairly passive, especially when compared to the highly active dominant person. Some outside observers might interpret this as a lack of ambition, but often this apparent lack of drive is really a desire on the part of the non-dominant person not to place himself in a competitive situation, where his abilities will be tested publicly. This attitude may reflect a sense of modesty, but it also can be due to a lack of self-confidence. Such people do not like being in circumstances where they might actually have to take aggressive action against someone which might cause that person to become hostile and fight back. They also do not like situations where the only way to get things done is by being forceful and very assertive.

If they are criticized for some reason, non-dominant people are apt to accept the criticism and to apologize. They usually try to avoid arguments, and if they find themselves disagreeing with someone, their strategy for manipulating the other person's behavior often involves sulking and pouting or acting extremely humble and hopeful.

At their best, non-dominant people are sensitive to the social demands made on them, and to the needs and desires of other people (especially those in authority). This means that they make every effort to fit into the ongoing activities, and to avoid friction and divisiveness. At their worst, people who are low in dominance will simply give in, accepting the direction and opinions of other people in most matters.

People who have medium-level scores on the dominance dimension tend to take a middle position in groups. While they do not try to take charge, they also will not let others boss them around. If leadership is forced upon people with a medium level of dominance, they will accept it (though not necessarily with great joy) and will usually perform competently and fairly when in a position of authority. When asked to join a committee or a team, people with mid-range dominance scores will accept this position and not try to be confrontational. They sometimes appear a bit inconsistent, since in some situations they feel self-assured and confident, and will take charge, while in other cases they yield to the authority of others—almost to the point of appearing meek or shy. As is the case with most mid-range personality traits, the behaviors of persons with medium levels of dominance seem to depend very heavily on the circumstances that they find themselves in.

Dominance is certainly an important personality trait that will help determine the dogs that will be most loved by any particular person. As was the case with extroversion, the pattern of dog breeds that fit best with a particular level of dominance depends on the person's sex. For the dominance dimension, however, we find closer agreement between the sexes than for any other personality dimension. The dogs that work best for people who are very high or very low in dominance are the same for men and women, and there is only one difference that occurs for medium-dominance people. Table 2 shows the dog groups that will be liked the best by people at all levels of dominance. Remember that a full listing of the dogs in each group is found in the Breed Groups appendix at the back of the book, and you might want to consult it to determine the specific breeds for each level of dominance.

ALL THE PRESIDENTS' DOGS

With the Self-Assured group coming out as the preferred dogs for people with highly dominant personalities, it is not surprising to find

TABLE 2

Dog groups that are most preferred by men and women with differing levels of dominance.

Dominance Score	Dog Groups For	
	Women	Men
High	Self-Assured Steady	Self-Assured Steady
Medium	Consistent Friendly	Friendly Clever
Low	Protective Independent	Protective Independent

that these are often the favorites of U.S. presidents.[1] In fact, more presidents have chosen dogs from this group than from any other group. Furthermore, Self-Assured dogs have often appeared at the White House in sets of two and three.

It is important to emphasize the word *chosen* in talking about the dogs of presidents. Presidents and other leaders of state are quite often given dogs as gifts, making it difficult to know whether a dog is living in the White House because the president likes it or because he is keeping it as a symbol and a courtesy. Thus, when John F. Kennedy began his term of office, he arrived with only one dog, but during his administration the White House dog population rose to nine. All additional dogs (except for puppies born at the presidential residence) were gifts.

Actually presidents are given all sorts of animals as gifts. Calvin Coolidge may have had the record for variety. In addition to dogs he was given cats, birds, a raccoon, a donkey, an extremely large white goose, a baby bear, a bobcat, a wallaby, a pair of lion cubs, an antelope, and even a pygmy hippopotamus. Coolidge kept virtually all of the dogs and cats and also kept the raccoon (which he walked around the White House on a leash). The other animals were sent off to various zoos.

Perhaps the most famous dog given to a president was Pushinka (the Russian word *pushink* means "fluffy"). A gift from Soviet Premier Nikita Khrushchev to Kennedy, Pushinka was supposed to be a symbol of the reduction in the cold war tensions between the Soviet Union and the United States. She was special because Pushinka was the daughter of the Samoyed named Strelka who rocketed to fame in the *Sputnik V.* I suppose that we could call Strelka a *canineaut,* since she became the first creature to survive orbital space flight. When the puppy arrived in Washington the Kennedy children immediately wanted to play with her. Unfortunately, Pushinka's acceptance into the president's household was delayed by several days. The U.S. Secret Service turned the dog over to the CIA, who then sent the dog to Walter Reed Hospital for examination. It was feared that Pushinka might have arrived with some sort of implanted transmitting device designed to spy upon the president's activities. The dog was poked, prodded, scanned with a magnetometer, tested with thermography, X-rayed, and even subjected to an early version of a sonogram. All that was found inside Pushinka was the usual "doggy stuff," so she was returned to the White House. Around a year later she gave birth to a litter of what JFK called "pupniks." Kennedy then used these puppies as gifts to other high-ranking people.

The specific dogs selected by presidents from the Self-Assured group have changed over time, reflecting the popularity of various breeds. Earlier presidents had a fondness for Fox Terriers (both Smooth and Wire) and occasionally would own more than one at a time. The presidents with these dogs included George Washington, Thomas Jefferson, Andrew Jackson, Rutherford B. Hayes, Calvin Coolidge, and Herbert Hoover. At least two of these presidents (Washington and Jackson) used their terriers in actual fox hunts, as well as keeping them as house pets.

Abraham Lincoln did not have a dog during his White House years, but he did have one before he came to Washington—a straight-legged, medium-sized terrier that was known commonly as the Fell Terrier. This breed was renamed around 1925 and we know it today as the Lakeland Terrier. Evidence for the affection that Lincoln had for his dog comes in a story that he used to tell. One winter the dog was playing along the banks of the Wabash River when the thin ice shelf gave way and the dog fell in. Lincoln was afraid that the dog might not be able to climb back out onto the slippery bank or that the ice-cold water might paralyze him before he could swim to safety. So without hesitation the future president waded into the freezing river to save his dog. He would end the story with the quip, "When I got him out he was near froze solid and shivering. He was shaking so hard that I wasted half a glass of whisky trying to aim it for his mouth. Must have got enough of it into him, though, since it did seem to bring him back to life."

Some people may be surprised to see Calvin Coolidge on a list of dominant personalities. Most histories talk of him as a warm, supportive, and not particularly imposing man who rose to be vice president and inherited his office on the death of Warren G. Harding. The parts of his administration that people tend to remember are associated with his ability to minimize problems, his pride in traditional institutions, and his emphasis on both security and faith. Because of this Coolidge was a popular president and became a national symbol of calm, steady, and practical leadership. His 1924 election campaign was based on the slogan "Keep Cool with Coolidge." This is only one facet of Coolidge, however; in fact it was a set of hard-line, dominant actions that catapulted him into the national spotlight in the first place. As governor of Massachusetts he called out the National Guard to forcibly quell two days of rioting and rampage that resulted when the Boston police force went on strike. Following the strike he refused to reinstate any of the police who had walked out. When a contingent of labor leaders called upon him demanding that he reverse his decision and offering threats if he did not, Coolidge refused, taking the tough stance that "there is no right to strike against the public safety by anybody, anywhere, any time." In so doing he clearly put his career on the line in a head-to-head confrontation with his opponents. These are not the actions of a nondominant person.

Coolidge had a Wire Fox Terrier named Peter Pan, which he had selected for himself. Peter Pan was quite wild and often became uncontrollably excited around visitors and White House staff members. Coolidge thought that this was rather amusing, and would sometimes warn visitors about his nipping by saying, "Be careful, Peter is one Republican in the White House who bites." On a warm summer day some visitors arrived, including a woman who was wearing a fairly full skirt made out of some very light material. It had a flowery print and was cinched with a cord-like belt with tassels which hung down in the back. We will never know whether it was the swishing of the skirt or bouncing of the tassels that caught Peter Pan's attention, but as the woman turned the Fox Terrier leaped at her skirt, catching some of the flimsy material in his teeth. There was a tearing sound, and a most revealing and embarrassing rip appeared. An aide resourcefully stepped in and wrapped his suit jacket around the waist of the flustered visitor.

This was all too much for Coolidge's wife, Grace. She insisted that Peter Pan be banished from the White House and sent back to the family home in Massachusetts. In order to maintain some peace and decorum in the presidential residence, Coolidge reluctantly agreed. For the rest of his term, the White House had only the dogs that Grace Coolidge preferred, namely Collies. Her favorite was a white one named Prudence Prim, which the first lady would dress up in floppy hats, trimmed in ribbons.

Among more recent presidents, the Self-Assured breed most commonly chosen has been the Scottish Terrier. Theodore Roosevelt had one named Jessie, who had one half-drooped ear that Roosevelt used to claim was "an old war wound." Later on, Ronald Reagan would also own Scotties. In his pre-politics days, when he was married to the actress Jane Wyman, Reagan owned two Scottish Terriers, which he claimed were among his all-time favorite dogs. One was appropriately named Scotch—the other was named Soda.

Dwight D. Eisenhower fits into the same pattern as Coolidge. Generally regarded as friendly, genial, kindly, and down-to-earth, he certainly was one of the most popular presidents of the last fifty years. Yet there is evidence that this apparent warmth may well have been simply a deliberately chosen style of dealing with other people. It is difficult to imagine a man who could rise to the rank of Supreme Allied Commander and then later to president without displaying a high degree of dominance.

People who worked with Eisenhower in the military described him as demanding and always in full control. He not only acted in a dominant manner but paid careful attention to the trappings of power and station. According to an article in *Time* magazine (June 19, 1944), he was "a strict disciplinarian with the troop formations under his command. He is a bear on uniform neatness, a bug on such items of military smartness as saluting." This article went on to note an incident which occurred when Eisenhower visited the Eighth Air Force headquarters and publicly reprimanded its commander, General "Tooey" Spaatz, although he was a fellow graduate of West Point. Spaatz's crime was that he had allowed himself to be co-opted by the casualness common to the Air Force and had banned saluting in the corridors as a "damned nuisance." Typical of a person high in dominance, Eisenhower would not tolerate any such actions that did not acknowledge status in the chain of command.

Dominance and control were powerful motives in Eisenhower's personality. According to some historians, when there was a conflict between compassion and the need to further his own goals, he was capable of abandoning any pretense of warmth in order to master a situation. An often-mentioned example of this was the reclassification of captured German soldiers as "disarmed enemy forces" rather than prisoners of war. The reason for this reclassification was that the level of rations required for prisoners of war was fixed by the Geneva Convention. If the Germans were not POWs, then their rations could be reduced to almost starvation levels, thus conserving allied supplies.

The breed of dog that Eisenhower most often chose as his companion was the Scottish Terrier from the Self-Assured group. He had a real fondness for these feisty little dogs throughout his life. In 1943, already the Supreme Commander, he was in North Africa, coordinating the allied operations that would finally wrest control from the Germans. He wrote to his wife, Mamie: "The friendship of a dog is precious. It becomes even more so when one is so far removed from home as we are in Africa. I have a Scottie. In him I find consolation and diversion . . . he is the 'one person' to whom I can talk without the conversation coming back to the war."[2]

The Scottie that Eisenhower mentioned was Caacie, who accompanied him back to England and continued providing companionship during his planning for the D-Day invasion. Once he had established his base at the allied headquarters on British soil, Eisenhower would have other company as well. There has been much speculation about his relationship with the woman assigned to him as his personal driver, Kay Summersby. Whether or not there was any truth to the gossip about a romantic involvement, they certainly did have a strong and warm friendship. Summersby came to know Eisenhower quite well and appreciated his fondness for Scottish Terriers. She gave him another Scottie, Telek, who could be company for both Eisenhower and Caacie (plate 8). In 1953, Eisenhower entered the White House as president. He brought with him yet another Scottish Terrier, this one named Spunky.

FDR AND FALA

The most famous Scottish Terrier in the history of all the presidents was owned by Franklin Delano Roosevelt. FDR was the longest-serving president in history, and during his four terms his actions were marked by dominance and decisiveness. He expanded the power of the federal government more than any other president. Everything he did had the characteristics of a "take-charge," high-dominance person. He frontally attacked the Great Depression with the package of public works programs and other economic initiatives that would come to be known as the New Deal. Consistent with his high dominance and need for control, he favored a strong military. When Britain felt threatened by increasing militancy on the part of Germany, he pushed through the Lend-Lease program to provide ships and military equipment, despite strong pacifist and isolationist feelings in the government. He also led the country through almost all of World War II.

FDR expected to be able to control every aspect of his political destiny, and when he was thwarted he fought back vigorously. Thus when the U.S. Supreme Court declared some of his economic measures unconstitutional, he attempted to change the very structure of that body to forward his goals. He instituted a plan to "reorganize" the court which would involve appointing six new members to the nine-man court. These six members would be hand-picked by him and would, of course, be strong supporters of the policies he favored. FDR gave in to massive political pressure against this initiative, but only following some new decisions by the court that opened the way for almost unlimited government regulation of the economy. Some historians have speculated that the court's decisions may have favored FDR's position because the justices themselves were feeling a bit threatened by the strong actions that he considered taking against it.

During his lifetime, Roosevelt had many Scottish Terriers. One was named Duffy; another, named Meg, made her mark in life by biting newspaper reporter Bess Furman on the nose. There were also several others, but the star of the group was Murray, the Outlaw of Fala Hill, who ultimately came to be called Fala by his master and the nation. Fala's doings were always news (plate 9). He was always around the president, providing companionship during the day and sleeping on the president's bed at night.

Fala seemed to sense whenever a press conference was about to occur. As soon as the doors opened to admit the reporters, Fala would dash in and settle himself at FDR's feet. He often did the same at cabinet meetings. During such events the president would sometimes casually reach down and gently touch the dog, who would then sit up so that FDR could reach him more easily.

In many ways, Fala became a sort of national symbol. Part of this was simply because he was seen so often with the president. However, there was also a quite deliberate use of the dog in a White House campaign to rally public sentiment in support of fund-raising activities associated with the war effort. One example of this was when Fala was made an honorary "army private" because of a cash contribution (of one dollar) that was made on his behalf to the war effort. The same option was offered to the public, whereupon hundreds of thousands of dogs across the country became army privates as well, with the resulting funds used to support military activities associated with the war.

Fala disliked being separated from FDR. When the presidential entourage was preparing to leave for Roosevelt's third inauguration, Fala hopped into the car beside his master. The president attempted to shoo him out of the car, but Fala just snuggled closer to him on the seat. Roosevelt laughed and said to one of the Secret Service guards, "Would you kindly check the credentials of this individual. If he does not have an invitation to be on the inaugural platform, please have him removed." A guard gently lifted the black dog out of the car and carried him back inside.

Fala was luckier on other occasions, since FDR did not like being separated from him either. The terrier frequently was the president's associate and companion at international meetings. He was with Roosevelt in 1941, aboard the U.S.S. *Augusta,* when FDR and Winston Churchill signed the Atlantic Charter. He was even photographed with the two state leaders and of course with Winston Churchill's Poodle, Rufus, who was there also.

Apparently during the election campaign of 1944, somebody associated with the Republican Party decided that the constant fellowship between FDR and Fala provided an opportunity to attack the president's credibility as a leader. A rumor circulated that FDR had squandered public resources by sending a U.S. Navy warship to retrieve Fala, who supposedly had somehow been left behind on an island off Alaska following a presidential visit. Unfortunately for his opposition, Roosevelt turned this whole incident against them in one of his national radio broadcasts.

Republican leaders have not been content with attacks on me, or my wife, or my sons. No, not content with that, they now include my little dog, Fala. Well, of course, I don't resent attacks and my family doesn't resent attacks, but Fala does resent them. You know, Fala is Scotch, and being a Scottie, as soon as he learned that the Republican fiction writers had concocted a story that I left him behind on the Aleutian Islands and had sent a destroyer back to find him—at a cost to the taxpayers of two or three or eight or twenty million dollars—his Scotch soul was furious. He has not been the same dog since.

On April 12, 1945, Fala accompanied FDR to Warm Springs, on Pine Mountain in Georgia. The president was feeling poorly that afternoon and was in bed with Fala lying on the floor across the room. At 3:35 Fala suddenly jumped up and stared in the direction of FDR. He gave a yip and a whimper and turned around quickly. He acted as if he was looking at something—following something—that was not visible to the human eye. Whimpering plaintively he raced across the floor, his eyes fixed on something in the air. Fala charged out of the room, down the short passageway, and, with his eyes still pointed skyward, crashed into the screen door. At that same moment the doctor pronounced that the president was dead.

Fala made the last trip with his master. They traveled from Warm Springs to the White House, from the White House to Hyde Park, and finally to the rose garden on the banks of the Hudson River.

JFK AND CHARLIE

Although we have come to view the Kennedy years in the White House as filled with dogs, the fact is that the only dog he had with him when he started his term of office was a Welsh Terrier named Charlie. For the record, Charlie was bought for Kennedy's daughter, Caroline. However, of all of the animals that would share the White House with JFK, Charlie was his favorite (plate 10).

Kennedy loved to swim and spent a lot of time in the White House pool. When he was at the pool, however, he liked to play with Charlie, so the poolside was littered with balls and floating toys for the president to toss into the pool for Charlie to fetch. Meanwhile, the Kennedy children played their own game at the pool. The object of their game was to toss a toy into the water and try to get close enough to their father so that when Charlie leaped after it in a burst of enthusiasm, he would land on the president. When he did there were gales of laughter from the children as JFK splashed about in mock distress over being hit by this furry missile. Charlie developed into such a good swimmer that he eventually became a great threat to ducks that would sometimes land in the fountains or pools surrounding the various presidential residences.

The word went out to the White House staff that in the whole Kennedy menagerie Charlie was the top dog. The terrier's naturally self-assured nature meant that he could get away with bossing the other dogs around in most instances; however, the staff was informed that if any problems arose, Charlie was to be protected and was assumed to be in the right. After a while Charlie developed a trick that did not endear him to the gardeners and outside workers around the White House. He would silently slip up behind a worker who was digging or planting. He would then pick a moment of vulnerability and make a quick rush at the man, nipping him in the seat of the pants or grabbing at his leg. This guerrilla operation was over in a second, with Charlie racing across the lawn in great excitement, well out of reach of his victims. One worker complained to his supervisor that Charlie had actually bitten hard enough to draw blood. "Leave it be," he was told. "If it was one of the other dogs we could do something, but when it comes to that one it's different. If it came to a choice of who would have to go, you would be packing to leave, not Charlie."

It is interesting how dominant individuals can draw comfort from these self-assured dogs. Take the time when Traphes Bryant,[3] the White House kennel keeper, found himself called to the president's office at the height of the Cuban Missile Crisis. Bryant describes the scene:

I was there in Jack Kennedy's office that day. Everything was in an uproar. I was ten feet from Kennedy's desk as Pierre Salinger [the Press Secretary] ran around the office taking messages and issuing orders while the President sat looking awfully worried. There was talk about the Russian fleet coming in and our fleet blocking them off. It looked like war. Out of the blue, Kennedy suddenly called for Charlie to be brought to his office.

The surprised kennel keeper raced out and was back in a few moments with the little terrier. The room was filled with a swirl of vital information, frantic aides, and fearful indecision. JFK sat in the center of it all, with the dog on his lap. "He petted the dog and it seemed to relieve his tension." After a while he signaled to Bryant to take Charlie out. JFK smiled as the dog was lifted from his hands, then leaned on his desk and said, "I suppose that it's time to make some decisions."

Charlie, however, was JFK's love, not his wife Jacqueline's. After the president was assassinated Jackie made it clear that she did not want the trouble or expense of having JFK's dogs around. So she got rid of almost all of them, including Charlie. The only dog that she kept was a Cocker Spaniel named Shannon, who had been given to them by the Prime Minister of Ireland, Eamon de Valera. It was widely believed that even this exception was made for diplomatic rather than for emotional reasons. Perhaps Jackie Kennedy simply did not have a dominant enough personality to find love and companionship in a Self-Assured dog such as Charlie.

Chapter Ten

Dogs for Trusting and Controlling People

The next personality trait that is important to us is *trust*. People who are high on this dimension we will call "trusting," while those who are low on this scale we will call "controlling." This dimension becomes quite important when we are dealing with dogs, since we often have to decide whether a situation requires trusting our dog's instincts or whether the dog's behavior must be manipulated or controlled. In addition, some breeds are more predictable and trustworthy than others.

People who are high on the trust dimension tend to be gentle and conventional. Obliging, modest, and straightforward in most of their interactions with other people, they are often described by people who know them as being "good sports." They readily follow directions and take orders from clearly designated leaders. There is general agreement that trusting people are not egotistical, and they are also seen as being believable and truthful in most situations.

It is exactly these trusting tendencies that make it less likely that these individuals will be successful in certain occupations where mistrust is an advantage and suspicion is called for. Thus we seldom find trusting people working as bank examiners, credit investigators, or quality control inspectors. They are very rare among financial speculators, stock or bond brokers, and even school principals. Trusting people are more comfortable in the arts, including music, performing, writing, and design and decoration. They are best in situations where any competitive aspects of their job involve direct evaluation of the quality of their accomplishments, rather than in situations where there is the potential for backbiting and betrayal. Trusting people are often simply too believing and can be lied to and manipulated by more unscrupulous people.

In structured situations, such as when a teacher is following a specified curriculum, or when someone is making phone calls and distributing literature for a fund-raising organization or political party, people high on the trust dimension tend to do well and are usually well received and well liked. They are capable of putting themselves in the background and working with a lot of energy for a cause, organization, or person that they believe in. When things get socially difficult, however, such as when a teacher has to deal with an irate parent who thinks that her child should be getting better grades, the trusting person does not do as well. A trusting person might not anticipate later difficulties, such as the parent taking the matter to the school principal, the school board, or even to the public press. Such actions would seldom cross their own minds, since they represent a violation of trust. This same attitude makes trusting people a marketer's dream, since they are apt to accept most claims made in advertisements at face value.

You know you have encountered a person who is high on the trust scale when you see that they have left their car doors or house unlocked, or perhaps have left their office door ajar, with keys dangling from the keyhole, while they have wandered down the hall to talk to someone. When the doorbell rings at home, they are apt to open the door without even first checking to see who is there.

These people make pleasant friends and lovers. They are seldom suspicious about the faithfulness of a spouse or close companion, even when they are away from home for extended periods of time. They take their friends at their word for most things. Thus, if a trusting person's friend offers to cut his hair, he may not even bother to ask if the friend has ever done it before and is any good at it. When trusting people get into disagreements they shy away from force-based tactics like profanity or shouting and even from more subtle coercion, like the "silent treatment." They also seldom hold a grudge for very long, and usually will eventually forgive people who have taken advantage of them.

Controlling people, who are low on the trust dimension, tend to be competitive and can be calculating or even manipulative. Others often describe them as crafty, cunning, wily, calculating, sly, and cocky. If you are a controlling sort, you are quite willing to put someone in their place if that person tries to get the best of you or push you around. When anyone annoys you, you can be pretty blunt in telling them what you think of them, even if the individual involved is your supervisor or some other person in authority. If you are slighted in any way you do not forget and ideas of revenge may fill your head for days or weeks after an incident. You may well act aggressively or impulsively if the opportunity to get even occurs. This tendency probably explains why individuals who are low on the trust trait are seldom found in occupations where conciliation must be used or advocated, such as among marriage counselors, personal counselors, and clinical psychologists, or where errors must be accepted from other people and not commented upon, such as among speech and physical therapists.

Perhaps because they are low on trust themselves, these individuals are quite good at manipulating other people, even if this requires deception. If necessary they can often bluff their way out of trouble, or "pull one over" on other people. When they are trying to manipulate the behavior of another person they will use every tactic possible, but their favorite is to deliberately act charming, helpful, and romantic. If that doesn't work they will resort to reasonable-sounding arguments which explain the costs of disagreement and benefits of agreement with their position. If these tactics don't succeed they will use more forceful methods—criticizing, cursing, threatening, or simply sulking or acting obstinate and ignoring the other person. The last tactic in their arsenal is to act humble and needy. They will use this tactic if the situation requires it, but since they have nothing but contempt for other people who act in a subservient manner, it is their tactic of last resort. With such an extensive set of social manipulation abilities, it is not surprising to find that these controlling people are often found among politicians at all levels of government, stock and bond agents, speculators of all sorts, and also among real estate sales people and in many of the other more aggressive marketing jobs, such as telephone marketing and solicitations.

People who are low on the trust dimension are often quite conscious of their desire to manipulate others. At their best they can become charismatic leaders, bringing together different factions in order to keep a country or an organization intact. Truth and honest dealing are not an issue in such matters; all that counts is the results, and these people can get results when dealing with other people. At their worst they can turn into con artists or swindlers. They have no compunctions about making friends with "the right people" simply for the advantages, prestige, or information that might come of it. These people want to have the control and the power over others that success will bring. On a basketball team the controlling person will often take a very long shot, since scoring will make him an instant star, even if he could pass the ball to another team member who may have a better chance at scoring. Thus at their worst, low-trust individuals care only for themselves and not for their social group.

People who are at the mid-range in trust will show aspects of both extremes. Sometimes they will tell untruths to get their way, while at other times they will be shocked and outraged by the lying of others. Whether they accept and trust others or manipulate them in a competitive way depends solely on the present circumstances. Such people are sometimes honest and straightforward, and at other times take advantage of the situation and even attempt to consciously manipulate others.

The trust dimension appears to be an important one in determining the breeds that will make us happy. Table 3 summarizes the dog breed groupings that will best fit the needs of men and women with different levels of trust. Remember that a full listing of the dogs in each group is found in the Breed Groups appendix at the back of the book. It is interesting to note that except for low-trusting people, the patterns for men and women are different on this dimension.

EMILY AND KEEPER

It is a sad fact that people who are very high on the trusting dimension frequently do not reach the pinnacles of power and fame. This is probably because on the way up a person is bound to make someone envi-

TABLE 3

Dog groups that are most preferred by men and women with differing levels of trust.

Trust Score	Dog Groups For	
	Women	Men
High	Consistent	Protective
	Protective	Clever
Medium	Friendly	Friendly
	Competent	Independent
Low	Steady	Steady
	Self-Assured	Self-Assured

ous, and a person with a highly trusting nature can easily be betrayed or deceived by an individual who wants to damage his or her reputation. Trust is also a factor when it comes to signing contracts or developing business or professional associations. The trusting person might not scan documents carefully for pitfalls or question the integrity of potential associates, and thus may end up with problems. When trusting individuals manage to achieve fame, they often do so because of accident or accomplishment in a realm that does not involve day-to-day social conflicts and competition. Thus a writer or artist of great skill may be very trusting and accepting and still may become famous simply because he or she writes or paints extremely well. Actually, this was more true of the past than the present, since both artists and writers today are more and more likely to be called upon to publicize their work. Such publicity often involves manipulating one's image and controlling other people and situations in a manner that might result in TV, radio, and print exposure and interviews. In today's environment it may be difficult for gentle and trusting people to make it on the basis of their personal skills. If we look back historically, however, we can find some instances where such individuals have succeeded.

We find an interesting example of such a highly trusting person in one of the three well-known sisters in the Brontë family.[1] Their father, Patrick Brontë, was an Irish-born Anglican clergyman who in 1820 became the rector at Haworth, which is surrounded by the moors of Yorkshire, England. He brought with him his wife, Maria Branwell Brontë, and their six small children. They had not lived there long when Mrs. Brontë died, as well as the two oldest children, Maria and Elizabeth. This left the father to care for the remaining three girls: Charlotte, the eldest; Emily, two years younger; and Anne, two years younger than Emily. In addition there was one boy in the family, Patrick Branwell. The task was too great for the father alone, so an aunt, Elizabeth Branwell, left her home in Cornwall and moved in with the family at Haworth to help care for the children.

Charlotte Brontë was to become the best known of the three girls. Her novels, of which the most popular was *Jane Eyre,* set a new standard in Victorian writing in terms of satiric realism. Her major innovation was the narration, which was delivered from the point of view of a woman or child. Her work is often cited by feminist writers as providing clear examples of the differences in the perception of situations by women and men. The struggle between societal expectations and restrictions versus the desires and needs of an independent woman is a recurring theme in her work.

Given the flavor of her writing it is not surprising to find that Charlotte was a strong dominant personality, and very controlling. She showed a remarkable degree of independence for that era, refusing three serious and respectable suitors who had proposed marriage to her before finally accepting the fourth. She assumed responsibility for the education and nurturance of her sisters, particularly Emily, who was so trusting that she tended to allow others to make most of her major life decisions for her. When her brother ran up large debts at the start of his career as an artist, Charlotte went to work in order to supplement the family's resources.

While Charlotte is not the focus of this story, it is interesting to note that she did have a fondness for dogs and, consistent with her dominant personality, the dogs that she most cared for were from the Self-Assured group. The family kept a terrier named Grasper—probably an early Scottish Terrier or Cairn Terrier, judging by the portrait Emily painted of him—and it was accepted by everyone that Grasper was really Charlotte's dog and that she had the greatest affection for it. Her fondness for terriers showed itself later on in her married life when she again had a terrier.

Anne Brontë, the youngest of the Brontë children, was not considered to be as brilliant as either Charlotte or Emily. She is best known for two novels, *Agnes Grey* and *The Tenant of Wildfell Hall,* both of which sold well but have not had much lasting impact. Tuberculosis cut her life short at the age of twenty-nine. Of the three sisters, she is described as the warmest and most gentle. As you will find in the next chapter, such people are very happy with dogs from the Friendly group, and it was from this group that Anne selected her pet, a Cocker Spaniel named Flossy.

The sister that we are most interested in here, however, is Emily Brontë. Emily is best known for her only novel, *Wuthering Heights,* a highly imaginative novel of love and passion, and also of hate and revenge, set on the Yorkshire moors. Emily also was an accomplished poet, and in 1845 Charlotte accidentally came across some of her poems. In discussing them, the sisters learned that all three of them had been writing verse. They decided to publish these poems jointly in a single volume, *Poems,* by Currer, Ellis, and Acton Bell, using pseudonyms because of fear that the work of female authors might not be taken seriously. They chose to use pen names all from the same family, and then each selected a first name that started with the same letter as her own. This book contained twenty-one of Emily's poems, and most critics agree that Emily's contributions were the only ones that showed any real poetic genius.

Emily was quiet and self-contained, low in personal dominance and extremely trusting and accepting. She prided herself on the fact that the controlling behaviors of Heathcliff and Catherine, the main characters in *Wuthering Heights,* were not drawn from any aspects of her own personality or experience. Charlotte recognized Emily's trusting nature and tried to protect her from people who might abuse her trust, and also to assist her in making decisions. When Charlotte obtained a teaching position at Miss Wooler's school at Roe Head, she took Emily with her as a pupil. Left to govern her own life most of the day, while Charlotte taught or tended to classroom-related tasks in the evenings, Emily felt uncomfortable, and soon returned home.

Emily's one great adventure away from Yorkshire was also due to her trusting acceptance of her sister's decisions. In order to keep the family together at home, Charlotte planned to open up a school for girls at Haworth. Therefore, she took Emily and went to Brussels so that both of them could learn the foreign languages and school management skills that they would need. Emily never questioned Charlotte's decisions and direction of her life. To do so would have required a display of more controlling behavior than she was comfortable with. Unfortunately, although the Brussels experience was interesting, the school never did really get started because Haworth was simply too far away from the major towns, and travel to it was inconvenient.

Emily Brontë had a favorite dog named Keeper. Consistent with a personality so high in trust (and perhaps, low in dominance), she favored a dog from the Protective group. There is some debate about the breed of Emily's dog. It was during the time when attempts were being made to cross Bulldogs with Mastiffs to produce more compact and faster guard dogs. These experiments led to the Bullmastiff, and by adding a bit of Great Dane to the mix the slimmer, lighter Boxer was produced. Some historians have claimed that Keeper was a Bullmastiff, while others have said that he was a Boxer. Although for our purposes it should not matter much, since both of these breeds are in the Protective group, a glance at Emily's watercolor pictures of Keeper leaves little doubt that he was a Boxer. He was fawn-colored, with a white blaze, and had a black mask on his chiseled, wrinkle-free head. Most importantly, his squarely built, muscular body and the long legs and narrow hips make this dog easily recognizable as a Boxer. Emily had shown a great interest in this dog before she owned it. She loved his independence, his fierceness, and his wild and stubborn nature. When she was given the dog it came with a caution. Emily was told that Keeper would be faithful to his friends, but no one should ever strike at him since it was in the nature of the breed to fly at an attacker's throat.

It may seem somewhat strange to find this delicate and fragile woman falling in love with a dog who is advertised to have such a savage nature. She would later write, "His growl is more terrible than the bark, menacing as muted thunder." Emily treated him with affection, and for Keeper she soon became the center of the universe. He would trot behind her on her long walks over the moors, only moving from his position when approached by a stranger or another dog. His protective instincts were strong, and Emily often had to salve his wounds when he decided that another dog had come too close and that she needed an active defense. To try to prevent such confrontations, Emily taught him to bark and growl on command. When cued to do so he could actually produce a roar that sounded much like that of a lion, and the sound was menacing enough to cause most people and animals to keep their distance. Emily's sister Charlotte actually used these behaviors of Keeper in the depiction of the savage dog Tartar in her novel *Shirley.*

One visitor looked at the slim woman and the great dog standing protectively beside her and, perhaps with a bit of disapproval, said, "I understand that most ladies tend to prefer lap dogs."

"Perhaps I am an exception," replied Emily.

The visitor did not know just how close to a lap dog Keeper could be for Emily. She would sit on a rug on the floor when she was reading, casually leaning against him, or draping an arm around his neck.

One evening the Brontës had a visitor—a man who was interested in Emily and hoping to develop some sort of relationship. Emily seated herself on their large sofa, with Charlotte on one side of her and the man on the other. While they spoke, Keeper walked across the room and forced his large body between Charlotte and Emily, and then settled down with his front quarters and head on Emily's lap. The space there was far too limited for his comfort, so he pressed forward, placing his paws and part of his head on the visitor's knee. Emily's heart was won by the man's acceptance of the situation; apparently she was too trusting to suspect that it was the closeness to herself that was inspiring her visitor to put up with the dog's antics.

Keeper slept in Emily's room at night and was allowed up on her bed at times, but he soon began to display an unacceptable daytime behavior. When he wanted to rest in comfort the big Boxer would steal his way upstairs and leap up on any available freshly made bed. It was bad enough to have this dog that the rest of the family did not trust, and viewed as ferocious, stretched out on their beds, but even worse was the trail of muddy footprints across the white bedspreads. Because the bed covers were white linen counterpanes and were difficult to wash and press, the parsonage's housekeeper became extremely upset at this "household fault" of Keeper's. Everyone in the family agreed that something had to be done. Emily announced to them that, despite their feel-

ings about the fierceness of Keeper and his breed, the next time this behavior occurred she would punish him so severely that it would never
happen again.

The moment of crisis came the very next afternoon. The housekeeper entered the parlor to tell Emily that Keeper was fast asleep on
her father's bed. Emily's face drained of color and she pressed her lips
tightly together as she stood up. Although the rest of the family were
concerned as to what would follow, they held their places while Emily
marched upstairs alone. A few minutes later she appeared at the head of
the stairs. Both of her tiny hands were clenched on the collar around
Keeper's neck, and she was dragging him behind her. The dog had his
legs set forward to resist any movement and he was growling in a low
menacing way as she pulled him down the staircase, one step at a time.
At every step she told him, "Bad dog. Bad dog."

Down the stairs the pair came, Emily dragging Keeper until they finally reached the place behind the stairs that had been designated as
Keeper's daytime napping area. At that point Emily released him and
began pounding him again and again with her small fists. All the time
she was hitting him she was sobbing, "Never, never, never, never, do
that again." The big dog stood there, utterly stupefied, until Emily collapsed onto her knees. She put her arms around Keeper's neck and
leaned her tear-streaked face against his forehead. Then, with as much
dignity and composure as she could muster, she stood up and led
Keeper to the kitchen, where she lovingly washed his dark face, mur-
muring, "You will be good now, won't you?"

Keeper did not bear a grudge, and he did stop sleeping on the beds
during the day. Emily never struck him again. The incident had simply
been too painful for one whose nature was so nonaggressive. She had
trusted Keeper not to turn on her, despite all of the warnings that she
had been given, and Keeper had proven to be worthy of that great degree of trust.

At the age of thirty, Emily, who had always been rather frail, contracted tuberculosis. On the last day of her life, she got out of bed in the
evening to feed Keeper and Anne's Cocker Spaniel, Flossy. Her sisters
tried to get her back into bed, but she insisted that it was her responsibility. That evening she died.

Keeper walked next to Emily's father at the head of her funeral pro-
cession and sat quietly through the graveside service. He then returned
to the house and lay down in front of the door to Emily's empty room.
When anyone walked by he would look up hopefully, and then whimper when he saw that it was not Emily. Three years later Keeper joined
Emily on what I hope is some soft white bed of dreams where he can
rest unpunished for eternity.

PRESIDENT NIXON AND KING TIMAHOE

I have already mentioned that individuals who are low on the trusting
dimension often have a set of skills that are very useful for politicians,
labor organizers, political lobbyists, advertisers, and campaigners for
various causes. Remember that people who are low on trusting also frequently have a skeptical and detached view of their social world. This
gives them the ability to use quite conscious strategies designed to manipulate the opinions of others. Psychologists sometimes refer to this
aspect of personality as *Machiavellianism.* The name pays homage to
Niccolò Machiavelli, a celebrated Italian political analyst, military theorist, historian, playwright, and diplomat. Machiavelli's most famous
work was *The Prince,* a manual outlining how a person in power can
control and manipulate the people around him by whatever means are
necessary.

Machiavelli's political advice ignores the usual ethical rules by which
people try to ensure mutual trust and fair play. He stresses that "it is
necessary for a prince, who wishes to maintain himself, to learn how
not to be good" so that he can pick and choose among all of the possible alternative behaviors so as to ensure that he gets his way. Machiavelli
would have agreed with statements like "The best way to handle people
is to tell them what they want to hear," "Anyone who completely trusts
anyone else is asking for trouble," "It is wise to flatter important
people," and "Only tell the truth if it is to your advantage to do so."
While such a philosophy suggests a cynical view of the world, it does
make for successful politicians and is helpful in any profession where
the opinions and behaviors of other people need to be influenced.

Dean Keith Simonton, professor of psychology at the University of

California at Davis, measured the Machiavellian tendencies in U.S. presidents from George Washington to Ronald Reagan. Of this whole group, by far the one who would score lowest on our personality dimension of trust (hence highest on Machiavellianism) is Richard M. Nixon.[2] In fact Nixon's score was so extreme that fewer than one person in a thousand would have such a low score.

Although one might question the ethics and wisdom of the series of decisions that eventually made Nixon the only U.S. president ever forced out of office before his term had ended, no one questions the fact that he was the consummate politician and a master at manipulating public opinion.[3] Evidence for Nixon's ability to influence and manipulate others appeared quite early in his life. At an age when most other children were still reading fairy tales, Nixon had already taken an interest in politics. While he was still in grammar school he joined a debating team and participated in his first public debate. In college his ability and desire to persuade and control other people continued to be evident. He was elected president of the freshman class, then president of his fraternity, then, in his senior year, president of the student body. After he graduated and entered the law school at Duke University, he was also soon elected president of the student body and in his last year he became president of the Duke Bar Association.

At the end of World War II, Nixon's controlling personality served him well in politics and eventually won him a Senate seat, the U.S. vice presidency under Eisenhower, and ultimately the office of U.S. President. It appears that it was Nixon's controlling tendencies that eventually ended his presidency. Just prior to the vote for his second term as president, Nixon, or associates acting on his behalf, arranged for a team of people to break into the Democratic National Committee headquarters in the Watergate Building to try to get campaign information that would allow him to better control the outcome of the election. Unfortunately for him, the men involved were arrested and charged with burglary and wiretapping. Influenced by his controlling tendencies, Nixon thought that he could cover up White House involvement. Although he was caught lying to investigators, as a true Machiavellian personality, he never admitted this breach of ethics. Instead he had his press secretary, Ronald L. Ziegler, simply tell the press that all previous statements issued by the executive branch regarding the Watergate affair were "inoperative." In a similar fashion, when he was finally forced to resign because of his involvement in the cover-up, his final statements never addressed any of the ethical issues, nor provided any apology or admission of guilt. He simply announced that he "no longer had a strong enough political base" with which to govern, and that this was his reason for leaving the presidency.

There is a well-known incident linking Nixon with a dog, which has led many people to believe that his preferred breed was a Cocker Spaniel, rather than a dog from either the Self-Assured or the Independent dog groups that our present data would suggest that he would favor. It was in 1952, just after the Republican Party had chosen Nixon as the vice presidential candidate to run with Eisenhower. Just a few days later Nixon's political career seemed doomed. A newspaper story in the *New York Post* was headlined "Secret Rich Men's Trust Fund Keeps Nixon in Style Far Beyond His Salary." There was immediate public outrage, and it looked as if Nixon would be dropped from the election ticket. In fact there was nothing secret or underhanded about the fund. Nixon himself was far from wealthy, and when he won his Senate seat a group of businessmen had publicly solicited a fund of around $18,000 to allow him to keep in touch with the voters in his home state while he was in the Senate and residing in Washington, D.C.

Nixon recognized that he could use the new medium of television to respond to the charges and to control public opinion. In a brilliant TV acting job, filled with pathos and humble family values, he denied that there was anything improper in his use of the money and pointed out, "My wife Pat does not have a mink. She wears only a respectable Republican cloth coat." The show-stopper came, however, when he admitted one gift that he had accepted—the family dog.

A man down in Texas heard Pat on the radio mention the fact that our two youngsters would like to have a dog. And, believe it or not, the day before we left on this campaign trip we got a message from Union Station in Baltimore saying they had a package for us. We went down to get it. You know what it was? It was a little Cocker Spaniel dog in a crate that he sent all the way from

Texas—black and white spotted. And our little girl Tricia, the six-year-old, named it Checkers. An' you know, the kids love the dog, and I just want to say this right now, that regardless of what they say about it, we're gonna keep it!

There were reports that many viewers, including Eisenhower's wife, Mamie, wept sentimental tears at this point, and some of Eisenhower's aides wiped their eyes a bit (remember this was 1952, when men were not supposed to cry in public). The speech was a political triumph. The movie producer Darryl F. Zanuck called to say that this speech was "the most tremendous performance I've ever seen," and when Eisenhower met Nixon on his return, he greeted him with the words "Dick, you're my boy." Nixon's career was saved, and for a while Checkers was the most famous dog in America.

Nixon appreciated the Cocker Spaniel for saving his career, but it clearly was his daughter Tricia's dog and not the breed that he would have chosen for himself. Long after Checkers had passed away, Nixon was elected president. When he arrived at the White House he came with two dogs: Pasha, a Yorkshire Terrier that belonged to Tricia, and Vicky, a Miniature Poodle that had been given to Pat Nixon. However, the dog that Nixon had always spoken of most fondly was an Irish Setter that he had had as a child. This dog had provided him with constant companionship during terrible times of illness and money problems that his family suffered through when he was growing up. Given Nixon's low trusting scores, an Irish Setter was appropriate, since this dog is in the Independent group, which is favored by people with his controlling personality.

Because Nixon so often spoke of his boyhood Irish Setter, the White House staff decided to purchase another to be his presidential dog. The dog arrived in January 1969 and was immediately christened King Timahoe after the little village in Ireland that Nixon's Quaker ancestors came from. King Timahoe was obviously Nixon's favorite (plate 11). The president kept treats in his desk drawer in the Oval Office, just for him. Nixon also would not allow anybody to punish the setter, even when he had badly chewed one of the carpets in the presidential office. In some of his few breaks from work, Nixon would ride around in a golf cart with the great red dog beside him. He once explained, "We're not really going anywhere, it's just that Tim likes to ride in the cart and I like to see him happy."

Nixon's affection for King Timahoe was so great that he was willing to put up with the displeasure of the U.S. Army for the dog's sake. Traditionally, White House pets are treated by the veterinarians at the Walter Reed Army Hospital. While this was good enough for the other family dogs, Pasha and Vicky, it was not good enough for the president's personal favorite. Much to the chagrin of senior army staff, Nixon had the dog sent to the veterinarian recommended by the dog's breeder. Each trip to the vet thus involved the White House kennel keeper taking the dog on a two-hour round-trip in one of the presidential limousines.

While King Timahoe was a well-loved dog, Nixon would not let that stand in the way of his Machiavellian attempts to manipulate other people. During his first term of office, the world's most eligible bachelor was Prince Charles of England. It was widely believed that Nixon had the idea that he could work his way into the circles of royalty if he could arrange a marriage between his daughter Tricia and Prince Charles. He therefore arranged a state visit for Charles, with Tricia as his hostess and escort. As the day of the prince's arrival drew closer Nixon circulated a message to the White House staff indicating that "during the Prince's visit, King Timahoe will be referred to only as Timahoe, since it would be inappropriate for the Prince to be outranked by a dog." All was for naught, since Tricia and Charles simply did not impress one another at all.

PICASSO AND KABUL

It is tempting to think that highly controlling people, who would score low on the trust scale, are mostly to be found in political or large business settings. Yet this personality can be found everywhere, even in the fine arts. Take the case of Pablo Picasso, probably the most famous artist of the twentieth century.

Picasso was born in Malaga, Spain, and was the son of a Basque drawing teacher named Blasco Ruiz and an Italian mother, Maria Picasso.[4] According to Spanish naming traditions his name was Pablo Picasso y Ruiz, and so he signed his earliest pictures. Before he died at the age of ninety-one, he would sign over forty-five thousand works. Given the fact that Rubens, with a whole "factory" of apprentices, turned out less than three thousand works in his lifetime, it is likely that Picasso was the most prolific major artist in history.

One professor of fine arts told me that Picasso had five passions: "his art, his ego, his image, his women, and his dogs, in that order." He always had to be in total control, and this served him well economically. Given his amazing productivity, in any world which had a logical law of supply and demand, works by Picasso ought to have been extremely cheap. Yet by carefully controlling his image and the public's evaluation of his stature, by skillfully influencing press coverage of his activities, by convincing critics and museum curators and gallery owners that his work was special and rare, Picasso became extremely wealthy and his reputation became enormous. Out of the production of one year (1969), he exhibited 167 oils and 45 drawings. The gross market value of that fragment of his output was about $15 million in 1970 dollars.

His interactions with women were strongly based on control. The number of women that he had relationships with is still a matter of dispute, but there were many. At times when he was married he would often have a mistress on the side. At times when he was unmarried he would frequently have, in addition to a mistress, another in the wings, plus numerous casual affairs. In all of these relationships he had to be in complete control. He characterized the women in his life as being "goddesses or doormats." They were goddesses until he had them enthralled, and doormats when they were under his spell.

Picasso would use whatever means needed to control those around him. In his dealings with women and lesser members of the art community, he would even resort to blackmail if needed. For instance, Picasso became interested in Irène Lagut, a minor artist and the mistress of another artist, Serge Férat, who was from a wealthy, aristocratic Russian family. Picasso desired her but she didn't respond to his advances, so he initiated an underhanded scheme to get Irène away from Férat. First he stole a nude photograph of her, which she had never shown to Férat. Picasso let her know that he had the photo and informed her, "This will be very useful one day." Irène later wrote that "when Serge's sister returned home from Nice, he [Picasso] went to her and said, 'Irène is a whore. For proof you only have to see what she wears when she gets photographed. She has cuckolded Serge. Even I have slept with her.'" According to Irène, "he did everything he could to have me thrown out into the street so that I would be forced to go and live with him. He's the vilest man one could possibly imagine."

Although Férat did not believe Picasso's claims at first, Picasso did not give up. He next showed the picture to Férat and repeated his fabricated story. His persuasive abilities were so good that Férat finally confronted Irène. He told her that it was useless to deny the charges, since Picasso himself had sworn that she had already slept with him. He told her to pack her suitcases and to leave. When Serge later returned to the studio there was a strong smell of gas and the door was locked from the inside. With the concierge's help, he broke in and found Irène passed out in front of the gas stove, in what had been a deliberate attempt at suicide. A doctor managed (with some difficulty) to revive her, and Irène managed to persuade Férat that Picasso's accusations were false and that they were part of a plot to get her away from him.

Undaunted by this new series of events, Picasso cleverly changed his tactics. In a series of notes to Irène, he professed his love for her and his regret that she had attempted such a rash action. Turning the tables on her, he tried to make her feel guilty and responsible for hurting him. He wrote in a note that by trying to commit suicide "you have caused me sorrow, much sorrow, but I do not hold this against you." This new tactic worked, and Irène wrote him a note to console him and to say that she was now fully recovered. This was followed by another exchange of notes, a rendezvous, and soon Irène was living with Picasso. She remained with him for only three years before being ejected to make room for another mistress.

Picasso's life was also full of dogs. He had many, of many different breeds, including terriers, Poodles, a Boxer, Dachshunds, a German Shepherd Dog, several Afghan Hounds, and numerous "random-bred" dogs. The dogs were part of his life and went everywhere with him. He gave dogs to his friends as gifts, in part to ensure that he would never be in their company without a dog. Often when a romantic relationship would break up, Picasso would leave all of his goods behind him and go off to live in a new place with a new woman. Usually he would arrange to have only a few things returned to him, generally including some of his recent paintings, some of his brushes and paint, and his dog or dogs. The rest was all left to friends or the woman whom he was leaving.

Picasso's dogs often worked their way into his art. One of his first pieces was a paper cutout of his terrier. Lump, a Dachshund, was drawn into several of Picasso's interpretations of Velazquez's painting *Las Meninas*. Freaky, a mixed-breed, is the subject of many drawings, while Kabul, his Afghan Hound, appears in several paintings with one of his wives, Jacqueline.

I got to meet Picasso once. The occasion was a reception held in honor of the unveiling of a large piece of public sculpture that had been commissioned by a university. Picasso had not actually carved the sculpture. If my memory serves me well, the carving was left to an assistant (I think he was Swedish) who worked from Picasso's drawings. The reception was one of those large formal affairs, with the guest list deliberately seeded with some people from the media so that the university could get some publicity out of this occasion. I no longer remember why I was invited; however, I was there with a few other academics, mostly from fine arts departments.

Picasso was already well into his eighties. I remember being surprised by how small and wiry he looked. What I remember most is his eyes—they were enormous in relation to his head, and at first glance they seemed almost black. By all accounts he lived a largely indoor life, yet his skin had that finely crinkled, leathery quality usually associated with people who have spent their lives exposed to the sun and wind. He was surrounded by dignitaries who were controlling the flow of people who wanted to meet him.

One of my colleagues leaned over to me and said, "We can go up and try to say hello, but he really only talks to important people or people who can do something for him."

"Well, I'd like to try," I said. "I wanted to ask him a question."

"About what?"

"His dogs."

My colleague looked at me as though I had the word "dumb" written on my forehead, but then shrugged and started moving toward the knot of "important people."

I noticed, that, in fact, he was quite right. Picasso said virtually nothing to the people paraded in front of him. When they were introduced to him he would not extend his hand, but nodded, sometimes making eye contact with them, sometimes not. Watching this scene, I knew that I would have little chance for even a minute-long conversation, but I thought that I would try.

I reasoned that I might have a little edge over some of the other people there, since I had recently read that, despite the fact he had lived in France for around fifty years, Picasso remained very proud of his Spanish heritage. At the time I spoke reasonably fluent Spanish (since then, living in Canada and learning French seems to have erased or distorted much of my ability in Spanish). As we moved closer, I quickly rehearsed the question that I intended to ask him—in Spanish.

Once I was in front of him, and my colleague had just given my name and gestured toward me, I quickly said, "Excuse me. I know that this occasion has to do with your art, but might I ask you a quick question about your dogs?"

On hearing his native tongue, he looked directly at me with the barest hint of a smile. "Certainly," he said.

"I have seen photographs of you with so many different breeds of dogs. Is there any one breed, or any one dog, that was your favorite?"

Now he did smile. "I have had so many," he started, and his dark eyes drifted upward. "Some were gifts, some I found. Breeds . . . I do not usually get the same breed of dog again. I want each to be an individual and I do not want to live with the ghosts of the other dogs. All except one. He was an Afghan Hound named Kabul. Since him I have had other Afghan Hounds . . . perhaps I am looking for his ghost. He is the only one that I sometimes think about."

He looked directly at me, and as he continued speaking his right hand was making lines and curves in the air, as if he were drawing something on an invisible canvas in front of us.

"Often, if he comes into my mind when I am working, it alters what I do. The nose on the face I am drawing gets longer and sharper. The hair of the woman I am sketching gets longer and fluffy, resting against her cheeks like his ears rested against his head. Yes, if I have a favorite it was my Afghan Hound, Kabul."

He smiled at me in a way that told me that my audience was over. As I thanked him and turned to leave I noticed that two dignitaries whom I did not recognize were staring at me, as though my brief foreign-language conversation represented some sinister plot or, at the very least, a major breach in protocol. I had my answer, however, and twenty-five years or so later, in light of our data, I understand why he chose Kabul. A man as controlling as Picasso would score very low on the trust dimension of personality. This kind of person would be very happy with a dog from the Independent group, which includes the Afghan Hound.

Incidentally, since then I have looked at Picasso's art in a different way. Now I always look at the noses and hair and wonder if the picture I am looking at has a bit of hound in it or not.

<< *Chapter Eleven* >>

Dogs for Warm and Cool People

The last interpersonal personality dimension that we have to deal with is *warmth*. Individuals who score high on this dimension are obviously called "warm," while those who score low on this trait are called "cool."

People who are high on the warmth dimension are usually described as sympathetic, kind, forgiving, soft-hearted, tender, charitable, and accommodating. In most of their social interactions, warm individuals come across as caring and helpful. These are the people who are most likely to provide emotional and material support for others who are in trouble, who need help, who are ill or emotionally vulnerable—in fact they are likely to try to help anyone (or anything) that is in trouble.

The occupations where we are likely to find the greatest number of warm individuals are those that involve providing personal assistance, service, and advice. Counselors of all sorts, including those who deal with marriage problems, vocational choices, or personal adjustment problems, fall into this category, as do clinical psychologists, speech therapists, psychiatrists, and a variety of other people in the mental health and social work disciplines. In some religious and clerical professions, particularly those which involve missionary duties, and in charity-related organizations you will find a high concentration of

< 141 >

warm people. Child-oriented professions, teachers at most levels but especially the lower grades, playground and youth camp staff often fit into this category as well.

If you usually try to help others out when they are having difficulty, even if it involves some disruption or discomfort to yourself, then you are acting like a warm person. If you are a warm person then you are also apt to do things for clubs or for social, political, and charitable organizations, and you won't think much about getting any public credit or acknowledgment for these activities. Some of the best ways to influence a warm person's behavior are by pouting, sulking, avoiding them, or not talking to them. Withdrawal of any attention or affection is quite painful for the person with a high degree of warmth. Warm people are also made very uncomfortable when someone shouts or curses at them during an argument. In such situations they are apt to try to find some form of accommodation to make the person less angry.

People who are low on the warmth dimension are much more self-oriented. Cool people tend to describe themselves in terms of their personal independence, their freedom from being influenced by the opinions of others, and their willingness to flaunt social conventions. People who are low on the warmth trait seldom seek advice or try to solicit support or help from family and friends. They are more likely to act the role of the lone wolf, keeping to their own plans and following their own desires. This focus on their own actions, with little thought for the responses of others, may make the cool person occasionally seem quite rude. Little courtesies, like opening a door for someone, providing assistance when someone is carrying a lot of packages, offering an elderly person a seat on a crowded bus, or even remembering to say good-bye before hanging up a telephone, are often forgotten or ignored.

If you are a cool person, then your friends or associates may often describe you as feisty, contrary, or irascible. To get your way you are likely to explode in an aggressive manner, criticizing the other person, using profanity or veiled threats if you think that these tactics will work. Sometimes you will deliberately sulk, use the "silent treatment," or act as if you are interpreting their actions as aggressive—as if they wanted to "put you in your place." The idea that people can be swayed by charm, compliments, and romantic actions seldom occurs to you.

When cool people engage in games or other forms of competition they are out to win, and if other people get hurt or upset during the process, that is just the way the world works. Cool people are also more likely to challenge the decision of a referee when it goes against them, and they are often the first to point out infractions (whether real or imagined) on the part of their opponents. Off the playing field, cool people are often the first ones to institute legal actions against other individuals.

People with cool personalities are concentrated in professions where a degree of cynicism or skepticism is helpful. Thus investigators of all sorts, whether private investigators, insurance investigators, or those who do credit checks, benefit from a cool personality. So do inspectors for quality control, safety, or construction, as well as financial analysts, cost estimators, government or corporate budget analysts, and those involved in things like inventory control. It is interesting that some forms of scientific research work, especially those areas where personal feelings must be kept out and people or animals must be viewed as data points rather than individuals, may often benefit from people whose personality is low on the warmth dimension.

People who are in the mid-range on the warmth dimension are much more likely to let the situation determine their responses. They tend to be selective, showing warm, supportive behaviors to people that they are familiar with, and more reserved and cooler behaviors to strangers. A person who is high in warmth will come into a new situation and start out being friendly, while one who is cool will start out as reserved and distant. People who are medium in warmth act much like a social mirror: if they are met with friendliness they will reflect it back, while if they are first greeted with coolness they will adopt a cool strategy in that particular situation.

A person with a medium score on warmth may also seem to be a bit inconsistent or unpredictable, sometimes responding with optimistic congeniality and at other times with a pessimistic detachment that may even appear uncaring. There is a positive aspect to this variability in their behavior, and that is that their moods and actions are much less extreme than those of people who score very high or very low on warmth. Even in their coolest moments, medium-warm people can still be swayed to help someone, or at least not to unduly harm them. Conversely, in their most friendly and helpful phases medium-warm people still monitor the situation and hold back just a bit to make sure that their behavior is appropriate for the present circumstances.

Warmth is an important personality dimension in determining the dogs that we will love and hate. Table 4 shows the dog groups that will be liked the best by people at all levels of warmth. Remember that a full listing of the dogs in each group is found in the Breed Groups appendix at the back of the book. This is one dimension where the differences between the sexes are quite large, with men and women preferring some fairly different breed groups at various levels of warmth.

JIMMY AND BEAU

The personalities that actors and actresses come to represent in the minds of the public are often quite different from the reality. Many movie vamps turn out to be quite modest and shy women in their private lives, while many heroic movie figures turn out to be quite ordinary people at home. One actor whose movie persona comes close to his real personality is Jimmy Stewart. The American Film Institute observed that James Stewart is an actor "so beloved by the movie-going public that they call him 'Jimmy,' just like a member of the family."

The roles that Stewart is identified with are usually those of ordinary

TABLE 4

Dog groups that are most preferred by men and women with differing levels of warmth.

Warmth Score	Dog Groups For	
	Women	Men
High	Protective Friendly	Clever Friendly
Medium	Independent Clever	Protective Independent
Low	Self-Assured Steady	Steady Consistent

men who, despite difficult situations, not only thrive, but do so with dignity, decency, and a lot of warmth. This is the essence of the characters that he played in his early work, such as director Frank Capra's *You Can't Take It with You, Mr. Smith Goes to Washington,* and *The Philadelphia Story* (which earned him an Academy Award). Such roles continued in the later part of his career, after he returned as a real-life hero from World War II. Even in high-tension films, such as the Alfred Hitchcock thrillers *Rear Window, The Man Who Knew Too Much,* and *Vertigo,* or in Otto Preminger's *Anatomy of a Murder,* the warmth of his real personality continued to be apparent.

Jimmy Stewart was born in 1908 in his parents' home in Indiana, Pennsylvania, a town that used to advertise itself as the "Christmas Tree Capital of the World." He and his two sisters lived in a loving family, and perhaps it was this wholesome upbringing that reinforced his naturally sociable and warm tendencies. Stewart was obviously quite bright and he graduated with honors from Princeton after majoring in architecture. Unfortunately it was 1932. The United States was in the midst of the Great Depression and there was little money for new buildings and little work for new architects. Stewart, however, was an accomplished accordion player, which ultimately determined the course of his life. On his graduation day from Princeton, he ran across Joshua Logan, who was also a Princetonian and who would go on to have a distinguished career as a movie producer. Logan invited Stewart to join the University Players in Falmouth, Massachusetts, as their "resident accordionist." He never returned to architecture.

When the show Stewart was playing in, *Good-bye Again,* went to Broadway, so did Jimmy, and his career path was set. Stewart ended up sharing a room with Henry Fonda, and both of them also shared dreams of becoming motion picture actors. Stewart's only prolonged break from acting occurred during World War II, when he volunteered for service with the air force and served as the command pilot on twenty combat bombing missions. After being promoted to squadron commander, he became operations officer, and later the chief of staff of his combat wing with the rank of colonel. His first film after the war is the role that comes closest to displaying his actual personality. The film is Frank Capra's *It's a Wonderful Life,* now an annual Christmas classic, in which Stewart plays George Bailey, a good warm man and an ideal-ist, who is contemplating suicide because he is in financial difficulty and feels that he is a failure. With the help of an angel, Bailey comes to see how significant and loved he has been, and how important he is to his family and his community.

Stewart married Gloria Hatrick McLean. At the time of their wed-ding she had already had two sons by a previous marriage, and later she and Stewart had twin daughters. Stewart was a warm and loving father to all four children. He and Gloria remained happily married for forty-one years, until her death. During that whole time he lived in the same house in Hollywood. He supported church and charitable activities and took time out from his busy professional schedule to head the fund-raising committee for his church for many years. He had a number of special loves for places and organizations, such as the Boy Scout move-ment. Although he had strong political views, he never let them affect either his work or his relationships with family and friends. At every opportunity his warm sociability always came through. People could rely on him to show up for charitable or community events, usually with Gloria by his side. He would even fly across the country just to re-turn to his hometown in Pennsylvania for special occasions.

His warmth was remarkable in a profession where people are often distant, self-protective, and even arrogant. His house was on the route traveled by many of the sight-seeing buses that take visitors past the homes of Hollywood stars. Unlike many film stars, who are continually annoyed by these intrusions into their neighborhoods, Stewart showed no such negative feelings at all. If he happened to be outside and visible from the street when a bus would pass, he would flash a friendly smile and casually wave his hand to the astonished and star-struck visitors.

Quite consistent with Stewart's warm personality is the fact that the dogs that he preferred were from the Friendly group. Specifically, the breed that he most preferred was the Golden Retriever. He had several during his life, and they were extremely important to him. While I was on a book tour a few years ago, I had the opportunity to meet with Jimmy Stewart. He was no longer the young Charles Lindbergh char-acter that I remembered from the film *The Spirit of St. Louis,* or the easy-moving character who became a hero in *The Man Who Shot Lib-erty Valance.* His age had begun to show on him, and he appeared almost fragile. He was slow moving and even slower talking than in the movies. However, when he started to speak about his dogs his face broke into a smile and the pace of his talking picked up. He told me:

When I married Gloria she already had a German Shepherd named Bello. He loved her a lot and, after a while he and I got along. Gloria really loves German Shepherds best of all, but sometime after we lost our second one, she decided that they weren't the breed of dogs that I needed. Anyway, she went out and got me this Golden Retriever named Simba, and it's been Goldens ever since for me.

We actually have three dogs now. Kelly and Judy are Golden Retrievers, and then there is Princess who is some kind of a mixed-breed that my daughter found and we sort of rescued. Princess had some behavior problems and I think that Kelly and Judy picked up some of her bad habits—figured that if Princess could get away with it so could they. We had met Matthew Margolis [co-author of a number of fine dog training books, such as When Good Dogs Do Bad Things, *with Mordecai Siegal] and Gloria liked him. He runs the National Institute of Dog Training. Kelly and Judy were not behaving. They didn't listen to anything we said, and they were always jumping up and barking and pulling on the leash—both were just imitating Princess, I think. Well, anyway, Matthew told us that he would have to take the dogs to his training kennel for six weeks to get them to behave. The reason that he wanted them at the kennel had something to do with "socialization" and other dog things like that. It was supposed to help their shyness and excitability. Gloria and I didn't like it, but she felt that we had to do something. Well that lasted just one day. You know I love my house, but without any dogs around it feels like some kind of mausoleum. I told Gloria, "Get those dogs back home because I can't put up with them not being here." Anyway, Matthew tried to set up a training program at the house, but it really didn't work so well. In the end we compromised. We broke the three dogs up into squads, so we could send one or two of them to school for short sessions, and still have one or two at home for company. I still didn't like it, even though we got to visit their school on weekends. Gloria made a lot of phone calls to make sure they were OK—to reassure me I guess.*

I suppose the truth is that I'd rather have a happy dog than a trained one. My dogs have never been good at things like "sit," "stay," or even "come." I think that we've given the tourists a few laughs, especially when the dogs hit the end of their leashes hard enough to drag Gloria down the street. I don't even mind it when the dogs jump up. Matthew showed us how to jerk the leash to correct that kind of thing. I suppose that it does have to be done—you know to keep them from knocking someone down or messing their clothes—but it seems kind of cruel to me. If my dog jumps up on me I figure that he wants to kiss my face and tell me that he thinks that I'm a really nice person. I don't believe that you should punish a dog for saying "I love you." When your dog's face is looking up at yours like that I think that you should tell him just how nice you think that he is too.

Gloria told me that Matthew says that we mother the dogs too much and that they'll never really be well trained. Well, they're a lot better now than what they were before, so some of the training must be working. The difference between "trained OK" and "trained perfectly" doesn't really matter all that much to me. I once did a film with Lassie. When that dog got excited it jumped all over Rudd Weatherwax [Lassie's trainer]. Now that's the smartest dog in the world. If the world's best-trained dog can jump around to show he's happy then my dogs should be allowed to do the same.

The truth is that it's just really hard for me to get to sleep without a dog in my bedroom. It's funny about that. I once had a dog named Beau. He used to sleep in a corner of the bedroom. Some nights, though, he would sneak onto the bed and lie right in between Gloria and me. I know that I should have pushed him off the bed, but I didn't. He was up there because he wanted me to pat his head, so that's what I would do. Somehow, my touching his hair made him happier, and just the feeling of him laying against me helped me sleep better. After he died there were a lot of nights when I was certain that I could feel him get into bed beside me and I would reach out and pat his head. The feeling was so real that I wrote a poem about it and about how much it hurt to realize that he wasn't going to be there any more.[1]

Jimmy Stewart paused and he stared wistfully off into space for a moment. The warmth of the man had been evident when he was speaking to me, and now the love that he still had for a long-gone dog was just as clear.

I later learned just how intense his feelings were for his dog Beau. At the time, Stewart was making a picture which was shooting on location in Arizona. One evening he got a phone call from his veterinarian, a Dr. Keagy, who told him that Beau was very sick. The dog was having trouble breathing and was in considerable pain, and it was obvious to Keagy

George Bush and his beloved
Springer Spaniel, Millie. Bush once
commented that while he was in the
White House Millie would share his
shower with him each morning.

Sigmund Freud with his Chow
Chow, Jo-Fi, who attended many of
his therapy sessions. Freud claimed
that he depended upon Jo-Fi's
judgment to tell him about his
patients' mental states.

Actress Jean Harlow and her Old English Sheepdogs. She once said, "I like any dog that makes me look good when it stands next to me."

Humphrey Bogart, who tried to live up to the image of the tough characters that he often portrayed in movies, had a fondness for tough and self-sufficient dogs, such as Boxers and Scottish Terriers.

Winston Churchill is the perfect counter-example to the claim that people pick dogs that look like themselves. Churchill was said to resemble a Bulldog or a Pug, but actually his favorite dogs were Miniature Poodles, such as Rufus, shown here.

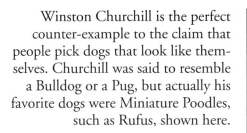

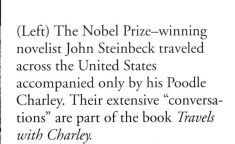

(Left) The Nobel Prize–winning novelist John Steinbeck traveled across the United States accompanied only by his Poodle Charley. Their extensive "conversations" are part of the book *Travels with Charley*.

For the Nobel Prize–winning playwright Eugene O'Neill, his Dalmatian, Blemie, filled the emotional void left by his unsuccessful relationships with his children. O'Neill purchased a four-poster bed for Blemie's personal use at night.

Dwight D. Eisenhower had a fondness for Scottish Terriers. During his campaign in North Africa he was accompanied by one named Caaci. When he was stationed in Britain as Supreme Allied Commander, his driver and friend, Kay Summersby, gave him another, Telek. Both are shown here.

Franklin Delano Roosevelt's favorite Scottish Terrier, Fala, became a national symbol during World War II. Fala also figured prominently in a smear campaign launched by Republican opponents during the 1944 presidential campaign.

While John F. Kennedy had many dogs during his White House years, the only one that he owned when he became president was a Welsh Terrier, Charlie. Charlie remained JFK's favorite and served as his "silent advisor" during the Cuban Missile Crisis.

Although the public has come to identify Richard Nixon with the Cocker Spaniel Checkers, who may have saved his political career, Nixon's favorite dog was actually this Irish Setter, named King Timahoe.

During her teenage years, Queen Victoria's favorite dog was a Cavalier King Charles Spaniel named Dash. The day of her coronation, the new nineteen-year-old queen arrived home after the ceremony, tossed off her weighty royal robes, and gave Dash a bath.

Queen Elizabeth II was given her first Corgi by her father, who was then still the Duke of York. She was only seven years old at the time, but the gift initiated her lifelong love for the breed.

Harry Truman seemed to have little fondness for dogs. Here, his daughter Margaret is seen with the Irish Setter Mike, whose tenure at the White House was very brief.

Lyndon Baines Johnson had a great fondness for dogs, and during his administration the White House was populated by a number of Beagles, a neurotic white Collie, and a mixed-breed terrier. When LBJ was photographed lifting one of his Beagles by the ears, however, it triggered a national furor.

In 1971, Elizabeth Taylor and Richard Burton lived on their boat on the Thames for their entire visit to England. They did so to avoid having to subject their Pekingese and Lhasa Apsos to the required six-month quarantine for dogs entering the country.

Writer E. B. White, who is probably best known for his children's classic *Charlotte's Web* and for his insightful and sometimes ironic commentaries in the *New Yorker* magazine, owned many breeds of dogs during his life. He often wrote about his love-hate relationship with his dachshund, Fred.

Elvis Presley's fondness for Bloodhounds may be related to his rock and roll hit song "You Ain't Nothin' But a Hound Dog"; however, he also kept a tiny Maltese named Foxhugh.

that he couldn't be saved. The vet was calling for permission to end Beau's life quickly. Stewart's wife, Gloria, had said that she couldn't make that decision since Beau was Jimmy's dog.

"I can't tell you to put him to sleep like this," Stewart said. "Not over the phone—not without seeing him. You keep him alive and I'll be there."

Stewart was always known as an easy actor to work with, one who never made excessive demands. So the director was taken aback when he asked for a few days off to fly home to see to his dog. The leave was granted and Stewart got to sit with Beau for a long while before making the decision. He later admitted that when he left the veterinarian's office he had to sit in his car for around ten minutes, just to clear his eyes of tears, so that it would be safe to drive home.

BYRON AND BOATSWAIN

One of the ways that a person can demonstrate a very low score on the warmth dimension of personality is through an inability to form meaningful and lasting close relationships with other people. One classic example of this type of personality is found in the talented but cynical and uncaring poet George Gordon Byron.[2] Byron was the son of a handsome but wayward sailor, Captain John "Mad Jack" Byron, who had squandered all of his wife's family money. Since he died when his son was only three, his profligate ways were not passed on to the future Lord Byron by example. His only legacy was to leave his family in relative poverty. At the age of ten, Byron unexpectedly inherited, not only a title, but also the estates of his great-uncle William, the Fifth Baron Byron. The properties included Newstead Abbey, in Nottinghamshire, which had been presented to the Byrons by Henry VIII.

Byron had been born with a slightly clubbed foot, and he limped a bit as he walked. This had provoked some ridicule when he was a child, and was always a source of embarrassment to him. Some of his biographers have suggested that this was one reason why he was so low on the warmth dimension and tended to hold himself aloof once he had the status and wealth to do so. On the other hand, this physical deformity was offset by the fact that he was quite handsome and could be socially charming when he had a desire or need to be.

Although lacking in warmth, Byron was not lacking in passion. He had numerous affairs but showed very little sustained affection for any of the women involved. Most of the women that he had sexual liaisons with appear to have been targets of opportunity. For example, because of the popularity of his poetry and his aristocratic position, he came into contact with Lady Caroline Lamb, and this intimate relationship was followed by one with another conveniently available socialite whom he had met at various occasions named Lady Oxford. Next there was Lady Frances Webster, who happened to be attracted to his work, and so forth. Propriety or even conventional morality had little influence on him. During the summer of 1813, Byron took advantage of his frequent meetings with his half-sister Augusta to start an affair, despite the fact that she was now married to Colonel George Leigh.

With the number and identity of his lovers threatening to become a public scandal, Byron sought to escape by marriage. He proposed to Anne Isabella Milbanke, but there was no love in this relationship, only a convenient refuge that would give him a more conventional and stable image. The marriage lasted only two years, but it was long enough to produce a daughter, Augusta Ada. Becoming a father did not stir any warmth in Byron. After her first year of life he never even saw Augusta again.

With the breakup of his marriage Byron left England, never to return. In Geneva he settled near the poet Percy Bysshe Shelley, who had eloped with Mary Godwin. Godwin's stepdaughter by a second marriage, Claire Clairmont, was living with them, and typical of Byron, she was convenient and became his next sex object. The Shelley party left for England, where at the end of the summer Claire gave birth to Byron's illegitimate daughter, Allegra. Byron had little more affection for this daughter than for his first. Later on he would send her off to a convent just to be rid of her.

Byron had moved on to Italy, and in Venice he carried on an affair with Marianna Segati, his landlord's wife. In Rome, his new sex toy was Margarita Cogni, a baker's wife. Then he met the woman who he felt would provide a focus for warmth and love. She was the Countess Teresa Gamba Guiccioli, who was only nineteen years old and was already married to a man in his fifties. Byron followed her to Ravenna, and she later accompanied him back to Venice. This "true love" lasted only three years (which was long for Byron). Byron's interest in the Greek revolution gave him an excuse to leave her, and just one year later, in Greece, he contracted the fever that would take his life at the age of thirty-six.

Although Byron is classified as a romantic poet, the tone of much of his writing is often distinguished by an absence of warmth or romance. His most famous work, *Don Juan,* is really a cynical satire. His other great work, *Childe Harold's Pilgrimage,* is a dark unhappy travelogue. There are certainly great insights and moments of poignancy, but as in the man, there is little warmth. In *Don Juan* we get lines like "Society is now one polish'd horde, / Form'd of two mighty tribes, the Bores and Bored." We also find comments like "Now Hatred is by far the longest pleasure; / Men love in haste, but they detest at leisure."

Given Byron's personality, it is not surprising that the dog that he was fondest of came from the group of Steady dogs. These include the Saint Bernard, Bulldog, Bernese Mountain Dog, and Byron's own dog, the Newfoundland. Byron's dog was named Boatswain (pronounced "*Bosun*"). He was a Landseer Newfoundland, which means that instead of the more common, all-black coloration, he was black and white.

Byron was around twenty years of age when he got Boatswain, and he developed a true fondness for the dog. He decided that the dog would come with him to Cambridge University, and would live in his college rooms with him. Byron already had a reputation as a bit of an eccentric; still, a dog living in the university was not considered acceptable to the other fellows of Trinity College. When they tried to prevent Boatswain from sharing Byron's residence, the poet launched a counterattack: he presented a trained bear as a candidate for a college fellowship. The press thought that this was quite amusing and might indicate something about the other members of the university if the bear was being offered as the "best and brightest of them all." The bear was rejected, but the fellows recognized that continuation of their objections would lead to a long and perhaps publicly humiliating battle. To avoid this, they agreed to allow the dog to stay.

At only five years of age, Boatswain had a sudden fit and died. His premature death was quite hard on Byron, who grieved more at his dog's loss than he would later grieve at the loss of his mother. To ease the pain of his loss, Byron invested 260 pounds sterling (a small fortune at the time) to construct a mausoleum and a monument for Boatswain. Not only was the dog to be buried in that crypt at Newstead Abbey, but he specified that Byron, himself, was to be buried beside his dog when his time came. This request was then formally entered into his will. Byron then composed an inscription which was placed upon the monument. In it he shows first his deep love for his dog, and second his rather cold and cynical view of the rest of humanity. The inscription is worth reading, so I have included it in its entirety below.

> Near this spot
> Are deposited the Remains
> of one
> Who possessed Beauty
> Without Vanity
> Strength without Insolence
> Courage without Ferocity
> And all the Virtues of Man
> Without his Vices.

> This Praise, which would be unmeaning flattery
> If inscribed over Human Ashes,
> Is but a just tribute to the Memory of
> "Boatswain," a Dog
> Who was born at Newfoundland
> May, 1803,
> And died at Newstead Abbey
> Nov. 18, 1808.

When some proud son of man returns to earth,
Unknown to glory, but upheld by birth,
The sculptor's art exhausts the pomp of woe,
And storied urns record who rests below;
When all is done, upon the tomb is seen,
Not what he was, but what he should have been.
But the poor dog, in life the firmest friend,
The first to welcome, foremost to defend,

Whose honest heart is still his master's own,
Who labours, fights, lives, breathes for him alone,
Unhonoured falls, unnoticed all his worth,
Denied in heaven the soul he held on earth—
While man, vain insect! hopes to be forgiven,
And claims himself a sole exclusive heaven.

Oh man! thou feeble tenant of an hour,
Debased by slavery, or corrupt by power—
Who knows thee well must quit thee with disgust,
Degraded mass of animated dust!
Thy love is lust, thy friendship all a cheat,
Thy smiles hypocrisy, thy words deceit!
By nature vile, ennobled but by name,
Each kindred brute might bid thee blush for shame.
Ye, who perchance behold this simple urn,
Pass on—it honours none you wish to mourn.
To mark a friend's remains these stones arise;
I never knew but one—and there he lies.

After Byron left England, and before his poetry made him financially secure, he ran up some large debts. To pay these he was forced to sell Newstead Abbey, and so his request to be buried beside his dog could never be honored. Byron never again established a warm, loving relationship with a dog. Because of this we can speculate that eleven years after Boatswain's death, while he was writing *Don Juan,* he must have momentarily thought back about that one warm lasting friendship of his life. In that classic poem he recalls a feeling that every dog owner knows and loves.

Tis sweet to hear the watch dogs' honest bark
Bay deep-mouthed welcome as we draw near home;
Tis sweet to know there is an eye will mark
Our coming and look brighter when we come.

Even a person as cold as Byron is capable of love. If not love for a human, then at least love for a dog—if he has selected the right dog.

Chapter Twelve

One Size Fits All

In the last four chapters I concentrated mainly on the dog breeds that suit people who are at the extremes (either high or low) on the interpersonal personality scales. In some respects these extremes are the aspects of our personality that make us unique. Thus if you were asked to describe someone you might say, "He is really just an ordinary average person, except for the fact that he . . ." and here you would pick out one of his extreme characteristics, maybe that he "is so warm and loving" or "is so hard working" or "has an air of dominance and leadership" or "is so intelligent." In other words, we expect most people to be at a medium or average level for most characteristics, and our attention is caught by those aspects of an individual's personality that are extreme and therefore distinctive.

Most people think that a person is rated medium on a personality trait because of having attitudes or displaying behaviors that are in the middle range all of the time. Thus a person who is rated medium on the warmth scale might be one who shows a moderate degree of friendliness to most people, never bubbling over with love and support, but also never ignoring people or showing open hostility. This is certainly one possible personality pattern. However, it is actually the less common of the two ways that a person can end up rated medium or mid-range on a personality dimension.

The more common way of ending up with a medium score on a personality trait actually involves averaging a number of extreme behaviors. Thus we might have a person who is extremely loving and friendly to those that he likes, and is very hostile and vindictive to those that he doesn't like. Or we might have a person whose attitudes seem to change erratically from day to day. On one day she is friendly and supportive, on another cold and uncaring. If, however, the number of warm and cold instances in behavior are about equal in number, such a person would also score as medium on warmth.

One of the interesting aspects of such "vacillating" personalities is that their behavior is not as unpredictable as one might think. These behaviors are often direct responses to the immediate circumstances, suggesting that people who are in the middle range on a personality trait are very responsive to their environment and the social climate that they find themselves in. These people are not simply leaves that are blown about by random winds of emotions. They are often quite consistent as to the conditions that produce particular patterns of behavior, and they often mirror the behaviors that they are confronted with. Thus, when they are met by people expecting trust and acting in a trusting manner, medium- or average-range people will respond in a trusting fashion. If met with suspicion, by people who are trying to control the situation, these people will feel their own level of suspicion rising and will develop a desire to control the situation themselves. In most situations, however, they will begin with behaviors which are mid-range and moderate in their intensity. The conditions that bring out the extremes of behavior in a person with medium scores on a trait are encountered relatively infrequently, so, in fact, most of the time such individuals act in a fairly average manner.

Are there dogs for people who score in the medium range on most personality measures? The answer is yes, if we use our rule of thumb that any dog group that shows up on two or more personality scales for an individual is a possible good fit. The majority of people score at the medium level on one or more of their personality characteristics, and so it is not surprising to find that the dogs that fit people with medium-level personality scores include many of the most popular breeds.

The group of dogs that most often comes up as suiting people with medium personality characteristics is the Friendly group. This group shows up in three out of the four personality scales for men and two out of four for women. It includes Labrador Retrievers, Golden Retrievers, and Cocker Spaniels, three of the breeds that are consistently in the top ten in popularity in North America. In fact, one recent survey that included statistics from fourteen different countries went so far as to proclaim that "the Labrador Retriever may be the most popular breed of dog in the world." The Friendly group works well for both men and women with medium scores.

When we look at the dog group that is in second place for average people, we find that there are significant differences between men and women. For women the best fit (coming out on three of the four scales) seems to be the Clever dogs. This group includes the Poodle and the German Shepherd, which are consistently found in the top ten list for breed popularity. In addition, for mid-range women, the Consistent group, which includes the Dachshund, Pomeranian, and Chihuahua (all in the top ten dogs in popularity), shows up on two of the four scales. The pattern for men with medium scores on the personality scales is a lot simpler than that for women. The only dog group that is mentioned more than once for men is the Friendly group, strongly suggesting that these breeds are the best bet for average men. However, every other group gets a mention in the mid-range for men. This can be interpreted as meaning that a man with an average personality might be a bit more accepting of more breeds of dogs than the average woman. The woman with an average personality seems to be a bit pickier about the dog breeds that she will accept, but also seems more capable of forming close bonds with the breeds that she does like.

The best-fitting groups of dogs for medium-scoring people include eight out of the top ten breeds in popularity. The reason that I point out the popularity statistics is that people tend to stick with the breeds that fit their lifestyle and their personality best. The flip side of this is that if you found a dog breed that just didn't work for you, you would probably never get another dog of that breed again. Although there are many factors that can inflate the popularity of a breed for a short time (such as another Disney release of a film production of *101 Dalmatians*), generally speaking we can take popularity of a breed as a rough measure of how well it fills the needs of most people. Thus if dog breeds came in measured sizes and styles, the dogs in the Friendly groups for both men and women, and the dogs in the Clever and Consistent groups for women, would probably be marked "One Size Fits All."

VICTORIAN DOGS

Most of the people who make their way into the public eye have at least some pronounced or extreme personality characteristics. This especially holds in the areas of entertainment, politics, and the arts. We expect our politicians to be dominant and controlling. We expect our actors and actresses to be extroverted. We expect artists such as painters and musicians to be extreme in their personalities, either excessively warm or excessively cold. Such expectations are often fulfilled because the media find extreme personality characteristics to be more interesting. A person with extreme values on some traits is more likely to be discussed in the media, and this coverage will often increase that individual's fame or notoriety.

There are still a few ways in which people with quite average personalities do make it into the public eye. These are often people with a particular skill, such as scientists, inventors, educators, physicians, or engineers. Often these are otherwise ordinary people whose abilities allow them to make a great discovery or complete an important project. Others become noticed because of chance circumstances or historical events. Examples of this might be the army captain heading an engineering unit who becomes nationally known because he is called upon to strengthen a failing dike system during a flood, or an airplane pilot who makes a spectacular landing with a damaged airplane, thus saving a couple of hundred lives. These people were singled out not because of their personality characteristics but rather for other reasons.

People with quite average personalities can also become well known because they belong to rich or powerful families, and achieve their own wealth and status because of these familial connections. This is especially the case for people who are in the position to assume a hereditary title or office. Let's consider one ordinary, average person who became the symbol of an era, and also kept dogs.

She was born Alexandrina Victoria, on May 24, 1819, in Kensington Palace, and eventually rose to the title of Victoria, Queen of the United Kingdom of Great Britain and Ireland and Empress of India.[1] She was not born to be queen, it was just that circumstances intervened. When George III became incompetent to rule, his son George IV became regent and then king. Unfortunately the only daughter of George IV, Princess Charlotte, died in 1817. This then started a race to see who would father the next ruler of England. In 1818, three of George III's sons, the dukes of Clarence, Kent, and Cambridge, immediately married to try to secure the succession. Edward, Duke of Kent, won the race with the birth of Victoria the next year. After his death, Victoria was still not the frontrunner for the throne; she was third in the line of succession to the throne after the Duke of York and the Duke of Clarence. The Duke of York died in 1827 and the Duke of Clarence eventually took the throne as King William IV. Victoria's chance to wear the crown should have ended there, but none of William IV's children survived their infancy. Thus it was a chain of chance events, not her personality and accomplishments, that led to Victoria's ascension.

The popular image of Queen Victoria is of a stern, domineering, overly moralistic, and controlling person. I was therefore quite surprised when four experts (three historians and a political scientist) rated her as average on all four of the personality dimensions. I called one of them back to get more information about this and he explained that, although Victoria showed memorable instances of extremely dominant and controlling behaviors, these were counterbalanced by instances of obvious acquiescence and submission. "She had flashes where her behavior was excessive or immoderate given the conditions," he said, "but these occasions were unpredictable and often her behaviors were contradictory. For instance, there was the time when she publicly cried in sympathy for the plight of one poor working man and his family. On the other hand, there are records of many instances where she was offered opportunities to do things that should have helped the poor working class as a whole, and she simply didn't respond, or flatly refused. Most of the time, if it weren't for the trappings of her office, we would have probably considered her behavior to be quite ordinary and middle-of-the-road. One expert on her life refers to her as an average and ordinary housewife who happened to win the throne." A look at Victoria's life shows that he is probably quite right.

She was a small woman who carried herself with self-assurance and had a silvery voice when she was young. Soon after taking the throne, Victoria married her cousin Prince Albert of Saxe-Coburg-Gotha. She had grown to know him well since his first visit to England, and had been corresponding with him for about four years. On his return visit to the English court in 1839, Victoria was strongly attracted by Albert's good looks and charm. Encouraged by her uncle Leopold (the King of Belgium), Victoria proposed to Albert just five days after he had arrived at Windsor.

Victoria's love for Albert shows incredible warmth and passion. "Without him everything loses its interest," she wrote. Later in life, after Albert's death, she established a warm personal relationship with the Scotsman John Brown, which she continued despite whispers of scandal and the advice of her ministers. She did not, however, show much warmth toward her nine children. Her secretary, Henry Ponsonby, once wrote, "Will the Queen never find out that she will have ten times more influence on her children by treating them with kindness and not trying to rule them like a despot?" Here we see some of those counterbalancing and contradictory sets of behaviors.

During her years with Albert, there were many parties, and Victoria would sometimes dance the night away. However, she really did not like the free ebb and flow of socializing as much as one might expect from these behaviors. Albert noticed that at times she needed structure in her social interactions in the shape of formalized rituals that would allow her to distance herself from others; as he put it, "she delights in Court ceremonies, etiquette and trivial formalities." Recognizing this introverted aspect of her behaviors, Albert encouraged her to build the royal residences of Osborne, on the Isle of Wight, and Balmoral Castle in Scotland. At these houses, Victoria delighted in their privacy and intimacy, yet welcomed visitors when they came. Obviously we have here someone who was in the middle range in terms of extroversion.

The idea of Victoria as a tough, unbendable monarch with great political skills is clearly wrong, though she certainly did like the trappings of power and dominance as much as she liked the formalities of court. Prime Minister Benjamin Disraeli forever ingratiated himself with her with several flattering imperialistic actions. When it looked as if Britain was going to lose control of the Suez Canal to the French, Victoria could not tolerate the prospect of this loss of power and prestige. Therefore she supported Disraeli's brilliant maneuvering, which led to the British purchase of slightly less than half of the shares in the Suez Canal in 1875. She was then delighted when he presented the canal to her as a personal gift, announcing, "It is just settled; you have it, Ma'am." She was even more thrilled when Disraeli had "Empress of India" added to her list of royal titles in 1876.

When necessary, Victoria could sometimes be politically quite effective and manipulative. She knew most of the major figures in the European aristocracy personally, both because of family ties that she and Albert had, and also because she married many of her children into the most important families in Europe. She was not above using the information and influence gained from these ties to exert political pressure. Sometimes Victoria's political maneuvering was quite adept. She did serve as an important mediating influence between the House of Lords and the House of Commons in order to bring about the compromise that resulted in the third parliamentary Reform Act in 1884.

Victoria was always image-conscious and often treated her personal and family relationships with the same exercise of power and manipulation that she used in politics. In some instances she seems to rival Richard Nixon in her Machiavellianism. Thus, after Albert's death, she used her authority as a mother to enhance her image as a queen. At the time of her Golden Jubilee she deliberately attempted to capitalize on her maternal image to impress upon the public that homage to the monarch was no less sacred than homage to a loved parent. Many of her children were going to give speeches on her behalf during the Jubilee, and she insisted on seeing and editing all of these in advance. She then instructed her secretary, Sir Henry Ponsonby, to inform her children as to her wishes. Writing in the third person (as usual) she noted, "The Queen approves of these answers, but always wishes the words 'my dear Mother' to be inserted. Not only on this occasion, but always. If Sir Henry thinks that it could come in any other place better, he can alter it. But the Queen wishes it should never be omitted when her children represent her."

So far I have painted the picture of a dominant and controlling person, but that is only half of the story. Victoria's displays of dominance were not very protracted, and she would often shift into the totally opposite pattern of complete acceptance and compliance. Thus, although her initial plans were to keep Albert out of government affairs, she was soon seeking his advice on every issue before making any decisions. One biography of Albert (by Daphne Bennett) is entitled *King without a Crown,* acknowledging his far-reaching influence on all of Victoria's state actions. She gave up most of the power and control of her daily life to Albert. It was said that Victoria "didn't put on a gown or a bonnet if he didn't approve it."

After Albert's death, Victoria still did not fully regain her own power of decision or seize full control of her life. In many cases she explicitly noted that she was seeking to come to the same conclusion "that Albert would have reached in this circumstance." It was often said that her testing point was then her "dear one's" point of view. As one might imagine, this would sometimes lead to odd and inappropriate decisions. Although she may have known what Albert's opinions were when he was alive, circumstances had often changed, and his point of view may have been based on considerations that were no longer relevant to the current period in English political life. With Albert gone, she easily turned over much of her authority to Disraeli, who simply accepted it, saying that it would be "his delight and duty, to render the transaction of affairs as easy to your Majesty, as possible." He assured Victoria that this was simply because she was already quite "overworked" and the queen readily went along with this.

While Victoria was extremely controlling in terms of her image and her children, she was not consistently as calculating and manipulative as some people have come to believe. She eventually gave up trying to influence her prime ministers, Lord Palmerston and Gladstone, despite the fact that she disliked both the men and their politics. In addition, Queen Victoria was strongly opposed to the concept of a "democratic monarchy" and in fact was deeply suspicious of democracy as a concept. Yet she did not show either the enthusiasm or the skill to fight it, so as her reign drew to its close, she found that the political power of the monarchy had begun to ebb away.

Victoria's overall pattern has no distinguishing, consistent peaks or valleys on any of the personality dimensions. Although she sometimes demonstrated an extreme on a particular characteristic, in another setting or at another time she could show the opposite. As I noted earlier, these varying behaviors are typical of people at the medium level on our scales.

If Victoria had a medium-range personality then we might expect her to have had a fondness for dogs in the Friendly group. This certainly turns out to be the case. Victoria's constant companion, and perhaps her only true friend during her teenage years, was her Cavalier King Charles Spaniel, Dash (plate 12). Cavaliers are small toy spaniels with a feathery coat, long, full spaniel ears, and a flowing tail. These dogs have a long history, and one of the earliest recognizable sightings of the Cavalier King Charles Spaniel is on the foot of the bed in Titian's portrait of the Venus of Urbino which was painted in the early 1500s. These dogs have had a long association with the British monarchy, being favorites of King Charles II, who originally popularized them and after whom they are named. King Charles I before him, and after him King James II and the Duke of Marlborough, also kept them. These dogs were also favorites of the ill-fated Mary, Queen of Scots.

Victoria loved Dash dearly and often mentioned him in her diaries. One entry in 1833 notes, "I dressed *dear sweet little Dash* for the second time after dinner in a scarlet jacket and blue trousers." (The emphasis is Victoria's.) Five years later, on June 28, 1838, the day of her coronation, the new nineteen-year-old queen arrived home after the ceremony, tossed off her weighty royal robes, gathered up her skirts, and scampered up to her room to collect Dash and give him his afternoon bath.

Six months later another entry chronicled a meeting with the prime minister, Lord Melbourne. Urbane, sophisticated, and quite gentle and likeable when around Victoria, Melbourne served as her mentor and private secretary during the early years. They developed a close friendship. He tried to build up her self-confidence and enthusiasm for her role as queen, while teaching her the basics of politics. The young queen wrote, "I sent for Dashy, who Lord Melbourne accused of having crooked legs, which I won't allow! We put him on the table and he was very much petted by Lord M. We gave him tea and Lord M said 'I wonder if lapping is a pleasant sensation'—for that is a thing we had never felt."

Sir Edwin Landseer, an artist who would achieve his greatest fame by painting dogs in dramatic poses, was called upon to paint a portrait of Dash. Pictures of Dash sitting royally on a tasselled cushion became a set piece for Victorian women to reproduce in needlepoint and embroidery. Many of these stitched pieces can still be found today in antique stores.

When Dash died Victoria was greatly saddened. She set aside a portion of the castle garden as a dog cemetery and then personally composed the epitaph for his gravestone.

> Here lies DASH, the Favourite Spaniel of Queen Victoria,
> By whose command this Memorial was Erected.
> He died on the 20 December, 1840 in his 9th year.
> His attachment was without selfishness,
> His playfulness without malice,
> His fidelity without deceit.
> READER, if you would live beloved and die regretted, profit by the example of DASH.

When Albert married Victoria he introduced her to his preferred breeds of dogs. His favorite dogs were Greyhounds, which come from the Independent group. This is consistent with two of his personality traits, namely his low trust score (which gave him the controlling tendencies that helped him be so politically astute) and his low extroversion scores. He also liked various terriers drawn from the Self-Assured group, which was predictable from his high level of dominance. However, despite her fondness and respect for Albert, Victoria never favored Greyhounds or terriers. She tolerated and respected these breeds, but never selected them for herself.

Victoria's fondness for dogs in the Friendly group never disappeared. Although she did not hunt, she surrounded herself with a large number of retrievers. Most of these were Labrador Retrievers, the most popular dog in the Friendly group, although she did have a Flat-Coated Retriever (also in the Friendly group), and there were several mixed-breeds, random bred, usually with some Lab in them.

Victoria was actually quite instrumental in popularizing another breed in the Friendly group, the Collie. At the time Collies were virtually unknown outside of Scotland, where Victoria saw them on her frequent retreats to Balmoral Castle. One Collie breeder put it this way: "Queen Victoria was responsible for taking Collies out of the pasture and putting them in the parlor. I suppose that if it weren't for her, a whole lot of Lassie movies would never have been made."

Victoria had several Collies. After Albert's death her favorite, named Noble, would often eat with her. This was not your casual "person at the table and dog bowl on the floor" dining, however. Noble was seated on a chair that was drawn up to the table. A dinner plate was placed on a linen napkin in front of him, and when Victoria ate she would place bits of food on his plate and Noble would delicately nibble at them. Beside the plate was a saucer of lukewarm tea, which he would gently lap at between morsels.

As Victoria grew older she began to prefer smaller, indoor dogs. This time she chose from another breed group that medium-scoring women have a high preference for, namely the Consistent dogs. One breed chosen from this group was also a gesture to Albert's memory. Albert loved all things from Germany, so in his honor she kept a number of Dachshunds.

Another dog that Victoria owned from the Consistent group was a Pekingese that she received as a gift. This breed of dog was virtually unknown in the West. They had been bred exclusively for the royal family and the high aristocracy in China, and it was a criminal offense for anyone else to own them, let alone export them.

Victoria got her Pekingese as a result of the Boxer War in 1860. When the capture of the Chinese Summer Palace by British and French troops seemed imminent, many of the court's Pekingese were slain by their keepers to prevent their capture by the Western troops. British soldiers came upon the scene while the last of the dogs were being butchered. Acting quickly, they managed to save five of them. Captain John Dunne took one of these dogs back to England and presented him as a gift to the queen, describing him as a "most affectionate and intelligent little creature" and also as "a souvenir of Your Majesty's far-reaching power." Victoria accepted the dog and named it "Lootie" since it was loot taken from the war. Sensationalized by the press as "the dog that had gazed upon two Empresses," Lootie was viewed by Victoria more as a symbol of British dominance than as a pet.

The small dogs from the Consistent group that Victoria eventually came to love most in her later years were Pomeranians. The Pomeranian is related to the Spitz family of breeds, the dogs often popularly referred to as "Huskies." It has a pointed face and prick ears, a full feathered tail carried in a gentle curl high over its back, and a full fluffy coat. Pomeranians are quite small today, weighing perhaps five to seven pounds. In Victoria's day they were quite a bit larger (up to thirty pounds), but the queen played a role in popularizing the smaller versions.

Victoria was not the first in the royal family to have Pomeranians. They were introduced to England by Princess Charlotte Sophia of Mecklenburg-Strelitz, a neighboring province of Pomerania, who had come to Britain to marry George III, Victoria's grandfather. Although Pomeranians were frequently seen around the palace, they did not catch the public fancy. In 1888 Victoria went to Italy to spend the winter, and in Florence she purchased four Pomeranians, all quite small. A sable red Pomeranian named Marco, who weighed only twelve pounds full grown, quickly became her favorite. She entered him and a female, Gina, in the earliest Cruft's dog shows, and won many ribbons and titles for them. The sight of the queen's tiny Pomeranians caused quite a stir, and soon breeders throughout the nation were trying to reduce the size of their dogs. Victoria herself set up a breeding kennel to perpetuate the line and to provide her with additional companions. Soon Marco and Gina were joined by Beppo, Fluffy, Gilda, Lulu, Mino, Nino, and others.

On January 22, 1901, after sixty-three years as queen, Victoria lay dying. She and the doctors knew that this was most likely her last day.

Propped up on a pillow, Victoria ordered that her current favorite Pomeranian, Turi, be brought to her. When the dog arrived, Victoria lightly slapped the covers and her attendants gently placed the little dog on the bed in the place that she had indicated. She began to stroke the dog, who snuggled close to her. Victoria paused for a moment and looked around her. "There is room for more than one dog," she said, "it is a very big bed." Turi licked her fingers and she produced the half-smile that indicated that she was at ease. A few hours later, Queen Victoria, the longest-reigning monarch in the history of England, was dead.

ELIZABETH'S DOGS

It is somewhat of an oddity that, fifty-one years after the death of Queen Victoria, another woman would take the throne who shares many of her characteristics, including her personality profile, and her preferences in dogs. With the official title of Her Most Excellent Majesty, Elizabeth II, Queen of the United Kingdom of Great Britain and Northern Ireland and of Her Other Realms and Territories, Head of the Commonwealth and Defender of the Faith, she lacks only Victoria's "Empress of India" to complete the picture.[2]

In her childhood Elizabeth, like Victoria, was not being groomed to assume the throne. As the niece of the Prince of Wales, she was a distant third in line for the crown (just as Victoria had been). Had things continued as everyone expected, she would have ranked increasingly further down the line as the years went by. Elizabeth's fate was ultimately determined by a chance meeting at a weekend house party in 1931, when the Prince of Wales (later Edward VIII) met an American woman, Mrs. Wallis Simpson. Five years later, in 1936, Edward abdicated the throne, and Elizabeth's father became King George VI. Thus Elizabeth Alexandra Mary Windsor became the heir presumptive, destined to succeed her father as the monarch. Again, much like Victoria, Elizabeth married a cousin, Lieutenant Philip Mountbatten of the Royal Navy, formerly Prince Philip of Greece and Denmark.

As one might expect of a person with her position, visibility, and wealth, there have been many analyses of Elizabeth's character and personality. Many of these have concluded that she is remarkable for being so unremarkable and that the striking feature about her is that she is so ordinary. Elizabeth's attitudes and behaviors are quite consistent with those found in an average middle-class English woman, which includes eating dinner from a tray while watching situation comedies on television, when her schedule permits. In terms of her personality she, like Victoria, is quite mid-range, according to four experts (three historians and a political scientist) who rated her using the Interpersonal Adjective Personality Scale. However, she arrived at this middle set of values in a different way. While Victoria achieved her medium personality ratings by alternating between opposite extremes, Elizabeth is ranked at the medium level on all four personality dimensions simply because she typically acts in a fairly middle-of-the-road, average fashion, given most sets of circumstances.

Some biographers have described Elizabeth as being a bit insecure, perhaps as the result of having been educated at home, rather than being exposed to a wider set of early social experiences in school. She received most of her schooling from her mother, with some assistance from her father and her grandmother Queen Mary. What these analysts are reading as insecurity, however, is simply the fact that she is not as extroverted, manipulative, or dominant as one might expect from a person holding an office with such apparent trappings of power. In the early years of her marriage she often allowed her husband, Philip Mountbatten, then the Duke of Edinburgh, to do most of the speaking on non-state occasions; but when it was pointed out to her that people expected the queen and not her husband to be in the forefront, she was clearly extroverted enough and self-confident enough to perform these functions.

As is the case with many people who have an average personality profile, Elizabeth has a strong desire for routine and structure in her life. The existence of set routines protects her from the unexpected and allows her to maintain a middle level of responses to most situations. Unfortunately, she can only impose structure on her own life and immediate environment. As the popular press is only too happy to point out, the structure that she has set up for herself does not protect her from random embarrassing activities by members of her family, their spouses, or their ex-spouses. Such events greatly disturb the queen's equanimity and, like most average people, she does not handle them all that well. For example, one day Prime Minister Harold Macmillan arrived at Sandringham, the royal family's English country residence. He was met by the Duke of Gloucester, who was quite upset. "Thank heavens you've come, Prime Minister," he said. "The queen's in a terrible state; there's a fellow called Jones in the billiard room who wants to marry her sister [Princess Margaret], and Prince Philip's in the library wanting to change the family name to Mountbatten." By the way, Elizabeth ended up seeking compromises on both of these issues, as might be expected given her personality. She did allow Princess Margaret to marry Anthony Armstrong-Jones, a commoner, upon whom she conveyed the title of the Earl of Snowdon. (The marriage ended in divorce—the first of many divorces in the family that Elizabeth would have to deal with.) Philip had his way with the name change only in part. All of Elizabeth's children, Prince Charles, Princess Anne, Prince Andrew, and Prince Edward, have the surname "of Windsor," but Elizabeth did create the hyphenated name Mountbatten-Windsor for other descendants who would not assume the titles of prince, princess, or royal highness.

Elizabeth presents the appropriate image for her position as monarch. She displays the formally expected signs and symbols of her station and her wealth when matters of state demand it of her, but such trappings are not necessary for her everyday life and the desire for display and exercise of power is not part of her personality style. Despite her wealth (estimated at around $15 billion), she drives across the moors at Balmoral in an old Land Rover, dressed casually in tweeds and sport clothes. She recycles sequins and beads from her old evening dresses to keep expenses down. When not engaged in affairs of state, she travels around the countryside, shopping, going to restaurants, and visiting dog and horse breeders. Her usual entourage is quite minimal and she demands neither recognition nor special treatment. Once Elizabeth was visiting a Norfolk tea shop when a woman walked up to her and said, "Excuse me, but you look awfully like the queen." Elizabeth smiled and answered, "How very reassuring."

Elizabeth began with quite modest ambitions. When still a child she confided to her riding teacher that she simply wanted to be a "lady living in the country with lots of horses and dogs." In many respects she has achieved these goals. As would be expected for a woman with medium-range personality traits, Elizabeth has a fondness for dogs from the Friendly group. She has a number of Labrador Retrievers, just as Victoria had. One documentary about the queen's life caught her playing with a black Labrador, smiling broadly as the dog bounced around, almost knocking her down with its exuberance. Her retrievers, like Victoria's, are seldom taken inside the palace. As inside dogs she—again like Victoria—has had several Dachshunds, drawn from the Consistent dog group, which also appeals to mid-range personalities. However, it is neither Labrador Retrievers nor Dachshunds that the public associates with Elizabeth. Rather it is her pack of Corgis, a dog breed drawn from the Clever group (plate 13). Clever dogs are the third group which our data showed as being compatible with women who have medium-level scores on the personality measures.

Elizabeth did not initially choose Corgis for herself. When she was only seven years of age, and her father was still the Duke of York, he bought her a Pembroke Welsh Corgi puppy with the impressive name of Rozavel Golden Eagle. He thought that it might be a good playmate for Elizabeth and her sister, Margaret. It certainly was a good friend to Elizabeth, and it fit so well with her temperament that it started her lifelong interest in the breed.

Corgis are a bright, interesting, and feisty breed. The Pembroke Welsh Corgi that Elizabeth favors is a long-backed, short-legged working dog that looks, at first glance, as if its head is a size too large for its body. The breed most likely came about from the crossing of some of the local breeds with Schipperkes, which had arrived in Wales with a group of Flemish weavers whom Henry I had sent for in 1107. The Pembroke Corgi has large erect ears, a sharp foxy face, and a docked tail. They are relatively small dogs, standing 30 cm (12 in.) at the shoulder, but have a substantial weight for their size at about 12 kg (26 lbs.). Bred as herding dogs, they drive cattle or sheep by nipping at their feet. Some dog experts maintain that this genetic tendency to nip in order to get what they want may have gotten out of hand. They report that there are now a large number of Corgis who will snap at anything or anybody if they get the least bit annoyed or excited. The queen herself actually suffered a severe bite when trying to break up a scuffle between two of her dogs in 1991.

The alternative explanation of the snappish nature of Corgis comes from the folklore about their origin. It is said that the first two Corgis were a gift from the fairies to a pair of children. Welsh legends claim that the fairies would use these little dogs for the same jobs that humans give to horses. They could pull little carriages, or serve as mounts for the little folk to ride into battle. If you look carefully, especially at the sable-colored Pembroke Corgis that the fairy knights preferred, it is said that you can still see the marks of the fairy saddle on their shoulders. Some say that the very name of the breed contains its fabled origin, since it combines the Welsh word for dwarf (*cor*) with the form for dog (*gi*) to produce *corgi,* or "dog of the dwarfs." The nippy nature of the dogs is supposed to be due to their being fairy gifts, since it is well accepted that the little folk do not give gifts without some kind of hidden mischievous aspect. So, the story goes, the playful little working Corgi was packaged with an unpredictable and not always controllable temper.

By the time Queen Elizabeth took the throne, the public duties of the British monarch were almost all ceremonial. Elizabeth, however, has a strong sense of responsibility, and began inspecting state papers daily and consulting with prime ministers. Around 1960, Harold Macmillan, who was then prime minister, got to know her well. He later wrote of Elizabeth, "She loves her duty, and means to be a Queen and not a puppet."

Her sense of duty and responsibility extends even to her dogs. She normally keeps about a half dozen Corgis in the palace at any one time. All of these "indoor" Corgis are females, and they bear names such as Diamond, Spark, Phoenix, Myth, Fable, Pharos, and Kelpie. Elizabeth insists on looking after these Corgis personally. This results in an *Alice in Wonderland* mixture of the ordinary and the exotic. Every afternoon that she is at home, a footman brings in a silver tray with a bowl of dry dog kibble, another bowl containing meaty dog food, a pitcher of gravy, and three large silver spoons. With these ingredients the queen then fills the bowls for each of her Corgis, mixing the contents to the dog's taste, and determining the quantity according to her estimate of the dog's needs. Afterwards, she often cleans up the dishes and the utensils herself.

The queen thinks about her dogs with much the same casual fondness that other people reserve for family members. A peek into Elizabeth's handbag reveals a few good luck charms, usually on dog or horse themes. Most of these have been given to her by her children. Whenever she is near any of her residences, her handbag also usually contains treats for the dogs. Every Christmas she gives each of her Corgis a stocking full of special treats.

Much like Victoria, Elizabeth seems to maintain her love for her dogs throughout their lives, and even beyond their lifetimes. She has carried on Victoria's tradition of having her dogs buried on the castle grounds. When one of the dogs dies it is placed in a grave in a place reserved as a canine cemetery. Each grave is marked with a headstone with the dog's name. One member of her household noted a time when the queen had gone out to visit this site. "I didn't know if there was a special dog that she was looking for," he said. "When I saw her do this she just slowly walked through the little burial plot, reading the names and pausing now and then to stop by a gravestone. She stooped down once to touch one of the grave markers and to brush something off of it. She looked sad and thoughtful, and finally left, without saying a word." The sad part about having a breed of dog that fits your personality perfectly is that when they leave us it hurts so badly.

Chapter Thirteen

No Dogs at All

While the major goal of this book is to show how you can match an individual's personality to a particular dog breed or group of breeds, there is another very basic question. Are there any patterns of temperament in people which suggest that the person would be happier without *any* kind of dog? This question is somewhat more difficult to answer than I thought it would be. In my survey, the vast majority of people who lived with a dog expressed a desire to own another one should that one die. People who had owned dogs in the past but did not have one at the moment also expressed strong yearning for a dog, often citing restrictive living conditions (such as apartments that did not permit pets) as the reason for not having a dog at this time. In total, 96 percent of the dog owners or former dog owners that I tested still wanted to live with a canine companion. Now some of these dog owners said that they would not like to repeat ownership of one or more of the breeds that they had lived with in the past, because of problems or personality clashes, but the vast majority still wanted a dog of some sort. This suggests that once exposed to a dog, most people can come to be very fond of them, and it may just be a matter of finding the right breed. In my survey there were, however, 1,564 people who had never owned a dog (or even a cat). It is possible to look at how their personality profiles differ from those of dog owners.

If we eliminate individuals who do not want to live with a pet because of cultural or religious restrictions or because of some sort of phobia, we find that the personality pattern for non–dog owners is relatively similar for both men and women. Generally speaking, these non–dog owners have somewhat extreme scores on the extroversion, dominance, and warmth scales. The trust scale seems to make very little difference in this case. To begin with, these individuals are extremely low on the extroversion scale, even compared with the scores that we usually call introverted. Among women, the non–dog owners are likely to score 13 or less, while men score 12 or less on extroversion. These individuals also tend to have fairly high dominance scores, with women typically scoring 26 or higher and men 29 or more. Finally, we have a pattern of very low warmth scores, with women averaging 16 or less and men 14 or less on this personality scale. This highly dominant, introverted, and cool personality pattern suggests that typical non–dog owners are very forceful and competitive people who are quite satisfied with their own company and do not feel much need to socialize unless it serves to advance them personally. They are not likely to go out of their way to make those around them feel comfortable and loved, nor are they apt to exert themselves very much to provide help and support for other people. This pattern of personality might also make it difficult for these individuals to develop and maintain loving relationships with human beings.

THE POET AND THE POODLE

One example of this personality pattern can be found in Johann Wolfgang von Goethe. Born in 1749, Goethe was one of the giants in the world of literature, making contributions as a poet, playwright, critic, essayist, and journalist. A productive writer—one complete collection of his work was published in fifteen volumes—Goethe was also a scientist, theater manager, and court official. His life, however, was filled with many frustrations due to his difficulty in dealing with intimate personal relationships. Despite his genius, Goethe's love life was an odd shambles of misplaced and poorly implemented affections which brought him little personal comfort.

When he was still quite young, Goethe developed a passionate attachment to a barmaid, Gretchen. This relationship only worked as a fantasy, and the reality turned into the first of a long series of rejections and botched relationships with women. While still at university, he wrote a series of poems and songs which became *The Book Annette* and *New Songs,* all inspired by the daughter of the wine merchant at whose tavern he usually stopped for lunch. While his passion was sufficient to produce literary compositions, no personal relationship ever came out of it. This seemed to be the typical course of his emotional life. An abortive love affair with Käthchen Shönkopf inspired his first two plays, but no lasting affection. Next, Goethe fell in love with a woman who was safely out of reach—Charlotte Buff, who was already betrothed to one of Goethe's friends. The affair ground to a nasty halt, but Goethe converted the abortive real-world events to a fantasy by writing a novel, *The Sorrows of Young Werther,* as a substitute for the real romance that he was denied. Next Goethe was betrothed to Lili Schönemann, the daughter of a rich banker. Although this relationship led to the lyric poem *On the Lake,* he simply allowed the engagement to lapse when he moved to Weimar.

His next passion was for Charlotte von Stein, the wife of a court official. Again, we have romance at a distance. He wrote her some 1,500 letters, and in these we can see that Charlotte was guiding him, teaching him the graces of society, dominating his thoughts, and filling his imagination with desire. Yet she insisted on a relationship governed by decorum and the conventional virtue of the time. She would consent to be Goethe's friend or even his "sister," but nothing more. For Goethe some plays and lyric poems came out of this relationship, but no loving intimacy. It would not be until 1806, when Goethe was fifty-seven, that he would eventually marry Christiane Vulpius, the daughter of a humble state official, and establish what we might call a conventional family relationship.

There is no evidence that at any time in his life Goethe ever owned a dog as a pet. In all of his extensive writing, he has very little to say about dogs. If he mentions them at all, it is only to complain about the "fearful noise that they make with their incessant yapping and barking."

Goethe's dislike of dogs was expressed in public when he was serving as the director of the Weimar Theater. At that time there was a very popular comedian by the name of Karsten, who had been appearing around the country in a play called *The Dog of Aubry.* Karsten's co-star was a performing Poodle who had become quite famous in his own right. When the owners of the Weimar Theater agreed to allow a production of that play, Goethe was incensed. He resigned his position as director because of this "affront." To explain his actions he wrote to a friend, the dramatist and historian Johann Schiller, in the form of an angry poem:

> *The theater stage is not a kennel*
> *Nor a home for curs.*
> *Enter poodle—exit poet:*
> *No artist to a dog defers.*

Goethe emphasized his negative feelings about dogs in *Faust.* In this play Faust, a disillusioned scholar, deserts his ivory tower in order to find the happiness that he feels he has been denied. He makes a pact with the devil, which results in a love affair with an ordinary village girl named Gretchen. The whole situation goes sour, however, leading to the death of the girl and a series of actions that bring Faust himself to the brink of total moral degradation. In Goethe's version of this story it is probably not accidental that the devil, Mephistopheles, decides to enter Faust's life disguised as a black Poodle, giving Faust the opportunity to label it "a mongrel of hell."

DOGS MEET THEIR WATERLOO

Another case that we might consider is that of Napoleon Bonaparte, the great military leader and Emperor of France.[1] Napoleon fits the pattern of our non–dog lovers quite well. Dominant, forceful, and ambitious, he was also quite self-contained and often possessive about his times of solitude. Although he was a passionate lover and could be loyal and generous as a friend or protector, he often had difficulty expressing affection or warmth to humans. When it came to furry animals, he had a benign tolerance for cats, which he considered elegant ornaments, and he allowed the artist François Gérard to paint a picture of him in a seated pose with a cat resting on his lap. However, this was done solely for the artistic effect that it created and the cat belonged to Gérard, not Napoleon. Toward dogs, especially the small companion dogs that were popular among the aristocracy and prosperous families in France, he showed even less warmth or interest.

Napoleon grew up under conditions that were bound to give him an independent, aggressive, and dominant personality. His father, Carlo, was active in the Corsican independence movement against the Genoese, and spent much of his time riding through the hills with the Genoese army firing at him. Carlo was more interested in teaching his sons about politics than having them spend time with pets. Napoleon, who was born the second of eight living children, grew up in a household that did not include a dog.

Napoleon was small for his age, and compensated for his size by becoming a fiery, hot-tempered youth. Despite his small stature, he became quite a fighter, often winning out over his brother Giuseppe, who was larger and more than a year older. The fiery temper and aggressive tendencies remained with him throughout his life (as did his small size).

Napoleon was quite young when he first became a general, and he found that most of the officers that he commanded were older than him. This made him uncomfortable. He had always had some difficulty socializing with people in authority or even with subordinates if they seemed not to recognize his rank and status. With this in mind, rather than follow his heart and seek a romance-based marriage, as a warm person might do, Napoleon made a "political" decision. It occurred to him that if he married a woman older than himself, he might appear to be somewhat older and more mature by association, and he might gain a little more respect from his officers, thus easing his difficult social interactions with them. Marie-Josèphe-Rose de Beauharnais, the widow of a rich young army officer, seemed to be the perfect catch because of her age and affluence, so Napoleon began to court her. An example of his dominant and controlling personality is perhaps given by the fact that, disliking "Rose," the name she was usually called, he informed her that he would henceforward call her Josephine, and proceeded to introduce her to others under the name by which we have come to know her.

Josephine spent her first fifteen years on the small French-controlled island of Martinique in the Antilles. She was the eldest daughter of an impoverished aristocrat who had a commission in the navy. In 1779 she married Alexandre, Vicomte de Beauharnais, and moved to Paris. Her personality was not particularly remarkable. She appeared to be quite mid-range in her dominance, sometimes showing streaks of stubbornness and sometimes coming across as extremely accommodating. She got along well enough in social situations, without either the flamboyance of a true extrovert or the discomfort of the extreme introvert. Her problem in social settings was that she was not very sophisticated, and Alexandre was ashamed of her provincial manners. Because of this, Josephine never had the opportunity to be presented to the court of Marie-Antoinette at Versailles.

Alexandre treated her more and more indifferently, and eventually she obtained a separation. With two children to support, and the possibility that at any time she might have her support cut off, she remained in Paris for several years, attempting to learn the manners and ways of the fashionable world in order to try to win back her husband's affection. In the meantime, Alexandre was caught up in the French Revolution and executed as an aristocrat. For Josephine, the match with the successful young officer Napoleon was a definite step toward security.

Given Josephine's medium levels for both extroversion and dominance, it is not surprising to find that the dogs that she preferred were mostly from the Consistent group. Her strong preferences were for miniature spaniels, such as the King Charles, but she also had a liking for Pugs, which are in the same group. It was probably her King Charles Spaniel, Fortune, who was sharing Josephine's bed on her wedding night with Napoleon. Napoleon was climbing into her bed, and with his typical commanding and unfeeling manner with people and animals, he shoved the small dog out of his way. The dog responded by biting the general's hand. Taken aback, Napoleon demanded that Josephine remove the dog from the bed. She declined to do so, noting that there was adequate room for both of them in the bed.

This incident, when preference over him was given to a mere dog, annoyed and upset Napoleon. It seemed to fester in his consciousness to such a degree that he often referred to it in passing to various confidants. Two years later, in 1798, Napoleon chained dogs all along the walls of Alexandria, Egypt. He explained that the dogs would provide an early warning of an attack and would also help to delay the enemy, and if a few dogs were sacrificed to slow any invaders, that would be little loss indeed. In fact, he noted, he could think of a dog that was probably resting on Josephine's bed at that very moment that he would be glad to see hanging from the end of an enemy lance.

Perhaps it was the very contempt that Napoleon had for dogs in general that led to his one recorded favorable commentary on a canine. Emmanuel, the Comte de Las Cases, to whom Napoleon dictated his memoirs in 1815 during his exile on the island of Saint Helena, transcribed Napoleon's recollection of the night after the Battle of Bassano, during his Italian campaign. The general was walking across the battlefield, which was covered with the corpses of those who had fallen just a few hours before. He remembered it this way:

We were alone, in the deep solitude of a beautiful moonlit night. Suddenly a dog leaped out from under the cloak of a corpse. He came running toward us and then, almost immediately afterward ran back to his dead master, howling piteously. He licked the soldier's unfeeling face, then ran back to us—repeating this several times. He was seeking both help and revenge. I don't know whether it was the mood of the moment, or the place, or the time, or the action in itself, or what—at any rate, it's a fact that nothing I saw on any other battlefield ever produced a like impression on me. I stopped involuntarily to contemplate this spectacle. This man, I said to myself, had friends, perhaps. He may have some at the camp, in his company—and here he lies, abandoned by all except his dog. What a lesson nature was teaching us through an animal.

What a strange thing is man! How mysterious are the workings of his sensibility! I had commanded in battles that were to decide the fate of a whole army, and had felt no emotion. I had watched the execution of manoeuvres that were bound to cost the lives of many among us, and my eyes had remained dry. And suddenly I was shaken, turned inside out, by a dog howling in pain!

It may well be that his emotion at that moment was driven by the fact that a dog, an animal that he held in contempt, was displaying nobility and loyalty beyond that shown by soldiers that he held in high regard. Perhaps this recollection came to mind because, only a few months before he dictated this passage, Napoleon's life had been saved by a dog. It was in February 1815 that he decided to end his voluntary exile on the island of Elba. This move would eventually result in a landing at Cannes, his return to Paris, his disastrous defeat at Waterloo, and his final confinement to the island of Saint Helena. All these events, which occurred within one hundred days, might never have come to pass, because of a misstep that Napoleon made when leaving Elba.

As Napoleon's boat pulled away from Elba, he stood by the gunwale for a last look at the island. The boat was pitching and surfaces were slippery. After a few moments the sailors noticed that Napoleon was missing—he had lost his balance and toppled into the sea. Unable to swim, he was floundering in the water when a dog came to his rescue. The dog was a large black and white Newfoundland, which was used by its fisherman owner to help tow lines to small boats and to recover fishing nets. The dog immediately swam to Napoleon and kept his head above water long enough for the sailors to turn the boat and come to his rescue. Napoleon made it back to the ship and proceeded on the path to his destiny. The dog, whose name we do not know, apparently returned safely to its owner.

When I think of this story I have the image of a great black and white dog standing on the shore with water dripping from him and his tail slowly swinging back and forth, looking out to sea and not caring that the person that he has just saved was one of the most famous men to have ever held his species in contempt. Dogs do not have to rationally justify their affection for humans—it is in their DNA.

If one believes in cosmic justice, or in the genetic transmission of memories, then one might also believe that dogs did not forget the insults and disrespect that they received from the Emperor Bonaparte in those earlier days. It appears that one member of the race of dogs would eventually avenge itself upon Napoleon's family, although this retribution was a long time in coming. It occurred in 1945, when Jerome Napoleon Bonaparte, the last of the original Bonaparte family in America, was walking his dog in Central Park in New York City. The dog became excited at something and darted across the path in front of him. This latter-day Bonaparte stumbled over the dog's leash and crashed to the ground, sustaining injuries that would eventually prove fatal.

HARRY HATES MIKE

I have already mentioned the fact that most of the presidents of the United States have been dog owners. However, there were some exceptions. Most of these exceptions were, at least politically, rather unexceptional characters, and the history books usually spend very little space talking about them. They include James Polk, Franklin Pierce, and Chester A. Arthur, none of whom did anything that elevated him to the status of a household name. Little is remembered about the politics of these presidents, and perhaps even less is remembered about their personalities, since they were not the focus of earth-shaking events. Because of this absence of the needed personal data, and the general lack of public interest in these figures, we will pass them by as useful examples.

There was one well-known president, however, who had an obvious lack of fondness for dogs. This was Harry S. Truman, who took over the presidency on the death of Franklin Delano Roosevelt.[2] Truman is considered to be one of the most dominant men ever to hold the presidency, and this tendency showed itself in his deliberate expansion of presidential powers. Implementing foreign policy in the cold war atmosphere, Truman began to assume more and more power at the expense of Congress. He committed U.S. troops to combat in Korea without prior congressional consent. He established the National Security Council and the Central Intelligence Agency, which he used as sources of advice and information. These agencies were responsible to the president and independent of the State Department and Congress. He also expanded the White House staff and the bureaucracy of the executive office. The president's Bureau of the Budget took over much of the planning that had once been under the jurisdiction of congressional committees. Ultimately, these actions gave Truman, and the presidents that have followed him, a much greater ability to function outside congressional restraints, especially in foreign affairs.

Truman's dominant and aggressive nature could also be seen in the way he exercised presidential authority. During the sitting of the 80th Congress, which was controlled by the opposition Republican Party, Truman used the presidential veto seventy-five times, more than any other president before or after him. The result was that virtually no major bill became law during that period, except the Taft-Hartley Labor Relations Act, which was passed over his veto.

Truman liked to cultivate an image of himself as basically warm and outgoing. He wanted to be known as a friend of the common man, and always pointed out that he was a former "dirt farmer" and men's clothing store owner. However, when he was a dirt farmer, nobody ever saw him in bib overalls. One relative of his pointed out that he sat in a wagon wearing a Panama hat, watching the plowing being done by hired hands. Afterwards he would pull a "rich man's car" out of the barn (a 1911 Stafford convertible with a brass-framed windshield and huge Prestolite lamps) and go to the city to socialize with politicians who he felt might advance his career. They certainly did. With the backing of Tom Pendergast and other big-city bosses, Truman entered politics and rose from the county courthouse to the Senate clubhouse and finally to the White House. Some of his biographers have argued that in his adult life, Truman virtually never sought company or social activity unless there was a political reason and some gain to be obtained.

Truman was definitely loyal to his close friends, but he had very few of them. In retrospect some historians have claimed that Truman, although expert at making people think that he was warm and caring, was actually quite cold. They argue that he seldom cared very much about the suffering of others if easing that suffering clashed with his political agenda. Some academics see a basic coldness in Truman's failure to give even minimal expressions of remorse over the number of noncombatant civilians who were killed when atomic bombs were dropped on Japan. Similarly, they argue that his stand on civil rights was forced by circumstances, rather than by any warm caring for the status of racial minorities.

Truman's temper was legendary, and he immediately sought vengeance for any perceived slight. Once a *Washington Post* music critic, Paul Hume, reviewed a concert by Truman's daughter Margaret. Hume wrote that her voice was "flat" and that he was mystified that people kept paying to hear her. After reading this Truman went on the warpath. He wrote a letter to the *Post*'s publisher, Philip Graham, which opened with "Why don't you fire this frustrated old fart and hire a music reviewer who knows what he is talking about?" He also wrote Hume, threatening him with bodily disfigurement and making comments on his ancestry.

Whenever anyone disagreed with Truman, he wanted revenge, often including humiliation. In one conversation with General Omar Bradley about General Douglas MacArthur (whom Truman dismissed from his command of the United Nations forces in Korea), he is said to have shouted, "The son of a bitch isn't going to resign on me, I want him fired!" With similar venom he described some other opponents—thus his replacement, Dwight Eisenhower, became a "pompous ex-army brat" and his vice president, Richard Nixon, was a "squirrel head" in some of his public statements.

To the extent that we can believe that these analyses reflect Truman's actual personality, then he certainly fits into the category of people who are not happy with dogs. The historical record confirms that this is the case. Truman had not been in the White House very long when he received a Cocker Spaniel, named Feller, as a gift. It came from a woman in Missouri who had been a Truman supporter, and who had been bothered by the fact that the president did not have a "first dog" to keep him company. She had chosen well, and Feller was a gentle, playful dog. Nevertheless, Truman was not at all pleased with this gift. According to press reports, the White House physician, Brigadier General Wallace Graham, was attending a member of the Truman household, and afterwards stopped to play with Feller for a moment. He was using the usual "What a nice puppy" phrasings and tones that we adopt around friendly dogs. The president looked at this scene with the same disdain that some people might reserve for a person trying to make friends with a line of ants on a picnic table.

"Do you like him?" he asked.

"Yes. He seems like a very pleasant little dog," General Graham replied.

"If you want him you can have him," Truman said.

Graham looked puzzled, and sputtered something on the order of "Are you sure, Mr. President? He was a gift to you."

"I didn't ask for him and I don't need him," Truman replied. "If he stays around for a while people will just get friendly with him and it will be more difficult for me to get rid of him later. Take him if you want him."

So it was that Feller found a new home. The press, however, responded quickly. One article appeared with a headline that would make some of today's tabloids proud—"Hard Hearted Harry Ditches Dog." There was a flood of letters from dog lovers all over the country. After reading one such note, Truman angrily crumpled it up, snapping to a nearby aide, "Stupid asses! Of what interest is it to them what I do with a dumb dog?"

Some members of Truman's administration took the negative press coverage more seriously, and wondered aloud if there shouldn't be a dog in the White House to give Truman even more of the "man of the people" image that he desired, and to stop the criticism evoked by Feller's quick departure. The postmaster general, Robert Hannegan, decided that he had the solution, and picked out an Irish Setter puppy with a good common Irish name—Mike. The puppy was ostensibly a gift to Margaret Truman, but Hannegan reasoned that its presence should allow the president to be seen and photographed as a warm-hearted man with a family and a dog (plate 14). This was not to be.

What Hannegan had not anticipated was the combination of Truman's quick temper and an Irish Setter's long and frisky puppyhood. The young dog bouncing around on the end of the leash trying to make a friendly acquaintance with White House guests was seen as "a damn nuisance" by the president. An unfortunate "accident," which stained an antique carpet, was met with an exasperated "Do we have to stand and watch while that moron of an animal vandalizes the nation's property?"

Margaret was genuinely fond of the dog, as were the White House staff. Careful attempts were made to keep Mike out of the president's sight in hopes that, over time, Truman would come to tolerate, if not to like, the dog. Unfortunately, neither the Trumans nor the presidential staff knew very much about dogs. Mike's regular feedings consisted of only raw meat. In addition, the staff and security personnel would occasionally feed him bits of candy. As one might expect from a diet of only meat and candy, the dog soon became ill and was eventually taken to a veterinarian. Then a call came from Walter Reed Hospital to give the president Mike's diagnosis. One newspaper report described the presidential side of the conversation as beginning with a typical Truman burst of anger. "Rickets! How the hell can a dog get rickets? . . . No, I don't know what he eats. . . . Well, look it here, if the dog is sick already is there any possibility that he might die in your office. . . . No, I am not ordering you to kill the damn dog! I am only saying that it might simplify things if the dog died of 'natural causes' while you were treating him. . . . Oh, alright, if several people have seen him already and said that his problem is not life threatening then I suppose that you have to send him back here."

Apparently Truman slammed the phone down and turned to an aide. "Find a home for the damn dog. Some place outside of Washington so Margaret won't be reminded of him." He then turned back to business as if the conversation had never taken place.

Within a very short time, Mike had been shipped off as a gift to a farmer in Virginia. Mike's exile received less media coverage than Feller's because of other, bigger issues that were occupying the country's mind at the time. What sparse notice there was, again had a critical tone. One columnist asked, "Can a man who is so lacking in tenderness and humanity that he can not establish an understanding with a loving puppy, be expected to have the charity and compassion to heal a divided nation?" When one such article passed across his desk, Truman glanced at it, quickly scanning its content. With his mouth tightly pursed he snorted through his nose, but made no comment other than to tear the column in half and drop it into his wastebasket. In all of Truman's extensive correspondence, his memoirs, autobiography, and oral biographical comments, I was unable to find any specific remark on either Feller or Mike. They were obviously minor annoyances in his life, much like a mosquito on a summer day. Once the mosquito is swatted and the annoyance is gone, the issue is of no further consequence, and certainly not worthy of a formal remark. Dogs were of little consequence to Harry Truman.

Truman did get one last kick at the canines, however. The situation was set up by Lyndon Baines Johnson, a president who loved dogs. LBJ filled the White House with Beagles. First there was Old Beagle, then Him and Her, then many of their puppies. In addition there was a neurotic, but still cherished, white Collie named Blanco and a terrier named Yuki. LBJ loved dogs so much that he had Christmas cards made up with a picture of the Beagle, Him, and the Collie, Blanco, standing next to the president. Each card was signed with Johnson's signature and the paw prints of the two dogs.

LBJ loved having the dogs around him and would often have the White House kennel keeper, Traphes Bryant, bring either Him or Yuki up to the presidential bedroom to spend the night. One night after a call from the president, Bryant tapped on the door of the bedroom and was told to come in. LBJ and his wife, Lady Bird, were in pajamas and lying in bed. The president took Yuki from Bryant and then turned to Lady Bird and said, "You know there is no one in the world I would rather sleep with than Yuki." The kennel keeper was already beating a hasty retreat from the presidential boudoir and unfortunately did not hear (or refuses to disclose) Lady Bird's reply.[3]

Johnson loved to show the dogs off to everybody. One day he was trying to please some photographers by getting the beagles to do a trick. LBJ was such a tall man that he really had to bend way over to get near a small dog like a Beagle, so as Him danced around, LBJ bent over and took hold of the dog by the most convenient handles, namely his large floppy ears. He apparently was thinking about a common Texas scene where farmers reach into a litter of young Beagle pups and lift them by their ears. This lift-'em-by-the-ears trick can only be done with young puppies who are still quite light. When a dog grows a little older it puts on more weight than the ears can comfortably support. For that reason, if old-time farmers grab a puppy by the ears and it starts to yelp, they let go and find another way to lift it, or simply grab a lighter puppy. In any event, LBJ grabbed Him by the ears and the dog yelped. Even when he heard the yelps it didn't dawn on the president that anything was really wrong. He just glossed over the situation with a casual comment that pulling its ears was good for a hound, and that everybody who knows dogs likes to hear them yelp because it means the dogs are paying attention.

The photographers loved it, and pictures of the yelping dog suspended by its ears appeared in virtually every major news publication (plate 15). Most of the articles were accompanied by comments of dog experts criticizing LBJ for hurting his dogs. The American Kennel

Club, the National Beagle Club, the American Society for Prevention of Cruelty to Animals, and several state and national veterinary associations all went on record to condemn this kind of behavior as harmful to the dogs. There were very few voices in support of LBJ's actions. One, however, was Johnson's predecessor as president, and fellow Democrat, Harry Truman. Asked for his opinion of this incident, this former president, who had shown no empathy or caring for the two dogs that had been his own temporary White House pets, sprang to LBJ's defense. He told reporters, "What the hell are the critics hollering about? That's the way to handle hounds!"

A smiling aide showed LBJ the report of Truman's comment, expecting that it would cheer him up, given the ongoing storm of disapproval. The president read it and burst out laughing. "I must really be wrong about this ear thing if Harry says it's OK. He don't know—or even like—dogs."

Chapter Fourteen

The Cat People

As this book was beginning to take shape and the data were being analyzed, I would often find myself chatting with friends and associates about the data and the results of my analyses. Inevitably, someone would ask, "Well, what is the personality profile of a cat owner?" Initially I had no intention to say much about cats at all. To be completely honest, cats are not my cup of fur. However, since the data that I collected contain some relevant material, I suppose that a brief digression to talk about the "cat people" might be useful.

In the lives of humans, cats and dogs have quite different histories. Dogs were domesticated at least fourteen thousand years ago, which is at least four thousand years before humans developed any organized agriculture. Dogs had the job of guarding human living quarters and were also supposed to assist in the hunt. With hunting the major source of food, dogs were important for their superior hearing and smelling ability which could help people find game that otherwise might go undetected. In addition, the dogs had great speed and the ability to hold game at bay, so they could be a vital asset in assuring the survival of our primitive ancestors. Because dogs had to work so closely with people, they had to be sociable and smart and willing to take instructions from humans, if the dog and human team was to prosper.

Cats, however, are a product of a much later time. The earliest evidence of a clearly domesticated cat was unearthed by archaeologist Alaine le Brun, who found their remains in Khirokitia, Cyprus, and dates them back to about seven thousand years ago. At that time the Agricultural Revolution was well in progress among humans.

Cats were simply not of any value to us until humans had progressed to a point where we were capable of farming efficiently. By "efficiently" I mean that the crops had to provide large enough quantities of harvested food to store for future use. Of particular importance was the grain harvest, since grains are so nutritious and naturally keep well for long periods without any special preservation. It is a good bet that, almost from the moment that humans switched from hunting to farming, they and their food stores became a very important part of the life cycle of teeming populations of rats and mice. Especially in cities and villages, where the food stores could be fairly large, rodents were probably viewed as a major threat to human subsistence since they consumed and contaminated so much food. Unfortunately people are simply not well suited to hunt for these nocturnal rodents. The task of stalking and eliminating all of them, or even sufficient numbers to prevent them from multiplying, is nearly impossible. Anything that would help to eliminate these rodent pests would have been viewed as a blessing from the gods.

Although we don't know the actual historical events, it is probably the case that somebody noticed that a few wild cats had been lurking around the grain storage areas, and that they had been killing and eating the mice. It must have then occurred to this observer that if he could encourage the cats to do even more of this it could go a long way toward preserving much of the harvest that was being lost to rodents. For cats the situation must have been heavenly. In this place where the two-footed beasts dwelled, breakfast, lunch, and dinner were scurrying all around them. No more stalking through the cold underbrush hoping to find a stupid fieldmouse that had strayed too far from its burrow. Now all that the cats had to do was to take a leisurely stroll in the general neighborhood of the food storage bins. There they would find a virtual delicatessen full of grain-fed rodents that were there for the taking. From this moment on, the fact that humans would breed and domesticate cats was assured. Success was guaranteed since the situation provided major benefits to both sides.

The value of cats was so immense that in some countries they were treated as if they were momentous gifts of the gods, if not gods themselves. In Egypt, cats were believed to have descended from the goddess Pasht, who was herself the daughter of the moon. One of the names associated with the sun god Ra was The Great Cat. Cats were treated as if they were members of the family, or at least valued possessions. When a cat died it was mourned with many of the same traditions that were observed at the death of a person. Family members would shave off their eyebrows, smear their hair with mud, and weep. When families could afford it cats were embalmed, mummified, wrapped in colored linens, placed in urns, and then buried near temples or in a designated cat necropolis.

Visitors to Egypt saw how efficient cats were in keeping the rodent population in check. Although it was illegal to take cats out of the country, the Phoenicians somehow managed to obtain a large number of these animals and sold them all through the Mediterranean area. Soon every country in Europe had domestic cats, preying on the fat rats and mice that lived in city food bins.

The relationship between cats and humans has always been quite different from the relationship between dogs and people. Both species have kept much of their wild heritage. In the wild, cats are usually solitary hunters and often are active mostly at night. Dogs in the wild are sociable animals that work in groups and are active between dawn and dusk. The dog's social needs are still such that without a master and a family, the dog seems unhappy—almost lost. Dogs will intrude on a person's ongoing activities if they are feeling lonely and want some company or play. Cats, on the other hand, are often invisible during the day, seeming only to appear in the evening, especially if that is when they are fed. Cats will occasionally engage in social activities or play with people, but their interest is limited. Usually, after only a few minutes cats will abandon the game and wander away. Dogs, on the other hand, will often engage in play, like fetching a thrown ball, for hours at a time, and it is usually the human that quits the game first.

Even behaviors that people take as being a sign of affection or sociability in cats, such as when they rub up against a person's leg, are not really meant as social gestures. Cats have special scent glands that are located on their temples, at the gape of their mouth, and at the base of their tail. Part of their grooming ritual actually involves rubbing these scents all over their body. Rubbing up against your leg marks you with the cat's scent, and declares you as part of its territory and one of its possessions.

Some people credit cats with more intelligence than dogs. If you ask such a person why cats don't obey human commands, or learn simple behavioral controls, such as keeping off of furniture or away from certain areas of the home, these people claim that it is because cats are "too independent." Dogs are, according to these people, "dumb, but servile and willing to be slaves." Numerous scientific studies have shown that cats are smarter than rats and dumber than dogs. Even if they are hungry and their lives depend upon doing things or solving problems to get food, cats still learn at a slower rate than dogs. In human terms, an average dog's intelligence is around that of a two-year-old child. A cat's intelligence lags by about six months, with an equivalent to the mental abilities of an eighteen-month-old child.

While this is relatively bright in comparison with many other animals on this planet, it still suggests, for instance, that cats would have great difficulty learning much human language. The smartest cats learn to understand and respond to about two dozen words or signals. Compare this to the ability of the average dog to respond to around 110 words or signals. There is a lot of evidence that cats often do not even recognize their own names, and have difficulty determining when messages are addressed to them. This would suggest that the cat's apparent "independence" when people try to get it to do something results, not from considered reasoning and contrary choice, but simply from the fact that he doesn't have the faintest clue as to what is expected of him.

The cat's behavioral traits have occasionally made people uncomfortable and led to bad outcomes for felines. In Europe the cat population suffered several centuries of abuse, torture, and even death, mostly instigated by the Christian church. The case against cats was based on the fact that they roamed the night when only evil things were around. In addition they had a tendency to disappear during the day, which might indicate that they were meeting secretly with demonic masters, or carrying out nefarious secret schemes and undermining human welfare. The silent comings and goings of cats came to be interpreted as spying. In addition there was the aloof disdain that cats seemed to show for humans, and their willingness to unsheathe their claws and draw human blood at the least slight. All of this was consistent with the idea that cats were agents of the Devil. After considering the evidence, Pope Innocent VII declared an inquisition against them. With the blessing of the church millions of cats were killed in horrific ways. They were often burned alive on religious feast days; they were crucified or ritually thrown from the tops of church towers as part of the war against the enemies of Christ.

Fortunately those times are past, and perhaps the only legacy that we have of that dark era is the superstition that black cats are associated with bad luck, at least in much of the Americas and Europe. I recently saw an extreme example of that superstition in operation. I was walking across my university's campus, with my Cavalier King Charles Spaniel, Wizard, on the leash beside me. Suddenly a young man came running up to me, in a state of agitation. He spoke with a heavy accent, and I later learned that he was a recent immigrant of Slovak heritage.

"Please help me," he pleaded. "I must get to my laboratory class."

I must have looked very puzzled. He gestured toward the chemistry building in front of us and said, "The cat—a black cat—has just crossed here and I cannot go over unless he comes back the other way to undo this curse. I cannot wait for so long, but you can help." Now he pointed to Wizard. "You know? You have a white dog, at least he is mostly white. He will do. Just cross in front of the building here— where the cat walked. It will erase the evil the cat leaves behind him and I can go past. Just walk beside me with the dog. I will show you where he stepped."

Wiz and I walked along beside the distraught man, and we traced an L-shaped path along two sides of the building. As we passed the last door on that side, the man blurted a quick "Thank you. Thank you so much. I must now run to class." Then he quickly crossed over the invisible line that we had traced and darted into the building.

I told this story to a colleague of mine who had spent two years doing research in England. He laughed and said, "That wouldn't happen in the part of Britain where I stayed. At least locally, black cats are supposed to be good luck there!"

I have lived with a number of cats over the years, none of whom actually belonged to me, but rather to loved ones. In my youth there was a gray cat with a white chest and a gray nose, named Dusty. He was pleasant enough but uninteresting to me in comparison to dogs. Next there was an odious, antisocial, purple Persian cat named Henry, who had nothing to recommend him other than the fact that he looked very handsome.

While I was still in graduate school, I rescued a Siamese cat whose pet name was Fu. She was scheduled for euthanasia after she proved to be too dumb to learn some preliminary simple tasks needed for a set of behavioral experiments being conducted by Charlie White, another psychology graduate student at Stanford University. The two of us shared the same graduate advisor, the well-known psychologist Leon Festinger, who is probably best known for his Theory of Cognitive Dissonance. Fu was incredibly beautiful and, at least for a cat, was very loving. I suppose that I just felt sorry for her and offered to take her. Festinger was sufficiently frustrated with the way the experiment was going that he had a strong desire to see the animal dead. She had certainly caused a lot of time and effort to be wasted. However, he had some affection for his own cat at home and was willing to relent under two conditions. First I had to take the cat out of the lab immediately, and second I had to promise that I would never tell him that she was happy in her new home, nor in fact ever say another word about her.

No pets were allowed in the student quarters where I lived. However, I smuggled the cat into the apartment, and the first chance that I got, I gave her to my parents on a trip home. Fu turned out to be a splendid addition to their household, which already contained a dog. My parents liked her so much that, when she died, they replaced her with another Siamese cat.

More recently there was the lovely but dopey gray striped cat, Willow, that my wife's daughter Karen brought with her when she lived with us for a couple of years. She was relatively friendly to people, but spent most of her time staring at blank walls or hiding from my Cairn

Terrier, Flint, who appeared to be planning some sort of malice involving her. Occasionally she would work her way out onto the roof of our house and have to be rescued.

At the moment I am living with an orange or "ginger" cat named Loki that was a gift to my wife from her daughter Karen. Our present cat actually earns his living. My little house in the city is quite old, with gaps in the foundation and numerous tiny access places that small animals can work their way through. In the fall, when the weather turns inclement, mice tend to find their way into the house and take up residence there. I don't like to put out poison bait or even mousetraps, because of my dogs. So Loki performs the function that cats were originally domesticated for, namely ridding our premises of rodents. In between hunting expeditions, the cat finds time to clean the ears of my Flat-Coated Retriever Odin, and he occasionally even spends time sitting near my wife or her mother, Jean, and purring.

I have always felt that having a cat as a pet is preferable to coming home to an empty house, but clearly inferior to having a dog. Cats are easy pets to own. They are almost instantaneously housebroken, and except for providing them with food and water, little other care is required. For the time and effort expended, cats are probably a good deal as a pet. They are handsome and do provide a bit of social contact. Dogs, of course, require much more attention, but the payoffs are much larger in terms of affection and interaction. Some of the differences between dog and cat owners may well reflect the amount of care that various personality types are willing to provide. Comedian Steve Martin once noted in an interview, "I like cats because I don't have to take care of them that much. Dogs are like having a kid."

My data sample included 1,223 cat owners. People who owned only cats seemed to be somewhat different from dog owners or people who owned both dogs and cats in terms of their personalities. People with both dogs and cats seemed to be much like people who own only dogs. This is consistent with the results that I got when I asked people who own only cats, "If you had adequate living space and there were no objections from other people in your life, and someone gave you a puppy as a gift, would you keep it?" Their answers were compared to what I got when I asked people who own only dogs the same question about a kitten. More than two-thirds of the cat owners (68 percent) said that they would not accept a puppy as a pet, while almost the same proportion of dog owners (70 percent) said that they would keep the kitten. This suggests that most people who own only a dog are potentially dog *and* cat owners, while most people who own only a cat are exclusively cat owners. You should keep this in mind, since from here on, at least for the purposes of this discussion, when I mention a cat owner I mean someone who lives only with a cat, while when I mention a dog owner I mean a person who owns only a dog or both a dog and a cat.

According to my data, cat owners were one-third more likely to live alone than dog owners and twice as likely to live in an apartment or flat. Being married, living in a house, and having children living in the home are all factors more often associated with dog owners than cat owners. A single woman was the most likely individual to have a cat. Of the people who grew up with cats as pets, 47 percent have cats today, while only 11 percent of people whose childhood years were spent with just a dog have only a cat as a pet.

The personality profile for the person who owns only cats is quite interesting. For both males and females we find that people who own only cats tend to be relatively introverted (low on extroversion), low in dominance, fairly trusting, and reasonably cool (low in warmth). I actually had experience with a person who fit this personality pattern perfectly, and long before I collected this data, I used to think of her as the prototypical cat owner.

Her name was Kim, and she was a university faculty member who taught literature. I knew her during my "years of chaos," between the end of my first marriage and my settling down with my present wife. We had met at a university committee meeting and enjoyed each other's company enough to get together now and then for lunch. Over time the nature of our meetings expanded to include dinner and the occasional movie or other event. While I greatly appreciated her intelligence and her wicked and cynical sense of humor, she was not particularly comfortable in social gatherings. One would have expected that such a bright and rather handsome woman would have had many friends and social relationships. Kim, however, preferred being by herself, and when faced with someone who offered her warmth and affection, she had difficulty opening up, and tended to back off in a fairly defensive and standoffish manner. She was not very dominant, and there were several instances in her academic life where her career would have advanced more smoothly if she had taken a strong stand with her department. Instead, she simply retreated and gave in to the demands put on her. She would often seek advice from her friends, and had such a trusting and accepting nature that she would almost always follow it. When she received conflicting advice from different people, she would become quite stressed and upset.

I knew that Kim liked cats, since on one weekend outing she suggested that we go to a cat show. I had been to many dog shows, but never a cat show, so I thought that it might be an interesting experience. The first thing that struck me when we got to the show was the smell. Dog shows do not smell, so I was surprised by the fetid odor that met us as we entered the door. Since one of the purposes for cat shows is to find good examples of purebred cats for breeding purposes, all of the animals in a show must be sexually intact animals. That means that they have not been spayed or neutered. Apparently most of this smell was due to some tomcats that were acting in a repulsive and territorial manner, marking and spraying everything and everyone near them. This stench was mixed with faint overtones of used cat litter and canned cat food. The second thing that struck me was the chaos. At a dog show you seldom if ever hear barking; at this cat show intervals of quiet would suddenly be broken by shrieks, hisses, and yowls erupting from one corner or another. Then, like a wave, the noise would move down one side of the building and up the other.

Another thing that I noticed as I scanned the scene was that there were first aid kits mounted on posts, placed strategically at thirty- or forty-foot intervals around the large hall. I was about to comment on this when a large woman standing near us suddenly let out a pain-laden shout of "Damn it!" I spun just in time to see her finish shoving a cat into a kennel. Then she turned and I saw that she was grasping one bleeding hand with her other. I stepped forward to ask if I could help.

"It's all right, dear," she said in a matronly manner. "He's just a bit annoyed. It's all these other cats, you know. The poor thing must think that I am about to trade him in for one of the others. Please excuse me now. I must get to the first aid kit."

As I looked around the hall it became apparent that one of the easiest ways to tell who the competitors were, as opposed to the spectators, was not to look for numbered armbands, as I would in a dog show, but rather to look at the backs of hands. Most of the competitors wore red streaks on their hands and arms from their angry pets. I wondered about just how mangled the poor cat judges must be, since they have to touch all of these cats to see if they are structurally and physically sound. The judges, however, seemed to be quite self-protective. If a cat showed any signs of aggression, a judge would calmly continue to stand several feet away, not moving forward until the cat was completely calm. If that didn't happen within a few moments, the judge would simply wave the usually bloodied competitor and the angry cat out of the ring. I saw one woman who had been ejected from the ring hugging her cat and trying to console it with "That nasty judge doesn't know how sweet you really are." Meanwhile the cat, whose paws were pinned against her buxom body, was howling with rage and trying to bite at her face.

Kim loved the show. She collected tons of literature and cat food samples. As I was driving her home she went through the brochures, reading me some interesting snippets. One of these said something like "Cats are particularly good for elderly and ailing people. These cat owners need not worry about what will happen to their pet should they become incapacitated or even should they die. They can rest assured that their cat will not suffer mental or physical anguish at such an eventuality. Unlike dogs, cats will not allow their grief about loss of their master to disrupt their lives. Their elderly owners can take comfort in the fact that their cat will readily transfer its affections to any new family that is willing to provide for it." Unlike Kim, who thought that this was high praise for the species, I was not impressed. The thought that any affection that cats have for the people who love and care for them can be sold to someone else for a plate of food does not recommend them to me as a companion.

At the time that I knew Kim, I was living in an apartment, and although she had visited my place once or twice, I had never been to her home. Then, one day, Kim invited me to dinner. When I asked if anyone else would be there she answered, "Just Byron and Shelley." This was not a couple that I knew, but I didn't ask questions.

I arrived at Kim's apartment at the appointed hour, carrying a bottle of red wine. The door opened and Kim ushered me into her living room. Now I knew that the salaries for assistant professors were far from sumptuous, but the furniture here seemed inordinately tatty. There were tiny rips and shredded edges on everything. Kim took the bottle from my hand, waved me toward the sofa, and told me that she would get me something to drink. As I approached the sofa I passed between two well-padded chairs which had their backs toward the door. As I glanced at them I immediately understood Kim's decor. On the seat of each chair was a white Angora cat. They were quite beautiful, with their long silky fur, so I reached over to pet one of them.

Suddenly there was an ear-piercing shriek from the open door to the next room. "No! Don't touch him!"

The warning was too late. There was a sudden white flash, and two parallel stripes appeared on the back of my hand and began to ooze blood. Kim raced over and took my hand. She looked disapprovingly at the cat and said in a schoolmarmish tone, "Byron, you are a naughty cat." The cat responded by curling up slightly and turning its head away from her, apparently preparing for a nap.

Kim moved me quickly into the bathroom, and I nearly tripped over the litter box. The tiny room smelled much like the cat show we had been at a few weeks earlier. She cleaned the wound and put antiseptic and a gauze-padded bandage on it. As she worked she explained. "I'm sorry that I didn't warn you about Byron and Shelley," she said. "They are often nasty to people that they don't know—especially men. You see, those chairs and that side of the room belong to them. Since they are in the apartment more of the time than I am, it only seems fair to give them some space of their own, and I just can't evict them from it when I get home, can I? They'll be much better after I've fed them."

Having completed her first aid treatment, Kim moved me to her kitchen and gave me the drink she had been preparing. As I leaned against the counter she reached into her cupboard and pulled out a tin of expensive imported sardines. "They're such fussy eaters. They won't eat cat food at all. They won't even eat some kinds of fancy fish, but they do like this."

As she was speaking Byron and Shelley appeared. They completely ignored me and moved in, out, and around, rubbing against Kim's legs and making an impatient guttural "Brrrrnnng" sound. When the two tiny china bowls were put down the cats circled them, as if checking to see if the contents were edible. Each cat then proceeded to nibble daintily at the food.

Kim was now explaining to me what she was making for dinner, indicating that we would begin with a special appetizer. She took an interesting dish from the refrigerator and announced in perfect Canadian French, *"Pâté de foie gras avec shallot et vin blanc."* She placed it on the tiny table in her dining alcove. The table had been set for two with an oversized silver candleholder containing a large white candle as the centerpiece. Kim fussed in the kitchen for a while and eventually asked me to open the bottle of wine. As we moved toward the table we were greeted with the sight of the hindquarters of two white cats, busily working away at the expensive pâté. Kim swiftly but gently lifted the protesting cats from the table and placed them on the floor. She glanced at the remains of what had been the neatly molded mound and said, "Well, they didn't eat very much of it. I'll scrape away the bad parts, but the rest should be OK. You know cats are very clean animals."

The way that I remember that night, I drank a lot of wine and ate very little pâté.

Several weeks later Kim and I met for lunch. In a fairly matter-of-fact way she told me that one of her cats, Byron, had gone missing. It had now been four days since she had seen him last. I was surprised by the relative absence of concern or emotion in her voice. Twice in my life one of my dogs has disappeared, though fortunately both were found. I thought that I treated the situations in a calm adult manner; however, everybody who came into contact with me during the search said that I was obviously grief-stricken, anxious, and perhaps on the verge of panic. Now this lovely blond woman, who let two cats virtually run her life and catered to their every whim, did not seem all that bothered that one of them was gone.

"I've done the usual things to get him back. I had a kid in the building put up signs around the neighborhood and called the SPCA. These sort of things happen—you know how it is with cats. They tell me there are sometimes raccoons and coyotes in the neighborhood and that they often catch people's pets. Then there are dogs and cars . . . I suppose if he isn't smart enough to avoid all that, or if he isn't bright enough to find his way home, then he's lost for good."

She stared across the room for a moment and then said, "If I have to replace him, I think that this time I'll get a black one. I was thinking about calling the new one Yeats—sort of keeping with the poet theme." At that she turned back to her sandwich and changed the topic of conversation to talk about a new book that she had just read.

I remember thinking that this appeared to be a fairly cold way to respond to the loss of a pet. Of course, had I known about this current set of data I would have understood much better.

Perhaps the most significant piece of data about the relative warmth of cat owners and dog owners comes from another question that I put on the survey form. It asked, "If your pet had a life-threatening problem and could be saved by a medical procedure, how much would you be willing to pay for its treatment?" The average amount that dog owners were willing to pay was almost twice as much as the amount that cat owners would pay ($1,183 versus $610). People who own both dogs and cats drew little distinction between them. They were actually willing to spend more money to save the lives of their cats than were people who owned *only* cats. There are two obvious ways to interpret these data. The first is that cat owners, despite their love for their cats, basically think that they are worth a lot less than dog owners think their dogs (and their cats if they have them also) are worth. The second interpretation is that the typical personality profile of people who prefer to own only cats is simply less warm and caring than is the personality profile of dog owners, and with that comes less of an inclination to help—even their cats.

Chapter Fifteen

Putting It All Together

From the previous chapters you should have some idea as to which breeds of dogs are preferred by people with different personality traits. However, when it comes to using your own personality profile to select the breeds that are best for you, you may still be a bit confused by the fact that each of the four personality traits may suggest different breeds of dogs. This may leave you thinking something like "On the basis of my dominance scores I need a dog from either the Protective or Independent group, while my extroversion scores suggest either a Friendly or Self-Assured dog and my warmth scores suggest . . ." and after a lot of musing you may well end up with "Damn it all, let's just get a Cocker Spaniel since they look so cute." There is no need for this, however. Actually, it is quite easy to put your scores together to see which dog breeds are best for you.

Of course, the first things that you need are your own personality scores—the ratings of high, medium, or low for the four personality traits, which I assume you have already computed. Next, let's give you a quick snapshot of how personality relates to the dog groups that people like best. We'll do this with a table that summarizes all the information that I've given you, so that all the important facts can be seen in one glance. Table 5 shows the dog groups that fit best with each scoring category for all the personality dimensions.

TABLE 5

Dog groups that are most preferred by men and women for all four personality dimensions and all levels of traits.

Relative Score	Extroversion		Dominance	
	Women	Men	Women	Men
High	Independent Protective	Clever Self-Assured	Self-Assured Steady	Self-Assured Steady
Medium	Consistent Clever	Friendly Consistent	Consistent Friendly	Friendly Clever
Low	Steady Self-Assured	Independent Steady	Protective Independent	Protective Independent

Relative Score	Trust		Warmth	
	Women	Men	Women	Men
High	Protective Independent	Protective Clever	Protective Friendly	Clever Friendly
Medium	Friendly Clever	Friendly Self-Assured	Independent Clever	Protective Independent
Low	Steady Self-Assured	Steady Independent	Self-Assured Steady	Steady Consistent

For each personality score, two dog breed groups are recommended. Simply count the number of times that each group of breeds is mentioned as being appropriate for you for the four traits. Since personality is a complex thing and you are measuring several aspects of it, you will certainly get several different recommended groups. This is because different aspects of your personality may be best suited by different types of dogs, and this is a normal outcome. However, the count that you have just made will easily allow you to choose the best dog breeds for your personality.

If a breed group is mentioned two times: Any category of dogs that is compatible with your personality scores on two or more dimensions is a reasonable candidate to fit in with your wants and needs. There may be occasional times when such a dog breed will exasperate you, but these should not be very frequent, nor should the problems be very intense. Most of the time you will find a dog from this breed group to be a welcome companion.

If a breed group is mentioned three times: A fit on three personality dimensions is a very strong match, and a dog selected from this group will be very strongly suited to your temperament. If we were arranging a marriage between humans, this degree of fit would be about as strong as we could ever hope for.

If a breed group is mentioned four times: This is a match made in heaven. If you can work out the details of size and activity level, which I will talk about in a moment, then a dog selected from this group is almost sure to fit into your life.

Some of you may have formed an initial fondness for a particular breed of dog based on its looks or its association with people or places that you feel warmly toward. If that dog's group is mentioned only once as fitting your personality profile, it might be the case that you and dogs from that group of breeds can get along reasonably well. However, there may be some rocky periods which could stress the relationship. Much as in human relationships, if the number and intensity of good experiences outweigh the number and intensity of the bad ones, a strong fondness can develop. With only one mention of the breed group, however, the likelihood of a good match is probably a cosmic roll of the dice. The result could well be a sort of love-hate relationship, with certain aspects of the dog's behavior that you really like and other aspects of its nature that you detest.

If a dog group is *never* mentioned in your profile, regardless of how much you like its looks or appreciate the stories told about it, your best advice is to stay away from this group of breeds. The likelihood that you and the dog will clash is very high indeed. Furthermore, there is a high probability that your disagreements with such a dog will be fairly intense. Presuming that you are looking for a companion, rather than a continuing challenge that may increase your stress level, selecting a dog from a different group seems wise.

As a hypothetical example, suppose you were selecting a dog for a man who is high on extroversion, high on dominance, medium on trust, and low on the warmth dimension. Checking the table, you can see that five different dog groups are mentioned as possible for him. The Clever, Friendly, and Consistent groups are each mentioned once, while the Steady group is mentioned twice and the Self-Assured group is mentioned three times. His best bet would be to select a dog from the Self-Assured group. A good second choice would be a dog from the Steady group. He should definitely avoid dogs from the Protective and the Independent groups, since they are not mentioned at all and would probably clash with his temperament.

A FEW EXTRA CONSIDERATIONS

Once you have isolated the group that fits with your personality, there are still a few choices to be made. After all, each of the dog groups has over a dozen different breeds, so how can you select among them?

The good news is that if you like one breed in any particular group of dogs, the chances are that you will like the others in that group. Take the case of the Academy Award–winning actress Elizabeth Taylor, known for such classic films as *Cleopatra, Who's Afraid of Virginia Woolf?, Butterfield 8,* and *Cat on a Hot Tin Roof.* To determine her personality profile I had four experts in film rate her personality. In the public's mind Liz Taylor has always been associated with Collies, since in her earliest appearances on the movie screen she was co-starring in films with Lassie. She appeared in the very first Lassie film, *Lassie Come Home,* and three years later in *The Courage of Lassie.* For her sixtieth birthday she was given a Collie puppy as a gift, and this puppy was in fact a great-grandchild (seven generations back) of Pal, the dog who played the original Lassie. When Taylor ended her marriage with construction worker Larry Fortensky (her eighth husband), this dog became an issue; Fortensky wanted it, but Taylor successfully sued for custody. Collies, however, have never been her first choice in dogs.

For many years Elizabeth Taylor lived with Pekingese, which is predictable from the fact that her personality profile suggests dogs from the Consistent group no less than three times. At any one time she would always have at least two dogs, and often more. Taylor was so fond of her Pekingese that she would go out of her way to accommodate them. Once, while she was married to actor Richard Burton, the two of them were supposed to co-star in a film that was being shot in

England, and she wanted to bring her dogs along. The problem was that England has a six-month quarantine period for any dog brought into the country. Taylor found a clever, if rather expensive, solution to this dilemma. She and Burton obtained a yacht and moored it on the Thames. They lived on board the boat for the entire time that the film was being made, along with her Pekingese dogs and a Lhasa Apso (also from the Consistent group) that she had newly purchased. In this way the dogs never needed to step on English soil, and so they avoided spending the usual time in quarantine (plate 16).

Taylor was always quite good with dogs, and was able to get along with them well. When she would call the dogs, or give them any commands, they would always respond to her, but they seemed to ignore Burton. This was an annoyance to him, since he also liked dogs. Then one day Burton showed up with a Pekingese named E'en So. The dog was blind in one eye and Burton claimed that he had "rescued it." Now E'en So was friendly enough, but Taylor seemed to have a lot of trouble communicating with it. She could never get it to respond as well to her as it did to her husband. The dog seemed to pay rapt attention to Burton when he spoke, but ignored Taylor. She could not figure out what she was doing wrong to be treated so shabbily by E'en So. It was some time later that Burton admitted that he had actually purchased the dog fully trained, but only to commands spoken in Welsh—a language that he spoke fluently, and Taylor spoke not at all.

Shortly after Taylor divorced Burton (for the second time) she not only went through a couple of new husbands but also changed her preferences in dogs. She added a new Lhasa Apso named Elsa. Lhasa Apsos are little dogs from Tibet, where they are known as Abso Seng Key, which translates to Bark Lion Sentinel Dog. This name pretty much sums up their functions; they were supposed to be watchdogs who sounded the alarm and they were also supposed to look like the celestial lion. As I mentioned earlier, Lhasa Apsos, like Pekingese, are also in the Consistent group of dogs.

Most recently Elizabeth Taylor's dogs have been beautiful white Maltese, which are again in the Consistent group. These are tiny dogs, eight to ten inches at the shoulder and weighing only around four to seven pounds, with a long silky coat that hangs to the floor. There are records of identifiable Maltese going back to 1500 B.C., when Phoenician traders brought them from Asia Minor. It was common for them to accompany sailors as pets and good luck charms on long journeys. Taylor's Maltese have names such as Sugar and Honey. During her period of convalescence following brain surgery, one of these dogs could be seen as her constant companion, nestled on her lap or beside her.

The important thing to note here is that over a more than thirty-five-year period, Elizabeth Taylor has had several different breeds of dogs that she has loved and pampered. She seems equally pleased with each of these breeds and has not abandoned any of them because of incompatibilities. This is exactly as we would have expected. Given that she liked the Pekingese, we could have also predicted that she would like the Lhasa Apso and Maltese since all are drawn from the same group of Consistent dogs. On the basis of this I would venture to predict that she would be equally happy with a Pomeranian or a Tibetan Terrier, which are also from that group. You must remember that your personality directs you to a group of dogs, not one specific breed.

While it is generally true that all of the dogs within a group will be equally acceptable to a person with the appropriate personality profile, there are two other aspects of the dog that you must consider. The first of these is the dog's size. In some of the breed groups the size variations can be quite large, as in the Steady group, which ranges from the small Beagle to the giant Irish Wolfhound. The choice of a big versus a small dog is often made simply on the basis of the available space in the person's living quarters.

If you live in a one-room apartment, a Great Dane or a Newfoundland is probably out of the question, while a Papillon or a Chihuahua will work quite well. However, big dogs can fit into smaller living quarters under some circumstances. I know a woman who lives in a one-bedroom apartment, with a small living/dining room, a kitchen, and a bathroom. Her pet is a tall, lithe Greyhound. She claims that the dog simply curls up in various tiny spaces around her apartment and that he is seldom underfoot.

In my own experience, however, a large dog is very noticeable in a small living space. When I am in the city, my home is a tiny house with not much more space than the average two-bedroom apartment. Odin, my Flat-Coated Retriever, stands around twenty-five inches at the shoulder and weighs around seventy-five pounds, and his presence is quite noticeable in that space. I often have to move him out of the way in order to cross a room. Similarly, my wife's aggravated bark of "Move it, beast!" is regularly heard when she finds it impossible to move through a doorway, open the refrigerator, or use the stove, because Odin's large black bulk is in her way. At such times I wonder about what kind of mental processes motivated me to get such a big dog. Things are different, however, when I am living at my farm. There the house is quite large, with high ceilings and a lot of floor space. At times when we are out there, I find myself looking at Odin and wondering if I should get another large dog to keep him company, since he seems considerably smaller in that context and never seems to be intruding into either my space or my wife's.

A dog's size has another aspect that may be more important than the actual space that it takes up. The issue is control—the smaller the dog, the easier it is to control. If a small dog gets into trouble you can simply pick it up and move it to a safer place. A six-pound Yorkshire Terrier may have the spirit of a tiger, but if you tug on its lead, even if you are only a tiny ninety-pound woman, the dog will follow you— whether it wants to or not. A big dog is usually considerably stronger as well as being larger. If an eighty-pound Golden Retriever decides that it wants to chase a squirrel, it can hit the end of the leash hard enough to knock that ninety-pound woman down and perhaps break her hold on the lead. In a battle of wills (which is what dog obedience training often turns into when the dog and its owner have different ideas as to who is in control) a 160-pound Rottweiler can be a formidable opponent. Therefore, your size and strength become an issue when selecting a dog.

The second important consideration, in terms of dog selection, is the activity level of the breed. Within each group there is a variation in the amount of activity that the dog engages in, and also the amount of exercise needed. For instance, the Friendly group includes the Cavalier King Charles Spaniel, who is quite happy sleeping most of the day on the sofa, and also the Springer Spaniels, who can remain in continuous motion for twelve hours at a time. The activity level that you select in a dog should be consistent with your own activity level. If you like to run, hike, and engage in other outdoor activities, a Bulldog is not for you while a Whippet or a Borzoi might work very well. If your desire for physical exertion is completely spent by changing the channels on your television, a Border Collie would be a disaster, while a Pug or an English Toy Spaniel could be excellent choices. Even if you have a perfect personality match with a breed, it is still important to make sure that your dog's activity level is similar to your own. Otherwise there will be daily hassles over the issue of exercise.

So, with these ideas in mind, let's take a real-life example and see how various dog breeds fit that particular personality.

THE WRITER AND THE DOGS

Let's use as our example the author and poet E. B. White.[1] Despite the fact that he won a Pulitzer Prize special citation, you might not remember who he is; but you probably have run into his work. White is the author of that marvellous children's classic, *Charlotte's Web.* That is the one about a pig named Wilbur who is in danger of being slaughtered. He is rescued by a wise spider named Charlotte, who weaves words of praise about Wilbur into her web, so that the farmer will see them and spare her friend. Two other time-honored children's books were also written by White, namely *Stuart Little* and *The Trumpet of the Swan.*

If you are not a reader of children's fiction, then you still may have encountered White's work. Millions of college students have used his tiny book *The Elements of Style* as either a textbook or simply a writing aid. This book was, ostensibly, based on some class notes provided for students by one of White's professors, William Strunk, Jr.; however, the end product is almost all White's. As of the time that I write these words, over 20 million copies of *The Elements of Style* have been sold, making it the most popular book on writing and writing style in history. It certainly is the only such book on my desk that still gets any degree of use. White had a simple philosophy of writing based on the insistence that words should communicate rather than confuse.

Elwyn Brooks White was the sixth child of a well-to-do piano manufacturer and grew up in a tree-lined suburb of New York City known as Mount Vernon. He was educated at Cornell University, where he was continually embarrassed by his given names. When some of his friends began calling him Andy (after Andrew D. White, Cornell University's first president), he gladly accepted this nickname. Later on, he adopted the practice of signing his pieces "E. B. White," thus avoiding any reference to his first name.

During his undergraduate years, White showed his literary ability and became the editor-in-chief of the student newspaper. After graduation White held jobs as a reporter, freelance writer, and advertising copywriter. Many of his employers didn't appreciate his whimsical and comic writing, and he was not happy with the restrictions that they put on him. Things changed, however, after White contributed a few essays to a new magazine called *The New Yorker.*

The editor of *The New Yorker* was Harold Ross. He was demanding and authoritative, but he knew good writing when he saw it. Ross was still trying to find "the voice" for his fledgling publication, and eventually offered White a staff position. White was very much his own person, and he was reluctant to commit himself to any job that required him to report to an office on a fixed schedule. Nevertheless, he did show up for an interview, and there he met Katharine Angell, the magazine's fiction editor. She had been the one who had suggested to Ross that he consider White as a staff writer. White would later remember his first impression of Katharine by saying that "she had a lot of black hair and the knack of making a young contributor feel at ease." He was destined to fall in love with her, and on the day that her divorce became official, he married her. This was one of those "happily ever after" marriages, which lasted for forty-eight years until her death in 1977.

Shortly after White joined *The New Yorker,* the humorist/artist James Thurber also became a contributing editor. White, Ross, and Thurber gave the magazine its character and its familiar tone. White's work was found all over every issue. One of his main jobs was to write the "Notes and Comment" section, which opened each week's issue. Under the general heading of "The Talk of the Town" White gave his observations on the passing scene. Though he often commented on political activities, he did not take any particular side on most issues. Often the pieces were caustic and ironic musings about current issues and personalities. The items in this section were supposed to represent the view of the magazine, so White used the plural in most of his writing, such as "we believe" or "we have heard." Describing how his work came to be, he noted, "We write as we please and the magazine publishes as it pleases. When the two pleasures coincide, something gets into print." White also contributed essays, poems, and editorials and was even called upon to edit and revise cartoon captions. Except for the longer essays and the poems, all of his work was unsigned, and although everybody in the publishing world knew that it was his work, this lack of personal recognition bothered him.

Despite the time-consuming nature of his duties for *The New Yorker*, White still found time to write pieces for other publications. For instance, he collaborated with James Thurber on a book entitled *Is Sex Necessary?*, a hilarious spoof on the many sex manuals being published at that time.

To be a humorist and commentator, especially for a widely read magazine like *The New Yorker*, one must be extremely self-confident. Often the target of a humorous or cynical commentary can be quite hostile and aggressive toward the writer in very public ways. The dominant and self-reliant nature of White's personality perhaps is most evident in the way he finally took control over his own life. He never did like having other people set schedules for him or tell him how to conduct his day-to-day activities. Therefore, one day he walked into Ross's office and told the flabbergasted editor that he and Katharine were moving to a forty-acre farm on the seacoast of Maine. There he intended to raise animals, such as sheep and chickens, and he would continue to write and submit his work by mail. (Later on he wrote a letter to Thurber in which he mused, "I don't know which is more discouraging, literature or chickens.")

Somehow White managed the task of both working the farm and writing at the same time. He continued to contribute to *The New Yorker*, and also began writing a monthly column called "One Man's Meat" for *Harper's* magazine. This column pleased him because it was signed and he obtained some regular recognition for his work.

Once out of restraints imposed by a routine office schedule White could write as he pleased, when he pleased. He produced the three children's classics that I mentioned earlier, as well as *The Elements of Style.* He and his wife edited *A Subtreasury of American Humor.* He also wrote an affectionate guidebook to New York and several books of poetry. In addition he collected many of his essays into books. All of this activity eventually earned him both a Laura Ingalls Wilder award and the National Medal for Literature.

E. B. White is of particular interest to us, not so much because of literary contributions, but because we know much about both his personality and his life history with dogs. This will allow us to demonstrate how to fit a personality profile to particular dog groups.

I have already mentioned that White showed evidence of a highly dominant personality in the way that he ran his life. He demonstrated the self-confidence that goes with that personality trait quite graphically during the 1950s. It was the time of the Communist witch-hunts headed by Senator Joseph McCarthy, when few people in the media had the courage to speak out against the smear tactics of the House Unamerican Activities Committee lest they themselves be accused of being Communist sympathizers. White ignored the implicit threat, and wrote several editorials about this situation. They were filled with his usual mix of deep thought ("The junior senator from Wisconsin has succeeded only in making the country less secure and in keeping America in an uproar just when it should have a firm grasp on itself") mixed with humorous barbs ("A couple of these committeemen don't know a fact from a bag of popcorn anyway").

White's high score on the warmth dimension can be seen in his personal relationships and in his writing. Once, in explaining his reasons for writing *Charlotte's Web,* he displayed just how warm and caring he really was. His problem revolved around the fact that he liked animals, and "a farm is a peculiar problem for a man who likes animals, because the fate of most livestock is that they are murdered by their benefactors. The creatures may live serenely but they end violently." White had kept several pigs, getting them in spring as weanlings and caring for them all through the summer and fall. The relationship bothered him, since each day he became better acquainted with his pig, yet he felt that the whole relationship would culminate with a piece of double-dealing on his part, knowing that its demise was drawing closer. As he put it, "I do not like to betray a person or a creature . . . Anyway, the theme of *Charlotte's Web* is that a pig shall be saved, and I have an idea that somewhere deep inside me there was a wish to that effect."

On the remaining two dimensions, White was quite average. He showed a mid-range trust score in the fact that he was not very accepting of other people's direction and manipulation and, at the same time, he felt uncomfortable trying to manipulate the people around him. This made him a terrible advertising copywriter. He was extremely loyal to his friends and, though he occasionally offered guidance and opinions, he never attempted to force his views upon them. When criticized by friends he felt hurt and betrayed, but he seldom changed his behavior or opinions on the basis of such criticism. All of this is the pattern of a medium level on the trust dimension of personality.

White also scores in the medium range on extroversion, not by being at the middle level at all times, but rather by swinging from one extreme to the other. He loved the solitude that he found on the farm, but he often complained of loneliness. He maintained a large circle of friends who often came to socialize with him, yet preferred to work in an empty boathouse where the sparse furnishing "sheltered" him and allowed him to be a "healthier man." Although he claimed that he panicked at the thought of public speaking, he was perfectly happy to read his works at various literary clubs. While cherishing solitude, he and his wife threw parties for special occasions where it was not unusual for over a hundred people to be invited. Overall, then, the extremes average out to a medium level on extroversion.

Let us then take a look at E. B. White's full personality profile using our four scales. As his biographers describe him, White was medium on extroversion, high on dominance, medium on trust, and high on warmth. Flipping back to Table 5 on page 201, we find that a personality profile of this nature suggests the Friendly group of dogs three times and the Self-Assured group twice, while the Consistent, Steady, and Clever groups warrant only one mention each. Thus we would expect White to have his warmest feelings about dogs in the Friendly group, and a lot of affection for dogs in the Self-Assured group, and mixed feelings about the other three groups. In his life he had many dogs, and the breeds are quite consistent with these predictions.

White's first loved dog was from the Friendly group. It was a Collie named Mac. White's comments on Mac show his feelings.

Out of the vast sea of assorted dogs that I have had dealings with, by far the noblest, the best, and the most important was the first . . . He was an old style collie, beautifully marked, with a blunt nose, and a great natural gentleness and intelligence. When I got him he was what I badly needed. I think, probably all these other dogs of mine have just been groping toward that old dream.

White remembered Mac's behaviors quite fondly.

I can still see my first dog in all the moods and situations that memory has filed him away in, but I think of him oftenest as he used to be right after breakfast on the back porch, listlessly eating up a dish of petrified oatmeal rather than hurt my feelings. For six years he met me at the same place after school and convoyed me home—a service he thought up himself. A boy doesn't forget that sort of association.

If he loved a Collie, why didn't he get another one? Apparently there were two reasons. First of all, White did not believe that breeding determined a dog's temperament (although today we know that genetics are definitely an important factor in determining a dog's personality). He claimed, "A really companionable and indispensable dog is an accident of nature. You can't get it by breeding for it, and you can't buy it with money. It just happens along." Second, he admitted, "I've never dared to get another collie for fear the comparison would be too uncomfortable."

Later on White had a Labrador Retriever and a large Springer Spaniel; both breeds also come from the Friendly group. Although he was happy with these dogs, he seems to have had more trouble with them simply because of their size and strength. He was never particularly strong, and his inability to control the larger dogs occasionally got him in trouble. For instance, in a note to the author and drama critic Alexander Woollcott, White admitted, "I have a spaniel that defrocked a nun last week. He took hold of the cord. I had hold of the leash. It was like elephants holding tails. Imagine me undressing a nun, even second hand." Thus it soon became obvious to him that he would be wiser to select smaller dogs that were easier to handle.

According to White's personality profile, the other group of dogs that should, and did, fit him best are from the Self-Assured group, which includes a large number of terriers. White had one named Jones, which he described as "a small, poorly shaped Norwich Terrier, a bundle of neuroses," yet he clearly was fond of him. "Jones is peppery, scrappy, canny, and semi-obedient. I think I can make a dog of him yet." There was also a Fox Terrier, Raffles. Then there was Susy, a West Highland White Terrier. Her acquisition showed that when his impulses turned to dogs, the self-assured terriers were high on his list. "I bought Susy from a woman in Southwest Harbor the other day when I was caught in a puppy-buying mood."

Perhaps his favorite dog, after the Collie named Mac, was a black Scottish Terrier named Daisy. She was continually with him, and he took her on many trips. He liked having her with him and hated to leave her in anybody else's care. When she died he wrote her an affectionate obituary:

Daisy ("Black Watch Debatable") died December 22, 1931, when she was hit by a Yellow Cab in University Place. At the moment of her death she was smelling the front of a florist's shop. It was a wet day, and the cab skidded up over the curb—just the sort of excitement that would have amused her, had she been at a safer distance . . . Her life was full of incident but not of accomplishment. Persons who knew her only slightly regarded her as an opinionated little bitch, and said so; but she had a small circle of friends who saw through her, cost what it did . . . She enjoyed practically everything in life except motoring, an exigency to which she submitted silently, without joy, and without nausea. She never took pains to discover, conclusively, the things that might have diminished her curiosity and spoiled her taste. She died sniffing life, and enjoying it.

With White's personality profile, as with most people's, there were several dog groups that were mentioned only once. As I have already noted, selecting a dog from a group nominated only one time for your personality type might work out, and you might have a good relationship. However, most people who make this kind of choice find that their association with the dog is often ambiguous, with definite highs and terrible lows. Under these conditions some qualities of the dog will be cherished, and others will be hated. In E. B. White's profile, the Consistent dog group appears only once. In this group you will find Dachshunds, and White had a pair of them. The first, Fred, was a classic reddish-chestnut color (plate 17). White didn't select Fred for himself, but purchased him from a Madison Avenue pet shop for his wife, Katharine, who had always loved the breed. Fred was a large, strong-willed, beer-drinking dog, who, although beloved by his mistress, produced the expected mixed feelings in White.

For a number of years past I have been agreeably encumbered by a very large and dissolute dachshund named Fred. Of all the dogs whom I have served I've never known one who understood so much of what I say or held it in such deep contempt. When I address Fred I never have to raise either my voice or my hopes. He even disobeys me when I instruct him in something that he wants to do. And when I answer his peremptory scratch at the door and hold the door open for him to walk through, he stops in the middle and lights a cigarette, just to hold me up.

White had a real love-hate relationship with Fred, and this was best expressed when he observed:

Next to myself [Fred] is the greatest worrier and schemer on the premises and always has too many things on his mind. He not only handles all his own matters but he has a follow-up system by which he checks on all of mine to see that everything is taken care of . . . He wants to be present in a managerial capacity at every event, no matter how trifling or routine; it makes no difference whether I am dipping a sheep or simply taking a bath myself . . . His activities and his character constitute an almost uninterrupted annoyance to me, yet he is such an engaging old fool that I am quite attached to him, in a half-regretful way. Life without him would be heaven, but I'm afraid it is not what I want.

E. B. White's life illustrates that a dog from a breed group mentioned three times as being appropriate for an individual's personality has the potential to be a stellar match—a dog that you remember fondly all of your life. A dog that is selected from a breed group mentioned twice is likely to become a good companion, fondly thought of, while a dog from a once-mentioned breed group has the potential to be loved, but the road to that affection may well be long and rocky.

Chapter Sixteen

The Right and the Wrong Dog

Finding the right dog for your personality will probably improve the quality of your day-to-day existence. As the author and dog expert Roger Caras has said, "If you don't own a dog, at least one, there is not necessarily anything wrong with you, but there may be something wrong with your life."

Some individuals, because of the nature of their current circumstances, their personality, or their life history, may have difficulty relating to other people. This difficulty may be temporary or long-term. Yet many of these same individuals can still relate to a dog—or at least to the right dog. For those who can, their dog may prove to be their major source of social contact and perhaps their only source of real affection. Such people will often show concern and affection for their dog which is deeper and more forgiving than anything they show for family, friends, or spouse. For example, consider a case that occurred in the town of Derry, New Hampshire, in 1991.

Pamela Smart was a twenty-three-year-old high school instructor described as having big brown eyes, Gainsborough ringlets, and a taste for heavy-metal music. The story goes that she invited a fifteen-year-old student, William Flynn, to watch a sexually explicit movie on video and then seduced him. She did this as part of a plan to convince Flynn and two of his friends to kill her husband, Greg, a twenty-four-year-old insurance salesman. Pamela Smart had decided to get rid of Greg rather than divorce him because she was worried that a divorce court might not only give her husband their condominium but, more importantly, she might lose possession of their dog. The plan worked. Flynn and his friends followed her instructions, and Greg was shot and killed.

Perhaps the most telling aspect of this story, at least for our purposes here, came from the boys after they were picked up by the police. All three of them pleaded guilty to second-degree murder, and during the trial they testified that Pamela Smart gave them explicit instructions about the dog. "I want you to lock him up in the cellar before you do anything," she said. "I don't want that dog to be upset or become frightened or neurotic because he saw something violent happen to a member of his family."

SIR ISAAC AND DIAMOND

Sir Isaac Newton was a person who never seemed to find comfort with people but did find solace with his dog.[1] Newton was, without doubt, the single most important figure in the scientific revolution of the seventeenth century. He discovered the law of gravity, and his three laws of motion have often been referred to as the basic principles of modern physics and mechanics. In addition he made contributions to optics and to our knowledge of the nature of light and created the mathematical system that we now call calculus. There is no doubt about the tremendous intelligence and intellectual drive in Newton, and similarly, there is no doubt that he was vengeful, vindictive, cold-hearted, and uncaring toward his fellow humans. His life seems to have been completely devoid of any love or affection.

Newton was a frail infant, and many people were surprised that he survived his first year. He never knew his biological father, who had died three months before his birth, and when Newton was two years of age he was taken from his mother. She had married again, this time to an affluent minister, Barnabas Smith, who felt little affection for a child that was not his own. Smith insisted that Newton be left with his grandmother and then took the child's mother to another village and gave her the responsibility of rearing his own three biological children. Newton remained separated from his mother for nine years, until Smith's death. Some psychologists have suggested that this early separation and estrangement from his parents is the reason for Newton's life-long inability to love. He certainly had a lot of anger toward his mother and stepfather, as is shown in some shorthand notes that he made about his life in 1662. In these he recalled "threatening my father and mother Smith to burn them and the house over them."

Newton's lack of tolerance, kindness, and forgiveness is best shown in his various scientific controversies. In these he assumed that the slightest negative comment on his work was really meant as a personal attack on him, which required, in Newton's mind, not only a cessation of any social contact with the person but vengeance and retribution.

Consider Newton's interactions with Robert Hooke. Hooke was a renowned scientist who, like Newton, worked in many areas including optics, chemistry, mechanics, and botany. Hooke's research resulted in the development of the balance spring for clocks and anticipated the development of the steam engine. He also developed the mathematical description of the compression of elastic substances which we now call Hooke's Law. Hooke had mildly criticized one of Newton's early papers on optics, and Newton, unable to distinguish between the normal give and take of honest scientific discussion versus personal attacks, had flown into a rage. In response he attempted to publicly humiliate Hooke.

Several years later, when Newton was studying the nature of gravity, Hooke attempted to establish a formal scientific correspondence with him. In a letter, Hooke suggested that Newton's analysis of one of his experiments was wrong and further suggested that it could be corrected if one assumed that gravity decreased with distance. Angered at the criticism, Newton did not respond to this letter, though he later admitted that it had started him thinking about some new experiments and analyses which proved to be quite important in shaping the law of gravity. Several years later, Newton included his revised discussion of gravity in the manuscript of his book *Opticks,* which he submitted to the Royal Society. When Hooke saw that the relationship that he had suggested to Newton was included in the manuscript, he raised the charge of plagiarism. Since Newton had never had the courtesy to respond to

Hooke's original letter to explain the situation, Hooke's reaction was understandable, even if not justified when all of the facts were known.

Newton's response to Hooke's charges shows us a lot about his personality. Hooke would have been quite satisfied, and would have readily dropped the charges, if Newton had simply included a few lines in the manuscript to acknowledge the fact that Hooke had been thinking along similar lines and that their correspondence had led to new experiments. This would have been a graceful gesture and a compassionate one, given the fact that Hooke was quite sick at the time and his illustrious career was clearly reaching its end. Furthermore, this warm gesture would have cost Newton nothing. Instead, Newton responded vengefully. He went through his manuscript and deleted nearly every reference to Hooke. He was so furious over this incident that he refused to publish his *Opticks* and also refused to accept the presidency of the Royal Society until Hooke was dead.

The fact that Newton was cold and unfeeling to others was shown many times during his tenure as leader of the Royal Society. While doing his astronomical calculations, he had occasionally called upon John Flamsteed, the Royal Astronomer, for assistance. Flamsteed had collected an incredibly rich body of important data which were not available elsewhere, and he had always provided the information when needed. However, in the 1690s, when Newton was working on his lunar theory, he again needed Flamsteed's data and became quite annoyed when he could not get all the information he wanted as quickly as he wanted it. Therefore, with no compunctions at all, Newton used his influence with the government to be named as chairman of the committee in charge of the Royal Observatory. He then seized Flamsteed's catalog of stars and tried to force its immediate publication so that he would have full access to the material. Newton would not listen to objections that he was, in effect, stealing the fruit of Flamsteed's lifetime of work. He broke agreements with Flamsteed whenever convenient for him, and finally was stopped only by a court action instituted by Flamsteed. As in the case of Hooke, Newton sought his revenge by systematically eliminating references to Flamsteed's help in any of his later work, although his calculations continued to be based upon the Royal Astronomer's data.

Another incident worth mentioning involved Gottfried Wilhelm Leibniz, the German philosopher and mathematician. We now know with certainty that Newton developed the mathematical system we know as calculus, and that Leibniz later developed the same system independently. Since Newton had never published his own work, and no one knew of it, when Leibniz's paper appeared in print it was the first public disclosure of the system and Leibniz received credit for it. In response Newton set about to destroy Leibniz's career and credibility. He wrote several articles attacking Leibniz but published them under the names of his students and disciples who, knowing the depth of Newton's wrath, never had the courage to publicly disapprove of this activity. Next, as president of the Royal Society, Newton appointed an "impartial" committee to investigate the issue. Having hand-picked a committee which he knew would censure Leibniz was not enough for Newton. Just to be sure of his vengeance, secretly, he personally wrote the report officially published by the society. Finally, to ensure Leibniz's condemnation Newton reviewed the report anonymously in the *Philosophical Transactions,* concluding that the investigation had been fair and that Leibniz had been malicious and unethical on all counts.

Newton had very few close relationships. His contacts with women involved only his unfortunate relationship with his mother, who had abandoned him, and, somewhat later, his guardianship of a niece. There is no evidence of any love interest in his long life. His relationships with men were also not very successful. Although he assumed the role of patron for a circle of young scientists, he did so with a magisterial attitude, treating them as disciples rather than friends. In fact, the only evidence of anything approaching love or caring that continued for any length of time is Newton's relationship with his dog.

Newton's dog was a cream-colored Pomeranian named Diamond, a good match given his low warmth and medium extroversion. As I noted when we discussed Queen Victoria, Pomeranians during that era were usually much larger than we have come to expect today, and it appears that Diamond was a medium-sized dog, weighing about thirty-five pounds (fourteen kilograms). In personality, however, they were quite similar to our contemporary Pomeranians. They are feisty little dogs who are quite protective, at least to the best of their abilities, and thus make good watchdogs. It was this quality that eventually got Diamond into trouble.

It was sometime after Newton had received his letter from Hooke, and while he was working on his revision of the law of gravity. It was after nightfall, and he was working by candlelight, while Diamond slept nearby. A knock on the door called Newton out of the study, and apparently Diamond awakened to the sound of unfamiliar voices. Her protective instincts were immediately aroused and she tried to get to her master. Unfortunately, the door to Newton's study was closed, so she was reduced to running wildly around the room, barking in excitement. On one circuit of the room Diamond apparently collided with a leg of Newton's small writing table. The shock of her collision caused the burning candle to tip over, directly onto the manuscript. There was little damage to the room, but the papers that Newton had been working on were completely destroyed.

When Newton returned to the room with the visitor he was shocked at the scene that greeted him. Yet instead of flying into a rage, he merely lifted the dog from the floor and said to her sorrowfully, "Oh Diamond, Diamond, thou little knowest what damage thou hast done."

The next day Newton explained to a fellow member of the Royal Society that his anticipated revision of the law of gravity would be delayed. "Because of Diamond I have had to begin much of the work afresh. I will not, however, rid myself of her, nor even punish her. She knew not what she was doing, and that which she did was for my protection and for love of my person. Her place remains at my side or against my feet when I lie abed."

This little Pomeranian, Diamond, thus may have been the only living thing who caused Sir Isaac Newton distress and did not incur his vengeful wrath.

THE POODLE HATERS

While we often develop a strong attachment and passion for a dog selected from a breed that fits our personality, the converse is also true. Being forced to live with or interact with a breed that is wrong for one's personality can bring out an equally intense disdain or even malice.

Would you believe that a web site has been created exclusively to show dislike for Poodles? This site is called "People Against Poodles." The opening page tells you that "People Against Poodles (PAP) is on your side. PAP is an organization dedicated to eliminating the poodle threat for the good of all other species inhabiting this planet." Later on it justifies the web site by noting, "Sure, other larger social issue problems may exist, but we of PAP feel that the change should begin here. When people are less irritated, they are less likely to turn to drugs. When people are not awakened at 4:30 in the morning by a yapping poodle . . . they are less likely to walk around with pent-up violence."

Supposed evidence for the harm that Poodles do is given in the form of scornful comments and observations. There is one section of the site that "describes incidents involving poodles that reveal their true nature." Various news items follow in which a Poodle bites someone or does something stupid or bizarre that causes a human or the dog itself injury, as in an article entitled "Fugitive Poodle Attacks Airport Worker." Another segment begins with the question "How should poodles be dealt with?" and goes on to suggest bizarre ways of actually killing Poodles.

Perhaps the most interesting aspect of this web location is the "Guest Book" where people can sign in and leave comments. The creator of this web site has sorted these into categories: "Poodle Haters," "Poodle Lovers," and "Vitriolic." One Poodle hater wrote, "I've always hated poodles! Thank you for showing me that I am not alone." Another said, "I have never encountered such a stunning example of common sense on any web site. Your views on the poodle species are indeed some of the most intelligent insights offered anywhere at any price. Good luck in your campaign against this furry demonic pest."

Most comments in the Poodle Lovers section are directed against Poodle haters in general with messages like "You are evil, evil, evil people!" Many comments, however, single out the creator of this web page for special censure: "I would like to offer my deepest sympathy to the pathetic person who maintains this web site. I can't even imagine how big of a loser you must be. I'm sure the only reason you are so disturbed about poodles is because they are both more intelligent and attractive than you. Regardless; all animals should be treated with respect and kindness as they unlike yourself have much to offer the world." And an occasional Poodle lover becomes enraged to the point of incoherence, as in: "I love Poodles you bastards, damn you !!!! damn you !!!! Damn you all !!!!!!!!! I hope you are all disembowled by a rampaging mob of rabif poddles." (The spelling and typographical errors are in the original message.)

MAX AND IDAHO

It may seem to you that the majority of people do not show either the extreme love for particular dogs that we saw in Elizabeth Barrett Browning for Flush, nor the extreme hate shown by People Against Poodles. For most of us, once we have found the right dog for our personality, we merely accept them into our homes and our lives. If we are not completely happy with a dog, we will probably not repeat that breed again. If we have found the right fit, when our present dog dies we will usually replace it with another, just like it, in the hopes of keeping the familiar warmth of that loved dog around us.

I once spoke with James J. Gibson, a well-known researcher in the psychological aspects of human perception, who spent most of his career at Cornell University. He told me a story about the distinguished psychologist Kurt Koffka, who is considered to be one of the founding fathers of Gestalt Psychology. Koffka always had dachshunds as his dogs. All of his dachshunds were the popular chestnut-colored, smooth-haired variety. In his lifetime Koffka had had seven such dachshunds (that Gibson knew of) and each of them had been named Max. One day when they were casually chatting Gibson asked the eminent psychologist, "Why do you name all of your dogs Max?"

Koffka replied, "The first one was named Max. When he died I got another, and I gave him a different name. Yet he looked like Max, and he acted like Max and sometimes I found myself calling him Max. So I said to myself, 'If he wants to be Max then he is Max.'"

At this point Koffka stopped and then resumed the conversation in a slow, bemused tone of voice. "I suppose that I wanted Max to live with me forever. That is the nice thing about a purebred dog—if you find one that you like, they are so much the same that you can have him again and again and they need never really die. So when I get a dachshund puppy who starts with the name Rolle or the name Jolly, I know that sooner or later they will turn into Max. That is because in their genes they are all Max, and that is who I wish to live with."

Sometimes the fit between a person or a family and a dog is perfect, and when that happens the bond between the human and the dog transcends our normal concept of a lifetime. In Koffka's case he managed to keep his favorite dog with him by seeking its reincarnation in a dog of the same breed and same look, and this is the path taken by many people who are happy with their dogs.

There was another time, however, when I encountered a person who had formed a powerful and unbreakable bond with his dog, and that had added a poignant element. This was the case of Ed and his dog Idaho. When I spoke to Ed he was three weeks shy of his eightieth birthday. He was living in a little house with his wife of fifty-six years, Jessie. We sat in his living room and he told me about his dog.

We got Idaho when she was just a puppy. Both Jessie and I could be described as easygoing people who were pretty much in control of our lives and we were looking for a dog that would be a playmate for the kids and a companion for us. Someone told us, or maybe we read somewhere, that a Labrador Retriever would fit that bill, so we looked for someone who breeds Labs.

We picked Idaho out of the litter because she was so friendly and accepting, and Jessie liked her chocolate color. The kids were playing with the pups and when they rolled her on her back and molested her, the way kids do, she didn't seem frightened or angry or even bothered. She just licked their hands and wagged her tail a bit.

Idaho was with us for thirteen years, which I am told is a good life for a Lab. She really was a friend. When Jessie got meningitis, and was stuck in bed and scared, Idaho would climb up there on the bed with her and just be there as company for her. When the kids came home she would lure them out of the house for a while so there would be some quiet. She was there for me too. When I didn't have Jessie to talk to because she was so sick, Idaho would come and sit next to me and kiss my face as if she was saying it would be OK . . . She was right, you know. Jessie did get better.

Anyway, the kids grew up and left us. Alan started college and Melinda got married. Idaho acted as though it was her job to remind us that we were still a family and weren't just two old people who were now alone. She kept the house full of love, I guess, and gave us the feeling that there was still someone that needed us.

When Idaho died I buried her in the backyard—in the corner near a snowball flower bush that she was always so interested in. We missed her, so we got another Lab and have stuck with the breed. Right now we have Lady, that brown pile of fur in the middle of the floor. [He smiled, and Lady looked up at the mention of her name, thumping her tail once or twice.]

Well, with the kids now both on their own, and with me retiring, we thought that it might be nice to get a smaller house, outside of the city, where it was quieter and things moved a bit slower, and that's how we ended up here. The last thing that I did at the old place was to dig Idaho up. The first thing I did here was to bury her in the corner of the yard. She's back there, where Jessie planted a snowball flower bush, like the one at the old house, to keep her company. I know that it seems like a dumb or crazy thing to do. You see I loved that dog and . . . [He paused and looked out the window and rubbed one eye with the back of his hand.] *It's just that I had promised that dog—swore it to her—that she would always have a home with me.*

I hope that the information in this book will help you to find your special breed of dog—your own Max or your own Idaho.

Chapter Seventeen

The Chosen Dogs

I n each of the previous chapters I gave a few examples of people who have selected dogs from the breed group that fit them best. I really wanted to be able to give you examples and stories of many more well-known and recognizable people who owned dogs from each of the seven groups, and even specific examples of people who owned dogs of each of the 133 breeds that fall into these groups. However, my editor decided that she did not want to publish the set of twenty-five volumes that would require. But to give you a flavor of what might have been in those volumes, I will give you a list of a group of celebrated people and their dogs. The people named come from many different walks of life. Some are kings, presidents, or politicians, others are actors, writers, artists, people in professional sports, some noted businessmen, TV personalities, and some prominent scientists.

The material presented here comes from various sources including biographies, histories, photographs, breed books, and various web sites and discussion groups on the internet. I tried to include some examples of eminent owners for every breed, and I have come reasonably close to this goal. Also, whenever possible, I have included the name of the dog that the celebrity owned. Sometimes the names tell us something about the feelings that the person has for that dog. Other times it tells something about the person themselves. If I have missed an interesting person, breed, or dog's name, feel free to contact me at the Psychology Department of the University of British Columbia (Vancouver, BC, V6T 1Z4, Canada) to correct my omission.

Perhaps, as you browse through the owners of dogs in the groups that best suit your personality, you will find people who are like you, who you feel a certain kinship with or similarity to. Even if you don't, it is sort of fun to find out the breed of dog that nestled at the feet of various rich, famous, or influential individuals.

GROUP 1: FRIENDLY DOGS

Bearded Collie

Bo Derek (actress, *10, Woman of Desire*): Molly and others

Tony Dow (actor, Wally Cleaver on TV series *Leave It to Beaver*): Magnolia

Molly O'Neill (*New York Times* columnist, cookbook author): Herschel, Betty Lou, Phoebe

Bichon Frise

James Arness (actor, TV series *Gunsmoke*): Matt, Miss Kitty

Barbara Taylor Bradford (novelist, *Angel, To Be the Best*): Gemmy

Mary Frann (actress, TV series *Newhart*): Panache

John Gavin (actor turned diplomat, *Psycho, Heidi*): Julie

Frank Gifford (TV sports announcer): Chablis, Chardonnay

Chick Hearn (sports announcer): owns several

Lainie Kazan (singer, actress): Ella

Aaron Spelling (TV producer, TV series *Dynasty, The Colbys*): Shelley and others

Tanya Tucker (country music singer): Lucy

Betty White (actress, comedian, TV series *The Golden Girls, The Mary Tyler Moore Show*)

Border Terrier

James Herriot (veterinarian, author, *All Creatures Great and Small, All Things Wise and Wonderful*): Bodie

Maxwell Knight (author, *My Pet Friends*): Teeny-wee

Brittany Spaniel

Susan Dey (actress, TV series *The Partridge Family, L.A. Law, Love and War*)

Cavalier King Charles Spaniel

William F. Buckley Jr. (editor, *The National Review;* TV host, *Firing Line*): Freckles and others

Charles I (king of England)

Charles II (king of England, for whom the breed was named)

Stanley Coren (psychologist, author, *The Intelligence of Dogs, Sleep Thieves, What Do Dogs Know*): Wizard

Victor Costa (clothing designer with Christian Dior): Dior

Armand Deutsch (writer, *Me and Bogie;* movie producer with MGM): Quizzical

Kirk Douglas (actor, *20,000 Leagues under the Sea, Spartacus, The Man from Snowy River*): Sparkle

Michael J. Fox (actor, *Back to the Future, Doc Hollywood, The American President;* TV series *Family Ties*): Rex

Mary Hart (host, TV series *Entertainment Tonight*): Pumpkin

James II (king of England)

Harris Katleman (entertainment executive): Mishka

Duke of Marlborough (John Churchill; the brown and white variety of the Cavalier is named after his home, Blenheim Castle)

Ronald Reagan (U.S. president): Rex—gift from William F. Buckley

Arthur Schlesinger Jr. (historian, author, *A Thousand Days: John F. Kennedy in the White House*): Polo, Molly, Sinbad

Mordecai Siegal (author; president of Dog Writers Association of America)

Frank Sinatra (singer, actor, *Robin and the Seven Hoods, The First Deadly Sin*)

Richard Thomas (actor, *All Quiet on the Western Front, Johnny Belinda;* TV series *The Waltons*): Henrietta

Victoria (queen of England): Dash (see plate 12)

Cocker Spaniel, English and American

JUNE ALLYSON (actress, *The Shrike, Best Foot Forward*): Heathcliff

LAUREN BACALL (actress, *To Have and Have Not, The Big Sleep, Key Largo*): Puddle, Droopy

CLARA BOW (early film actress, *It, Man Trap*): Diablo

ANNE BRONTË (author, *Agnes Grey*): Flossy

ELIZABETH BARRETT BROWNING (poet, *Sonnets from the Portuguese*): Flush

GEORGE BUSH (U.S. president): C. Fred Bush

ROGER CARAS (author, *Celebration of Dogs* and many other animal books): Peter

LESLIE CHARLESON (actress, TV series *General Hospital*): Freeway

WILLIAM COWPER (18th-century English poet, *The Task, The Diverting History of John Gilpin*): Beau

A. J. CRONIN (author, *The Citadel, The Judas Tree*): Sally

MAZO DE LA ROCHE (Canadian author, best known for the Jalna series)

PHYLLIS DILLER (comedian): Mr. Deeds

ERNEST HEMINGWAY (writer, *The Sun Also Rises, The Old Man and the Sea*): Blackie

KATHARINE HEPBURN (actress, *Guess Who's Coming to Dinner?, The Philadelphia Story, On Golden Pond*): Mica and others

KAREN HORNEY (psychologist): Blackie

ARTE JOHNSON (comedian, TV series *Laugh-In*): Kleine and others

JOHN F. KENNEDY (U.S. president): Shannon—gift from prime minister of Ireland, Eamon de Valera

ROBERT KENNEDY (U.S. attorney general, senator): Freckles

GAYLE KING (TV talk show host)

SUGAR RAY LEONARD (Olympic and world champion boxer): Max, Thunder

LIBERACE (pianist, flamboyant entertainer): Chow Mein

HAROLD LLOYD (silent screen and early talkies comic actor): Bobby, Captain

FRED MACMURRAY (actor, *Double Indemnity, The Absent-Minded Professor;* TV series *My Three Sons*): Jack

FREDRIC MARCH (actor, *The Best Years of Our Lives, Inherit the Wind, The Iceman Cometh*): Coco

GARRY MARSHALL (director, *Pretty Woman;* TV series *Happy Days, Mork and Mindy*): Linus

CATHY RIGBY McCOY (Olympic gold medal gymnast): Molly

RICHARD NIXON (U.S. president): Checkers (actually his daughter Julie's dog)

KENNY NORMAN (pro sports, Atlanta Hawks)

VITA SACKVILLE-WEST (British novelist and poet, *The Edwardians, The Land*)

LAWRENCE SANDERS (author, *The First Deadly Sin*): Feets

TOM SELLECK (actor, *Three Men and a Baby, Mr. Baseball;* TV series *Magnum P.I.*): Topper

FREDERICK SHERMAN (rear admiral, aircraft carrier U.S.S. *Lexington* at Battle of the Coral Sea): Admiral Wags

FRANK SINATRA (singer, actor, *Robin and the Seven Hoods, The First Deadly Sin*): Miss Wiggles

KATE SMITH (singer, radio and TV show host; best known for her versions of "God Bless America" at sporting events): Sport

AARON SPELLING (producer, TV series *Dynasty, The Colbys*)

STEVEN SPIELBERG (film director/producer, *E.T., Jaws, Schindler's List*)

CHARLOTTE MAILLIARD SWIG (owner of Fairmont Hotel chain): Stevie Wonder

ELIZABETH TAYLOR (actress, *Butterfield 8, Cleopatra, Who's Afraid of Virginia Woolf?*): Spot

CHARLIZE THERON (actress, *That Thing You Do, 2 Days in the Valley*): owns several

STROM THURMOND (U.S. senator): Lady, Tramp

HARRY S. TRUMAN (U.S. president): Feller—unloved gift from a woman in Missouri

BRENDA VACCARO (actress, *Midnight Cowboy, Once Is Not Enough*): Brentwood, Rosie and others

EDWARD O. WILSON (biologist, psychologist; Pulitzer Prize winner, *Sociobiology*): Toby

OPRAH WINFREY (TV host): Solomon and others

HENRY WINKLER (actor, director, *Night Shift, An American Christmas Carol;* TV series *Happy Days*): Spunky

VIRGINIA WOOLF (writer, intellectual, feminist, and publisher): Othello

Collie

EDGAR RICE BURROUGHS (writer, Tarzan series): Rajah

PIERRE BURTON (author, *Yukon, The Last Spike*): several

CALVIN COOLIDGE (U.S. president): Rob Roy, Bessie, Oshkosh, Foxy, Prudence Prim (actually these were the favorites of his wife, Grace)

DORIS DAY (singer, actress, *The Pajama Game, Midnight Lace*): Daisy

BO DEREK (actress, *10, Woman of Desire*)

JUDY GARLAND (singer, actress, *The Wizard of Oz, A Star Is Born*): Eddie

GEORGE V (king of England): Heather

MARK HARMON (actor, *The Presidio, The Deliberate Stranger;* TV series *St. Elsewhere*)

HERBERT HOOVER (U.S. president): Glen

LYNDON B. JOHNSON (U.S. president): Rover (his first dog), Blanco

ART LINKLETTER (radio/TV broadcaster and author): King

WALTER MONDALE (U.S. vice president): Bonnie

MARILYN MONROE (actress, *Some Like It Hot, Bus Stop*): Muggsie

J. P. MORGAN (banker, founder of U.S. Steel, philanthropist): owned several

PAUL NEWMAN (actor, *Butch Cassidy and the Sundance Kid, The Color of Money*): Smokey

NICHOLAS II (czar of Russia): Iman was his favorite of many.

JACK PICKFORD (silent movie star, *Tom Sawyer, Exit Smiling*): Prince

BEATRIX POTTER (author, *The Tale of Peter Rabbit*): Kep

DICK SCHAAP (author, theater critic, sportscaster): Max

ROBERT SCHULLER (clergyman/author, TV series *Hour of Power*): Deacon

RANDOLPH SCOTT (actor *Last of the Mohicans, Ride the High Country*): Bob

SIR WALTER SCOTT (author, *Ivanhoe, Rob Roy*): Royal

SUSAN STRASBERG (actress, *Picnic, Sweet 16*): Sunshine

ALBERT PAYSON TERHUNE (writer of many dog stories): Argus, Break, many others

VICTORIA (queen of England): Noble

CASPAR WEINBERGER (U.S. secretary of defense, Reagan administration): Kiltie

E. B. WHITE (author, *Charlotte's Web*): Mac

Curly-Coated Retriever

WILLIAM TECUMSEH SHERMAN (U.S. Civil War general): Loyal

English Setter

GROVER CLEVELAND (U.S. president)

JOHN STEINBECK (Nobel Prize–winning author, *Of Mice and Men, East of Eden*): Toby

Field Spaniel

HENRY VI (king of England)

JAMES I (king of England)

JAMES II (king of England)

Flat-coated Retriever

STANLEY COREN (psychologist, author, *The Intelligence of Dogs, Sleep Thieves, What Do Dogs Know?*): Odin

GEORGE V (king of England)

VICTORIA (queen of England)

Golden Retriever

JANE ALEXANDER (actress; head, National Endowment for the Arts): Cody, Liberator

PAMELA ANDERSON (actress, TV series *Baywatch*): Star

BILL BLASS (clothing designer): Brutus, several others

JIMMY BUFFETT (popular singer, "Margaritaville"): Cheeseburger

MARY CHAPIN-CARPENTER (country and pop singer, songwriter)

JAMIE LEE CURTIS (actress, *Halloween, True Lies*): owns several

NEIL DIAMOND (popular singer, "Sweet Caroline," "I'm a Believer"): Sol

PHYLLIS DILLER (comedian): Gemina

SHANNEN DOHERTY (actress, TV series *Beverly Hills 90210*): Clancy Muldoon, others

JERRY DOUGLAS (actor, TV series *The Young and The Restless*)

JIM EDGAR (governor of Illinois)

BRUCE FOGLE (author, *Pets and People, Dog's Mind*, other animal books): Honey

GERALD FORD (U.S. president): Liberty and others

INDIRA GANDHI (prime minister of India)

FRANK GIFFORD (TV sports commentator): Charlie

DEIRDRE HALL (soap opera actress, TV series *Days of Our Lives*): Molly

GUS HALL (head of U.S. Communist Party): Yuri

MARIETTE HARTLEY (actress, *O'Hara's Wife, No Place to Hide;* TV host *Today, The Morning Show*): Daisy

BOB HOLLAND (CEO, Ben & Jerry's Homemade, Fortune 500 company): Mad Max

BO HOPKINS (actor, *Midnight Express, The Ballad of Little Jo*): Candy

RON HOWARD (actor, TV series *Happy Days;* director, *Splash, Cocoon*)

STACI KEANAN (actress, TV series *Going Places, My Two Dads*): Fatty, several others

JOHN LARROQUETTE (actor, *Blind Date, Richie Rich;* TV series *Night Court*): Pluto

JOEY LAWRENCE (actor, *Gimme a Break, Blossom*): Jack

TIMOTHY LEARY (psychologist and LSD advocate): Bo

MARY TYLER MOORE (actress, *Ordinary People;* TV series *The Mary Tyler Moore Show*): Dash

MICKEY MORANDINI (pro baseball player): owns several

BILL MURRAY (actor, *Ghostbusters, Groundhog Day*): Bark

PAUL NEWMAN (actor, *Butch Cassidy and the Sundance Kid, The Color of Money*): Lucky

JACK NICKLAUS (professional golfer): Lady, Bear, White Paws

KIM NOVAK (actress, *Picnic, Vertigo*): owns several

BOBBY ORR (Hall of Fame ice hockey player)

ARNOLD PALMER (professional golf star): Rieley

MICHAEL PARÉ (actor, *Eddie and the Cruisers, The Last Hour*): Cody

SARA PARETSKY (author, the V. I. Warshawski mystery novels)

NORMAN VINCENT PEALE (clergyman/author, *The Power of Positive Thinking*): Buff

GREGORY PECK (actor *Moby Dick, To Kill a Mockingbird*)

DENNIS QUAID (actor, *The Big Easy, Great Balls of Fire*): Fawn Hall

RONALD REAGAN (U.S. president): Victory

CHRISTOPHER REEVE (actor, *Superman*): It is his assistance dog.

DAN REEVES (professional football coach): Hondo and others

ROBIN RIKER (actor, TV series *Thunder Alley*)

JOAN RIVERS (comedian, TV series *Live with Regis & Kathie Lee*): Callie

MORLEY SAFER (TV journalist): Goldie, Dora

TED SANN (CEO, BBDO, Fortune 500 Company): Dudley

JERRY SEINFELD (actor, TV series *Seinfeld*)

MAURICE SENDAK (children's author/artist, *Where the Wild Things Are*): Io

JANE SEYMOUR (actress, *Live and Let Die, Lassiter;* TV series *Dr. Quinn, Medicine Woman*): Crispin

MARC SINGER (actor, *Beastmaster, Watchers 2;* TV series *V: The Series*): Rufus

DAVID SOUL (actor, *World War III, The Key to Rebecca;* TV series *Starsky & Hutch*): Dublin

JAMES STEWART (actor, *It's a Wonderful Life, Harvey, Anatomy of a Murder*): Barron, Kelly, Judy, Beau

PAUL TSONGAS (U.S. senator from Massachusetts)

JACK WAGNER (actor, TV series *General Hospital*): Elvis and others

CLAY WALKER (country singer)

BETTY WHITE (actress, comedian, TV series *The Golden Girls, The Mary Tyler Moore Show*): Dinah

JAMES WHITMORE (actor, *Black Like Me, Battleground, Give 'em Hell, Harry*)

JERRY WIGGINS (psychologist, creator of the Interpersonal Adjective Personality Test)

OPRAH WINFREY (TV host): Arizona and others

DAVID WOLPER (movie and TV producer, TV mini-series *Roots*): Sunshine

Keeshond

HELOISE (helpful hint and advice columnist and author): Sheeba

LIBERACE (pianist, entertainer): Gretel

Labrador Retriever

DOC AND KATY ABRAHAM (horticultural writers; syndicated column, *Green Thumb*): Mirabelle

ANNE (princess of England): Laura

KAREN BLACK (actress, *Five Easy Pieces, Nashville*): Minnie

BILL BLASS (clothing designer): Burnaby

J. BRYAN III (author, *Hodgepodge*): Dixie

BARBARA CARTLAND (English romance novelist, author of over 250 books): Duke

CHARLES (crown prince of England): Harvey

GARY COLLINS (TV personality): Florence

KEVIN COSTNER (actor, *Field of Dreams, Dances with Wolves, Wyatt Earp*): Rosalita

ED COX (Texas oilman and art collector): Rocket

SHERYL CROW (rock star): Scout

TOM CRUISE (actor, *Top Gun, A Few Good Men, Mission Impossible*): Joseph

BARRY DILLER (film and TV producer; president, Paramount Pictures; CEO, Twentieth Century Fox): Whip

PHYLLIS DILLER (comedian): Skipper

SHANNEN DOHERTY (actress, TV series *Beverly Hills 90210*): Precious Penelope

HARRISON FORD (actor, *Star Wars, Raiders of the Lost Ark, Airforce One*)

GEORGE VI (king of England): Mimsy and others

DEIRDRE HALL (actress, TV series *Days of our Lives*): Max

BILL HARRIS (gossip commentator and TV personality): Diamond

TOM HAYDEN (political activist, author, co-founder of Students for Democratic Action): Taxi

JAMES HERRIOT (veterinarian/author, *All Creatures Great and Small, All Things Wise and Wonderful*): Dan

MARJORIE HOLMES (religious writer, *I've Got to Talk to Somebody, God; Two from Galilee*): Ben

BO HOPKINS (actor, *Midnight Express, The Ballad of Little Jo*): Bogie

ROGER HORCHOW (mail order entrepreneur): Valentine

PAUL IRWIN (president, U.S. Humane Society): Zack

HARRIS KATLEMAN (entertainment executive): Trillion

HENRY KISSINGER (U.S. secretary of state): Amelia

VIVIEN LEIGH (actress, *Gone With the Wind, A Streetcar Named Desire*): Jason

STEPHEN MACHT (actor, *The American Dream, Flight #90: Disaster on the Potomac;* TV series *Cagney and Lacey*): Jagss and others

KARL MALONE (pro basketball player): Tosshie and others

BARBARA MANDRELL (country singer): Boomer

GEORGE MCGOVERN (U.S. senator, presidential candidate): Atticus

SCOTT MCNEALY (CEO, Sun Microsystems, Fortune 500 company): Miyake

CHRISTA MILLER (actress, TV series *The Drew Carey Show*): Skye

MARY ANN MOBLEY (Miss America, TV personality): Florence

EARL OF MOUNTBATTEN (of England): Kimberly

GEORGE PLIMPTON (writer, *Paper Tiger*): Ernie

RICHARD PRYOR (actor, *Silver Streak, Stir Crazy, Harlem Nights*): Brother

DENNIS QUAID (actor, *The Big Easy, Dragonheart, Wyatt Earp*): Dave—shared with Meg Ryan

RONALD REAGAN (U.S. president): Millie

KEITH RICHARDS (rock musician with the Rolling Stones)

RENEE RICHARDS (tennis player): Houdini

DIANA RIGG (actress, *The Hospital, Evil under the Sun;* TV series *The Avengers;* TV host *Mystery*): Bonnie

JOAN RIVERS (comedian, TV series *Live with Regis & Kathie Lee*): Apollo

MEG RYAN (actress, *Sleepless in Seattle, Restoration*): Dave—shared with Dennis Quaid

NORMAN SCHWARZKOPF (U.S. general during the Gulf War): has owned several

ARNOLD SCHWARZENEGGER (actor, *Terminator, Conan the Barbarian, Eraser*): Conan

FRANK SINATRA (singer, actor, *Robin and the Seven Hoods, The First Deadly Sin*): Leroy Brown

SYLVESTER STALLONE (actor, Rocky and Rambo films): Flipper

VICTORIA (queen of England)

E. B. WHITE (author/poet, *Charlotte's Web*): Moses

JACK YOUNGBLOOD (pro football player): Jet

MORT ZUCKERMAN (publishing executive): Stockman

Nova Scotia Duck Toller

JAMES E. CREIGHTON (first president, American Philosophical Association)

Old English Sheepdog

EMILY CARR (Canadian artist)

JEAN HARLOW (actress, *Dinner at Eight*) (see plate 3)

LAINIE KAZAN (singer, actress): Nana

JEANETTE MACDONALD (actress, *Naughty Marietta, Indian Love Call*):
   Captain

CHARLES OSGOOD (broadcast journalist): Everett, Cecilia

FRANKLIN D. ROOSEVELT (U.S. president): Tiny

KATHARINE ROSS (actress, *Butch Cassidy and the Sundance Kid, The
   Stepford Wives*): Samantha

JOAN VAN ARK (actress, TV series *Knots Landing*): Boulder

Portuguese Water Dog

CARLOS RUIZ CAMINO (legendary bullfighter whose career lasted 19
   years)

CHARLES OSGOOD (broadcast journalist): Tony

Soft Coated Wheaten Terrier

JERRY DOUGLAS (actor, TV series *The Young and The Restless*)

EUGENE ROCHE (actor, *Slaughterhouse-Five, The Late Show;* TV series
   Perfect Strangers, Julie): Duffer

LOUISE SOREL (actress, *When Every Day Was the Fourth of July, Get
   Christie Love!;* TV series *The Don Rickles Show*): Jiggs

TORI SPELLING (actress, TV series *Beverly Hills 90210*): Sammy

Springer Spaniel (English and Welsh)

STEVE ALLEN (TV talk show host, composer of over 2,000 songs; actor,
   The Benny Goodman Story): Mr. T.

DAVID BATES (artist): Clovis Lee

JIMMY BUFFETT (popular singer, "Margaritaville"): Spring

GEORGE BUSH (U.S. president): Millie, Ranger (see plate 1)

ROGER CARAS (author, *Celebration of Dogs* and many other animal
   books)

MISHA DICHTER (concert pianist): Mercedes

CURT GERLING (newspaper publisher/columnist; author, *Freckles and
   Betsy*): Freckles, Betsy

RUTHERFORD B. HAYES (U.S. president)

PATRICIA MCPHERSON (actress, TV series *Knight Rider*): Sam

JAYNE MEADOWS (actress, *David and Bathsheba;* regular panelist, TV series *I've Got a Secret*): Mr. T.

JAMES MONROE (U.S. president): bought for his daughter Maria

NORMAN VINCENT PEALE (clergyman/author, *The Power of Positive Thinking*)

FRANKLIN D. ROOSEVELT (U.S. president)

MEL TORMÉ (singer, songwriter, "The Christmas Song"): Spooky

Vizsla

WILLIAM FOX (founded Fox Film Corp. which eventually became Twentieth Century-Fox Studios)

GROUP 2: PROTECTIVE DOGS

Akita

DAN AYKROYD (actor, *Blues Brothers, Ghostbusters*)

AMANDA BEARSE (actress, *Married . . . with Children*): Sakki

CHER (singer, actress, *The Witches of Eastwick, Moonstruck*)

CHRIS GREEN (pro football player): owns several

DAVE HOLLINS (pro baseball player): Jake

EVANDER HOLYFIELD (heavyweight boxing champion): owns seven

HELEN KELLER (advocate for the handicapped): Kamikaze, others

JOHN KRUK (pro baseball player): Head

SONNY ROLLINS (jazz saxophonist)

BYRON SCOTT (pro basketball player): Fuji, others

O. J. SIMPSON (football player turned actor): Kato

ELVIS STOJKO (champion figure skater): has two

PIA ZADORA (singer): Toky, others

Boxer

HUMPHREY BOGART (actor, *Casablanca, The African Queen*): Harvey

EMILY BRONTË (English novelist, *Wuthering Heights*): Keeper

NAT KING COLE (singer, "Unforgettable," "Ramblin' Rose," "Too Young"): Mr. Pet

STANLEY COREN (psychologist, author, *The Intelligence of Dogs, Sleep Thieves, What Do Dogs Know?*): Penny

Douglas Fairbanks Jr. (actor, *Gunga Din, Catherine the Great*)

Diane Fossey (naturalist, played by Sigourney Weaver in *Gorillas in the Mist*): Cindy

Jodie Foster (actress, *Taxi Driver, Bugsy Malone*)

Steffi Graf (tennis pro): Ben

Sonja Henie (figure skater)

Charlton Heston (actor, *The Ten Commandments, Planet of the Apes*)

Billie Holiday (jazz and blues singer)

Alan Ladd (actor, *The Great Gatsby, The Carpetbaggers*): Jezebell

Rocky Marciano (world champion boxer)

David Niven (actor, *Around the World in Eighty Days, The Guns of Navarone*): Phantom

Carroll O'Connor (actor, *In the Heat of the Night;* Archie Bunker in TV's *All in the Family*)

Dorothy Parker (writer and critic): Flic

Pablo Picasso (artist): Jan

Sylvester Stallone (actor, best known for Rocky and Rambo roles): Gangster

Andy Williams (singer, "Days of Wine and Roses," "Moon River"): Barnaby Rudge

Robin Williams (actor, *Hello Vietnam, Jumanji*): has a white Boxer

Briard

Charlemagne (king of the Franks/emperor of the Romans): first recognizable versions of this breed

Bullmastiff

Laraine Day (actress, *Foreign Correspondent, The High and the Mighty;* TV series *Dr. Kildare*): Igor

Gary Larson (cartoonist, *The Far Side*): Murray

Sylvester Stallone (actor, best known for Rocky and Rambo roles): Butkus

Jane and Michael Stern (authors, *Encyclopedia of Bad Taste, Dog Eat Dog*)

Mike Tyson (heavyweight boxing champion): Mel Gibson

Bull Terrier

ROBERT ALTMAN (director, *M*A*S*H, Nashville, The Player*)

FRED ASTAIRE (dancer/actor, *Funny Face, Silk Stockings, Finian's Rainbow*)

FRANCIS BARRAUD (artist, painted "His Master's Voice," seen on RCA Records): Nipper

DON CHERRY (hockey player/coach, sports broadcaster): Blue

MICHAEL J. FOX (actor, *Back to the Future;* TV series *Family Ties*): Burnaby

MAXWELL KNIGHT (author, *My Pet Friends*): Bill

GERALD MCCLELLAN (middleweight boxing champion): owns four

GEORGE PATTON (WWII general): Engelbert, Willie

THEODORE ROOSEVELT (U.S. president): Pete

SIR WALTER SCOTT (author, *Ivanhoe, Rob Roy*): Camp

LATRELL SPREWELL (pro sports, Golden State Warriors): owns several

JOHN STEINBECK (author, *Of Mice and Men, East of Eden*): Angel

JAMES THURBER (writer, humorist, *The Secret Life of Walter Mitty, My Life and Hard Times*): Rex

Chesapeake Bay Retriever

PEE-WEE HERMAN (aka Paul Reubens, actor, *Pee-Wee's Big Adventure;* TV series *Pee-Wee's Playhouse*)

MARYLAND (U.S. state, one of the few to name a state dog)

CARL RENSTROM (inventor of the bobby pin)

THEODORE ROOSEVELT (U.S. president): Sailor Boy

Chow Chow

BIJAN (fashion designer for the very rich): owns several

CALVIN COOLIDGE (U.S. president): Blackberry, Ruby Rough, Tiny Tim

WALT DISNEY (animator, film producer, *Snow White, Lady and the Tramp*): Sunne

SIGMUND FREUD (psychologist, founder of psychoanalysis): Jo-Fi and others (see plate 2)

KELSEY GRAMMER (actor, TV series *Cheers*)

JAMES HAMPTON (actor, *The China Syndrome, Hangar 18*): Cucci

DAVID LLOYD GEORGE (British prime minister): Bandy, Beauty, Chong

KONRAD LORENZ (Nobel prize–winning animal behaviorist and author, *King Solomon's Ring*)

DOTTIE MOCHRIE (pro golfer): owns several

MERLE OBERON (actress, *The Scarlet Pimpernel, Wuthering Heights*): Luke

RINGO STARR (drummer for the Beatles): Yang

MARTHA STEWART (author, cookbooks, decorating and design books): Max and others

SALLY STRUTHERS (actress, TV series *All in the Family*): Chuckie, Eddie, and others

UMA THURMAN (actress, *Pulp Fiction, Batman and Robin*): Muffy

DMITRI ZHILINSKY (Russian artist)

Gordon Setter

SIR WALTER SCOTT (author, *Ivanhoe, Rob Roy*): Finette

DANIEL WEBSTER (American statesman and orator)

Komondor

GENE TUNNEY (world heavyweight boxing champion): Pannonia Pandur

Kuvasz

MATHIAS I (king of Hungary): bred a large pack of them

Puli

KENDALL HAILEY (author, *The Day I Became an Autodidact*): Puli

Rhodesian Ridgeback

EMILIO ESTEVEZ (actor, *Mighty Ducks, Repo Man, The Breakfast Club*): Rowdy

WHOOPI GOLDBERG (actress, *The Color Purple, Ghost;* TV series *Star Trek: The New Generation*): Rutger

JOHN JAMES (TV actor, *Dynasty, The Colbys*): Camille

KATHY KEETON (publisher, *OMNI* magazine): Grundy

GRACE KELLY (actress turned princess, *High Noon, High Society*): Fanny

Rottweiler

KAREEM ABDUL-JABBAR (basketball star): Spencer

SID CAESAR (comedian, TV series *Your Show of Shows*): Conus

MICHAEL CAGE (pro sports, Cleveland Cavaliers): Bruno

MICHAEL COLES (politician; CEO, Great American Cookie Co.): Ally

ELVIRA (aka Cassandra Peterson, campy TV horror movie host and screen vampire): Bela, Brahm

CARRIE FISHER (actress, *Star Wars, The 'Burbs;* writer, *Postcards from the Edge*): Sweetie

BRIAN AUSTIN GREEN (actor, TV series *Beverly Hills 90210*): Cube

ELTON JOHN (rock singer, songwriter, "Don't Let the Sun Go Down on Me," "Rocket Man")

JOHN LARROQUETTE (actor, *Blind Date;* TV series *Night Court*): Max

STAN LEE (comic book artist and writer, Marvel Comics publisher): Vera

CLIFF NELSON (actor, TV series *Coach*): Pluto

KENNY NORMAN (pro sports, Atlanta Hawks): owns four, all attack-trained

ADRIAN PAUL (actor, TV series *Highlander*): owns five

SALLY JESSY RAPHAEL (TV talk show host)

JACK SCALIA (actor, TV series *Dallas*): Nitro and others

CURT SCHILLING (pro baseball pitcher): owns three

CARRIE SNODGRESS (actress, *Diary of a Mad Housewife*): Bandit

GREG VAUGHN (pro sports, Milwaukee Brewers)

HERSCHEL WALKER (pro football player): Al Capone

BRYANT YOUNG (pro football player)

Schnauzers (Standard and Giant)

BROOKE ASTOR (socialite and philanthropist): Maizie

BO DEREK (actress, *10, Woman of Desire*): Tough

ERROL FLYNN (actor, *Adventures of Robin Hood, Charge of the Light Brigade*): Arno

OTTO GRAHAM (Hall of Fame football quarterback): Little Otto

HELOISE (helpful hint and advice columnist, author): Sauvignon and others

BRUCE LEE (actor, numerous martial arts films): Riff

SUGAR RAY LEONARD (Olympic and world champion boxer): Kiki
STEVE MCQUEEN (actor, *The Great Escape, The Cincinnati Kid*)
BOB WATERFIELD (pro football star): Maggie

Staffordshire Bull Terrier, American Staffordshire Terrier

ANNE BANCROFT (actress, *The Graduate, The Turning Point*)
MEL BROOKS (director/comedian/writer/actor, *Blazing Saddles, Young Frankenstein, Robin Hood: Men in Tights*): Pongo
JOHN F. KENNEDY JR. (celebrity son of U.S. president): Friday

Weimaraner

DEAN CAIN (actor, TV series *Lois and Clark*): Mocha
DICK CLARK (TV personality, TV series *American Bandstand, TV Bloopers and Blunders*): Molly
DWIGHT D. EISENHOWER (general and U.S. president): Heidi
WILLIAM WEGMAN (photographer): Man Ray, Fay Ray

GROUP 3: INDEPENDENT DOGS

Afghan Hound

GARY COOPER (actor, *High Noon, Sergeant York*): Zora
JACQUES-HENRI LARTIGUE (photographer/painter, *Diary of a Century*)
PABLO PICASSO (artist): Kabul—his favorite dog

Airedale Terrier

EDGAR RICE BURROUGHS (writer, Tarzan series): Tarzan
HARRY CAREY (actor, *Mr. Smith Goes to Washington, Red River*)
TY COBB (Hall of Fame baseball star)
RICHARD CONDON (author, *Prizzi's Honor, The Manchurian Candidate*): Fiona, others
CALVIN COOLIDGE (U.S. president): pre–White House dog
A. J. CRONIN (author, *The Citadel, The Judas Tree*): Blix
OLIVIA DE HAVILLAND (actress, *The Heiress, Hush Hush Sweet Charlotte*): Shadrack—gift from director John Huston
BO DEREK (actress, *10, Woman of Desire*): Harum Scarum
WARREN G. HARDING (U.S. president): Laddie Boy

VICKI HEARNE (author, *Animal Happiness, Bandit*): several

JAMES EARL JONES (actor, voice of Darth Vader)

PAUL MUNI (actor, *The Story of Louis Pasteur, The Last Angry Man*):
Simon

RENEE RICHARDS (tennis player): Tennis-ee

THEODORE ROOSEVELT (U.S. president): hunted with one in Africa

RONNIE SCHELL (actor, TV series *Gomer Pyle*): Ethel, others

JOHN STEINBECK (Nobel Prize–winning author, *Of Mice and Men, East
of Eden*): had mixed feelings about the breed

JAMES THURBER (writer, humorist, *The Secret Life of Walter Mitty, My
Life and Hard Times*): Muggs

JOHN WAYNE (actor, *True Grit, The Shootist*): Duke—from which
Wayne got his nickname

WOODROW WILSON (U.S. president): Davie, Sandy

Alaskan Malamute

VIDA BLUE (pro baseball pitching star)

JUDY COLLINS (singer, "Send in the Clowns"): Kolya, Smoky

SUSAN CONANT (author, the Holly Winter mystery novels)

DOM DELUISE (comic actor, *Robin Hood: Men in Tights*)

IAN DUNBAR (dog trainer and author)

MELISSA GILBERT (actress, *The Diary of Anne Frank, Penalty Phase;* TV
series *Little House on the Prairie*)

HERBERT HOOVER (U.S. president): Yukon

CHERYL LADD (actress, *Now and Forever, Millennium;* TV series *Charlie's Angels*): Abel

GEORGE LUCAS (film director, producer, *Star Wars,* Indiana Jones
films): Indiana Jones

DANIEL PINKWATER (writer/commentator, National Public Radio program *All Things Considered*): Arnold

LOWELL THOMAS (author, radio and TV news commentator, *Good
Evening, Everybody: From Cripple Creek to Samarkand*)

ROBIN WILLIAMS (actor, *Good Morning Vietnam, Jumanji, Mrs. Doubtfire*)

American Water Spaniel

WILLIAM TAPLIN (author, *The Sportsman's Cabinet,* one of the earliest great dog books in English)

Black and Tan Coonhound

ANDREW JACKSON (U.S. president)

Borzoi

ALEXANDRA (queen consort of England)
JANE ARDMORE (author, *The Self-Enchanted*): Kemo
THEDA BARA (early film actress, *A Fool There Was, Cleopatra*): Belva
BO DEREK (actress, *10, Woman of Desire*): Russia
MICHAEL DOUGLAS (actor, *Wall Street, Fatal Attraction, Disclosure*)
DON JOHNSON (actor/singer, *Guilty as Sin, Tin Cup,* TV series *Miami Vice*)
LAINIE KAZAN (singer, actress)
KONSTANTIN KUSMINSKY (poet, editor)
ZUBIN MEHTA (conductor/music director, New York Philharmonic Orchestra; Israel Philharmonic)
NICK NOLTE (actor, *48 Hours, Lorenzo's Oil, Mulholland Falls*)
WARREN SKAAREN (screenwriter, *Batman*)
ROD STEWART (rock singer, "Tonight's the Night," "Do You Think I'm Sexy?")

Chinese Shar-Pei

FREDDIE GERSHON (producer, *Grease, Saturday Night Fever;* author, *Sweetie, Baby, Cookie, Honey*): Cookie

Dalmatian

JANE ALEXANDER (actress; head, National Endowment for the Arts)
DICK CLARK (TV personality, TV series *American Bandstand, TV Bloopers and Blunders*): Lucille
MICHAEL J. FOX (actor, *Back to the Future, Doc Hollywood, The American President;* TV series *Family Ties*): Bosco
MARJORIE HOLMES (religious writer, *I've Got to Talk to Somebody, God; Two from Galilee*): Belle

MAXINE KUMIN (poet, Pulitzer Prize winner): Gus

EUGENE O'NEILL (playwright, Nobel Prize winner, *Mourning Becomes Electra, Long Day's Journey into Night*): Blemi (see plate 7)

CHARLES OSGOOD (broadcast journalist): Cleo

CONNIE SELLECCA (actress, TV series *The Greatest American Hero, Hotel*)

LINDA GRAY SEXTON (novelist): Rhiannon

BOBBY SHORT (singer, pianist): Chili

RICHARD SIMMONS (fitness guru): Ashley and others

ADLAI STEVENSON (governor of Illinois, candidate for U.S. presidency, U.S. representative at the United Nations): King Arthur

JOHN TESH (musician, TV personality)

JERRY WIGGINS (psychologist, creator of the Interpersonal Adjective Personality Test): His relationship with the dog was a disaster.

Foxhound (American and English)

ALEX COLVILLE (Canadian artist)

ANDREW JACKSON (U.S. president)

THOMAS JEFFERSON (U.S. president)

JAMES MADISON (U.S. president)

GEORGE WASHINGTON (U.S. president): Vulcan and others

German Shorthaired Pointer

GROVER CLEVELAND (U.S. president)

ROBERT B. PARKER (author, Spenser mystery novels): The fictional detective Spenser has a dog of this breed as well.

EFREM ZIMBALIST JR. (actor, TV series *77 Sunset Strip, The FBI*): Zimmie

Greyhound

ALBERT (prince, husband of Queen Victoria): Eros—his favorite

CHEOPS (Egyptian pharaoh circa 3770 B.C. who built the great pyramid of Giza): Abakaru

COLETTE (French novelist, *Gigi, The Cat*): Lola

GEORGE ARMSTRONG CUSTER (general, Battle of Little Big Horn): Blucher, Byron

BO DEREK (actress, *10, Woman of Desire*): Bolero, China and others

RUTHERFORD B. HAYES (U.S. president): Grim

SIR EDWIN HENRY LANDSEER (English artist, famous for dog pictures): Brutus

LOUIS XI (king of France): Chermai

CHARLES OSGOOD (broadcast journalist): several, all racetrack rescues

RICHARD II (king of England): Mathe

SIR WALTER SCOTT (author, *Ivanhoe, Rob Roy*): Hamlet

Harrier

ANDREW JACKSON (U.S. president)

Irish Setter

BRIGITTE BARDOT (actress, *And God Created Woman, Viva Maria*): Pat-apon

CHIP BLOCK (founder, *Games* magazine): Buddy Boy

ERMA BOMBECK (author, *Motherhood: The Second Oldest Profession, The Grass Is Always Greener over the Septic Tank*): Arlo

JIMMY DURANTE (comedian, singer, "You Gotta Start Off Each Day with a Song"; actor, *Jumbo*): King

MERV GRIFFIN (TV talk show host): Patrick and others

OLIVIA NEWTON-JOHN (singer, "Let Me Be There," "I Honestly Love You"): Jackson

RICHARD NIXON (U.S. president): King Timahoe (see plate 11)

RONALD REAGAN (U.S. president): Peggy

FRANKLIN D. ROOSEVELT (U.S. president): Marksman—dog of his youth

WILLIAM HOWARD TAFT (U.S. president): Trevor

HARRY S. TRUMAN (U.S. president): Mike—disliked by Truman (see plate 14)

E. B. WHITE (writer, *Charlotte's Web*): Beppo, Brownie

T. H. WHITE (writer, *The Once and Future King*): Killie

Irish Water Spaniel

WILLIAM TAPLIN (author, *The Sportsman's Cabinet,* published in 1804, one of the earliest great dog books in English)

Norwegian Elkhound

HERBERT HOOVER (U.S. president): Weejie

VITA SACKVILLE-WEST (British novelist and poet, *The Edwardians, The Land*): Freya

Otterhound

ELIZABETH I (queen of England)

HENRY II (king of England)

HENRY VIII (king of England)

JAMES I (king of England)

RICHARD III (king of England)

DONALD SUTHERLAND (actor, *M*A*S*H, Klute, Six Degrees of Separation*)

Pointer

GEORGE ARMSTRONG CUSTER (general, Battle of Little Big Horn): Ginnie

BENJAMIN HARRISON (U.S. president)

T. H. WHITE (writer, *The Once and Future King*): Quince

Saluki

MUHAMMAD (the prophet of Islam)

VITA SACKVILLE-WEST (British novelist and poet, *The Edwardians, The Land*)

Samoyed

JAMES GARNER (actor, *Murphy's Romance, Maverick;* TV series *Maverick, The Rockford Files*): Rocky

JIMMY McNICHOL (actor, *The Fitzpatricks, California Fever*)

JULIE PARRISH (actress, *Good Morning, World*): Natasha

PATRICK WAYNE (actor, son of John Wayne, *Mustang Country, An Eye for an Eye*): Sandy

Siberian Husky

SID CAESAR (comedian, TV series *Your Show of Shows*): Sascha

EDWARD VII (king of England): Luska

PAUL IRWIN (president, U.S. Humane Society): Huxley

KATE JACKSON (actress, *Making Love, The Stranger Within,* TV series *Charlie's Angels*): Catcher and others

RONALD REAGAN (U.S. president): Taca

MORDECAI SIEGAL (author; president, Dog Writers Association of America): Quentin

EDDIE VELEZ (actor, *Extremities, Repo Man*): Dino and others

GROUP 4: SELF-ASSURED DOGS

Affenpinscher

PAUL EHRLICH (German Nobel Prize–winning bacteriologist, laid the foundation for understanding of immunity)

Australian Terrier

GORE VIDAL (writer, *Myra Breckinridge, Lincoln*): Rat—gift from Paul Newman

Basenji

SALLY ANN SMITH (author, *Candle, A Story of Love and Faith*)

COURTNEY THORNE-SMITH (actress, TV series *Melrose Place*)

Brussels Griffon

ESTHER RUDOMIN HAUTZIG (author, winner of Jane Addams Children's Book Award and Lewis Carroll Shelf Award): Jasper

Cairn Terrier

JOY ADAMSON (author, *Born Free*): Pippin

STANLEY COREN (psychologist, author, *The Intelligence of Dogs, Sleep Thieves, What Do Dogs Know?*): Flint

A. J. CRONIN (author, *The Citadel, The Judas Tree*): Sandy

SHELLEY DUVALL (actress, *Popeye, The Shining*): Digby and others

EDWARD VII (king of England): Hamish

GEORGE V (king of England): Bob

DAVID HASSELHOFF (actor, TV series *Baywatch, Knight Rider*): Toto

J. EDGAR HOOVER (FBI director): Cindy and several others

GEORGE KENNEDY (actor, best known as Patroni in the Airport films): Blyme

BERT LAHR (actor, cowardly lion from *The Wizard of Oz*): Merlin

MARY KATE MCGEEHAN (actress, TV series *Falcon Crest*)

LIZA MINNELLI (singer, actress, *New York, New York, Cabaret*): Lilly

BILL MURRAY (actor, *Ghostbusters, Groundhog Day*)

DUKE OF WINDSOR (former Prince Edward): Cora and several others

Fox Terrier (Smooth and Wire)

LUCILLE BALL (comic actress, *Mame;* TV series *I Love Lucy*): Tinker Toy and others

ADMIRAL RICHARD E. BYRD (polar explorer): Igloo

KARL ČAPEK (author/dramatist, *Meteor, An Ordinary Life*)

ROGER CARAS (author, *Celebration of Dogs* and other animal books)

AGATHA CHRISTIE (mystery writer, best known for Miss Marple and Hercule Poirot): Peter

CALVIN COOLIDGE (U.S. president): Peter Pan

STANLEY COREN (psychologist, author, *The Intelligence of Dogs, Sleep Thieves, What Do Dogs Know?*): Tippy

EDWARD VII (king of England): Caesar

AVA GARDNER (actress, *Mogambo, Night of the Iguana*): Lucky

GEORGE V (king of England): Happy

GEORGE GERSHWIN (composer, *Rhapsody in Blue, Porgy and Bess*): Tony

MICHAEL GRAY (actor, TV series *The Brian Keith Show*): Buzzy and others

ALDO GUCCI (fashion designer)

THOMAS HARDY (writer, *Far from the Madding Crowd*): Wessex

RUTHERFORD B. HAYES (U.S. president)

HERBERT HOOVER (U.S. president): Ben, Big Ben, Sonny

ANDREW JACKSON (U.S. president)

THOMAS JEFFERSON (U.S. president)

JEROME K. JEROME (author, *Three Men in a Boat, The Idle Thoughts of an Idle Fellow*): Peter

JEAN KERR (humorist, author, playwright, *Please Don't Eat the Daisies, The Snake Has All of the Lines*): Kelly

DAVID LLOYD GEORGE (British prime minister): Grock

EDMUND LOWE (actor, *What Price Glory, The Last Hurrah*): Joey, others

MARTINA NAVRATILOVA (tennis player): K.D.

PAUL NEWMAN (actor, *Butch Cassidy and the Sundance Kid, The Color of Money, Nobody's Fool*): Harry

MAUREEN O'SULLIVAN (actress, *Pride and Prejudice, Hannah and Her Sisters*): Junior

SAKI (real name H. H. Munro, Edwardian British writer, *Reginald, Beasts and Super Beasts*): Gillie

ALFRED SLOT (novelist/children's fiction writer): Freddie

CHERYL TIEGS (model): Martini

GEORGE WASHINGTON (U.S. president)

E. B. WHITE (author, *Charlotte's Web*): Raffles

EDWARD O. WILSON (biologist, psychologist; Pulitzer Prize winner, *Sociobiology*)

JOANNE WOODWARD (actress, *The Three Faces of Eve, The Glass Menagerie, Mr. & Mrs. Bridge*): Harry

Irish Terrier

MAZO DE LA ROCHE (Canadian author, best known for the Jalna series): Badger

EDWARD VII (king of England): Jack

WILLIAM LYON MACKENZIE KING (prime minister of Canada): Pat, Pat II, Pat III

EUGENE O'NEILL (playwright, Nobel Prize for literature, *Long Day's Journey into Night, Mourning Becomes Electra*): Irish Terrier and others

Jack Russell Terrier

AMANDA BEARSE (actress, *Married . . . with Children*): Buster

SANDRA BULLOCK (actress, *Speed, While You Were Sleeping*): Luigi Deflorio

MARIAH CAREY (rock and roll singer, "Vision of Love"): Jack

CHARLES (crown prince of England): Pooh, Tigger

MICHAEL DOUGLAS (actor, *Wall Street, Fatal Attraction, Disclosure*):
Reggie
SARAH FERGUSON (duchess of York)
AUDREY HEPBURN (*Roman Holiday, Breakfast at Tiffany's*): Penny
JAMES HERRIOT (veterinarian, author, *All Creatures Great and Small, All
Things Wise and Wonderful*): Hector
JACQUES-HENRI LARTIGUE (photographer/painter, *Diary of a Century*)
BETTE MIDLER (singer/actress/comedian, *The Rose, Ruthless People*):
Puddles

Kerry Blue Terrier

JOHN HUSTON (director/producer/actor, *The Maltese Falcon, The African
Queen, Prizzi's Honor*): Jennifer
EVELYN KEYES (actress, *Gone With the Wind, The Seven-Year Itch*)
GENE TUNNEY (world champion heavyweight boxer)

Lakeland Terrier

SKITCH HENDERSON (band leader, TV personality): Sir Rex
ABRAHAM LINCOLN (U.S. president): At that time it was commonly
called the Fell Terrier.

Manchester Terrier

AGATHA CHRISTIE (mystery writer, best known for Miss Marple and
Hercule Poirot): Bingo and others
IAN FLEMING (author, best known for James Bond novels)

Miniature Pinscher

MICHELLIE JONES (world champion triathlete, only woman to win
back-to-back world titles): owns two

Norwich Terrier and Norfolk Terrier

OSCAR DE LA RENTA (clothing designer): owns several
LILY TOMLIN (comedian and actress, *Nashville, 9 to 5*): Tess
E. B. WHITE (writer, *Charlotte's Web*): Jones

Schipperke

LUCILLE BALL (actress, *Mame;* TV series *I Love Lucy*): Ginger

Schnauzer (Miniature)

BO DEREK (actress, *10, Woman of Desire*)

ROBERT DOLE (U.S. senator, presidential candidate): Leader

ARTE JOHNSON (comedian/actor, *Love at First Bite;* TV series *Laugh-In*)

TOMMY LASORDA (professional baseball manager): Austin

Scottish Terrier

LIONEL BARRYMORE (actor, *Grand Hotel, Duel in the Sun*): Johnny

HUMPHREY BOGART (actor, *Casablanca, The African Queen, The Caine Mutiny*): Sluggy and others (see plate 4)

EVA BRAUN (mistress of Adolf Hitler): owned two

BETTE DAVIS (actress, *What Ever Happened to Baby Jane?, The Whales of August*): Meg

PHYLLIS DILLER (comedian): Joe

ELINOR DONAHUE (actress, TV series *Father Knows Best*): Mary Elizabeth

PHIL DONAHUE (TV talk show host)

DWIGHT D. EISENHOWER (WWII general and U.S. president): Spunky, Caacie, Telek (see plate 8)

ZSA ZSA GABOR (actress/author, *Moulin Rouge, How to Catch a Man*): Mishka

DUSTIN HOFFMAN (actor, *The Graduate, Kramer vs. Kramer, Rain Man*): Sandy

BERT LAHR (comic actor, cowardly lion in *The Wizard of Oz*): Barry

DOROTHY PARKER (writer and critic): Daisy

BEATRIX POTTER (author, *The Tale of Peter Rabbit*): Sandy

RONALD REAGAN (U.S. president): Scotch, Soda—pre-politics dogs owned with Jane Wyman

FRANKLIN D. ROOSEVELT (U.S. president): Duffy, Fala, Meg and others (see plate 9)

THEODORE ROOSEVELT (U.S. president): Jessie

MARLO THOMAS (actress, *Free to Be . . . You and Me;* TV series *That Girl*)

JAMES THURBER (author, humorist, *The Secret Life of Walter Mitty, My Life and Hard Times*): Jeannie, Black Watch, others

E. B. WHITE (author, *Charlotte's Web*): Daisy

CHRISTINE TODD WHITMAN (governor of New Jersey)

JANE WYMAN (actress, *Johnny Belinda, Magnificent Obsession*): Scotch, Soda—owned with Ronald Reagan

Shih Tzu

YUL BRYNNER (actor, *The King and I, The Magnificent Seven*)

BETTY BUCKLEY (actress, *Cats, Sunset Boulevard*): Bridget, Gemma, Jessie

OLEG CASSINI (fashion designer): Mr. Flinton

CIXI [Tzu Hsi] (dowager empress of China)

PHYLLIS DILLER (comedian): Fang

ELIZABETH (England's queen mother): Choo Choo

ZSA ZSA GABOR (actress, author, *Moulin Rouge, How to Catch a Man*)

BILL GATES (computer genius, founder of Microsoft)

GEORGE VI (king of England)

GEORGE KLEIN (TV show host)

DALAI LAMA (religious leader of Tibet)

GREG MADDUX (professional baseball player): has two

Silky Terrier

MIKE DOUGLAS (TV talk show host): Lucy

Welsh Terrier

EDWARD VIII (king of England): Gwen

JOHN F. KENNEDY (U.S. president): Charlie was JFK's favorite dog (see plate 10)

West Highland White Terrier

JIMMY BUFFETT (singer, "Margaritaville"): Alice

CHARLES DARWIN (biologist responsible for the theory of evolution)

BO DEREK (actress, *10, Woman of Desire*): Gunn

JOAN FONTAINE (actress, *Rebecca, Suspicion*): Carnoustie

ALFRED HITCHCOCK (movie director, *Psycho, Vertigo*): Sarah

HENRY KRAVIS (merger mogul): Pookie

PABLO PICASSO (artist): Klipper

Tom Weiskopf (pro golfer): Whiskers

E. B. White (author, *Charlotte's Web*): Suzy

Yorkshire Terrier

Jim and Tammy Faye Bakker (TV evangelists): Corky

Richard Basehart (actor, *Moby Dick;* TV series *Voyage to the Bottom of the Sea*): Katie and others

Erma Bombeck (author, *Motherhood: The Second Oldest Profession, The Grass Is Always Greener over the Septic Tank*): Murray

Richard Burton (actor, *Becket, Who's Afraid of Virginia Woolf?*): Sally

Mariah Carey (rock and roll singer, "Vision of Love"): has several

Johnny Carson (comedian and talk show host): Muffin and others

Eva Gabor (actress, *Gigi;* TV series *Green Acres*): Baby, Googie

Joe Garagiola (baseball player, TV sportscaster): Sassy, Sweetie

John Gardner (author, *October Light, Mickelsson's Ghosts*): George

Alex Haley (author, *Roots, The Autobiography of Malcolm X*): Buttons

George Hamilton (actor, *Love at First Bite, Your Cheating Heart*): Mitzi

Julie Harris (actress, *The Member of the Wedding;* TV series *Knots Landing*): Teresa

Audrey Hepburn (actress, *Roman Holiday, Breakfast at Tiffany's*): Famous

Carol Lawrence (actress, singer, *West Side Story*): Miss Mouse

Rush Limbaugh (radio and TV political satirist and commentator)

Barbara Mandrell (country singer): Tasha

Maureen McGovern (singer, composer, "The Morning After"): Nicodemus, Rocky

Demi Moore (actress, *A Few Good Men, Indecent Proposal*): Henry— shared with Bruce Willis

Tricia Nixon (daughter of U.S. president): Pasha

Roman Polanski (writer/director, *Rosemary's Baby, Chinatown, Tess*)

Joan Rivers (comedian, TV series *Live with Regis & Kathie Lee*): Spike

Marcia Rodd (actress, TV series *Trapper John, M.D.*): Feather

Marina Sirtis (actress, TV series *Star Trek: The Next Generation*): Skilaki

ELIZABETH TAYLOR (actress, *Butterfield 8, Cleopatra, Who's Afraid of Virginia Woolf?*): Daisy, Thomas à Becket and others

MEL TORMÉ (singer, composer, "The Christmas Song")

ARTHUR TREACHER (British character actor, talk show sidekick to Merv Griffin): Belle

TOMMY TUNE (dancer, choreographer, director, *Bye Bye Birdie*): Ophelia

BRUCE WILLIS (actor, *Die Hard*): Henry—shared with Demi Moore

DARRYL F. ZANUCK (producer, *The Grapes of Wrath, The Longest Day*): Lisa, Tina

GROUP 5: CONSISTENT DOGS

Bedlington Terrier

DOROTHY PARKER (writer and critic): Wolf

Boston Terrier

WARREN G. HARDING (U.S. president): Hub

EARL HOLLIMAN (actor, *The Biscuit Eater, The Solitary Man;* TV series *Policewoman, T. J. Hooker*)

RICHARD KILEY (actor, *Man of La Mancha*): Joey

MASSACHUSETTS (U.S. state, one of the few to name a state dog)

DOROTHY PARKER (writer and critic): Woodrow Wilson

VINCENT PRICE (actor in many horror films such as *The Raven*): Happy

JOAN RIVERS (comedian, TV series *Live with Regis & Kathie Lee*): Lulu

YVES ST. LAURENT (clothing designer): Moujik

Chihuahua

PAULA ABDUL (popular singer, "Cool Hearted")

JOSEPHINE BAKER (U.S.-French singer and dancer originally with Folies Bergère)

RED BUTTONS (actor, *Sayonara, Pete's Dragon*)

XAVIER CUGAT (Latin band leader): He often had one in his pocket.

BILLIE HOLIDAY (jazz and blues singer)

SUGAR RAY LEONARD (world champion boxer): Lulu

MADONNA (singer, actress): Chiquita

JAYNE MANSFIELD (actress, *Will Success Spoil Rock Hunter?, It Takes a Thief*)

WINK MARTINDALE (TV game show host): owns several

MARTINA NAVRATILOVA (pro tennis player)

ROSIE O'DONNELL (TV talk show host): Buster, Valentine

MICKEY ROURKE (actor, *Body Heat, Angel Heart*): owns several

MURIEL SIEBERT (CEO, Muriel Siebert & Co., Fortune 500 company): Monster Girl

GERTRUDE STEIN (writer, *Three Lives*): Pepe

LIV TYLER (model and actress): Banana

Chinese Crested

GYPSY ROSE LEE (actress, burlesque striptease artist)

Dachshund

MATTHEW ARNOLD (Victorian British poet, *Culture and Anarchy*): Geist and others

BROOKE ASTOR (socialite and philanthropist) Fafner

LOUIS J. CAMUTI (veterinarian/author, *Park Avenue Vet*): Baron, Heidi

TRACY CHAPMAN (singer, songwriter, "Talkin about a Revolution"): Mini

CLAIRE CHENNAULT (U.S. Air Force general, WWII): Joe

JOAN CRAWFORD (actress, *Mildred Pierce, What Ever Happened to Baby Jane?*)

GEORGE CUKOR (movie director, *Camille*): Amanda and others

MARION DAVIES (actress, girlfriend of publisher William Randolph Hearst): Gandhi

DORIS DAY (singer, actress, *The Pajama Game, Midnight Lace*): Rudy and others

JAMES DEAN (actor, *Rebel Without a Cause, Giant*): Strudel

MAURICE COUVE DE MURVILLE (French prime minister): Xenophon

PATTY DUKE (actress, *The Miracle Worker, Valley of the Dolls*)

DAVID HASSELHOFF (actor, TV series *Baywatch, Knight Rider*): Sissy

FRED HAYMAN (perfume designer, Giorgio): Giorgio

RITA HAYWORTH (actress, *The Lady from Shanghai, Pal Joey*): Knockwurst and others

WILLIAM RANDOLPH HEARST (publisher): Helen and several others

DAVID HOCKNEY (artist)

JOHN HOUSEMAN (producer, actor, *Paper Chase*): Jasper and others

HENRY JAMES (novelist, *The Turn of the Screw, Daisy Miller*): Max

WINONA JUDD (country singer)

KURT KOFFKA (gestalt psychologist): He had a series of seven, all named Max.

CAROLE LOMBARD (actress, *My Man Godfrey*): Commissioner

DOROTHY PARKER (humorist, short story writer, wit, critic): Eiko von Blutenberg—later called Robinson

PABLO PICASSO (artist): Lump

ROSAMUNDE PILCHER (author, *The Shell Seekers*)

WILLIAM POWELL (actor, best known for the Thin Man series): Fritzie

PRISCILLA PRESLEY (actress, *The Naked Gun;* TV series *Dallas*)

VINCENT PRICE (actor in many horror films): Hansie and others

ERWIN ROMMEL (German general in WWII, famous for his tank battles)

ISABELLA ROSSELLINI (model, actress)

LIZ SMITH (newspaper and TV gossip columnist): Calypso, Odysseus

ADLAI STEVENSON (governor of Illinois, candidate for U.S. presidency, U.S. representative at the United Nations): Merlin

LIV ULLMANN (actress in Ingmar Bergman films such as *Cries and Whispers*): Pet

VICTORIA (queen of England): Deckel

MARIA VON TRAPP (whose story inspired *The Sound of Music*)

ANDY WARHOL (artist): Amos, Archie

E. B. WHITE (author, *Charlotte's Web*): Fred, August (see plate 17)

P. G. WODEHOUSE (author, *The Butler Did It, Bachelors Anonymous*): Rudolph, Towser

FAY WRAY (actress, *King Kong, Murder in Greenwich Village*): Mr. Deeds

Dandie Dinmont Terrier

DOROTHY PARKER (writer and critic): Timothy

SIR WALTER SCOTT (author, *Ivanhoe*)

English Toy Spaniel (King Charles)

Marie-Josèphe-Rose de Beauharnais (Napoleon's wife, best known as Josephine)

Mary (queen of Scots)

Richard Wagner (classical composer, best known for the operas that make up the Ring Cycle): Peps, Fips

French Bulldog

Christine Elise (actress, *A League of Their Own, Body Snatchers;* TV series *Beverly Hills 90210*): Swifty

Douglas Fairbanks Sr. (actor, *Mark of Zorro, Thief of Bagdad*)

Maurice Maeterlinck (author, Nobel Prize winner, *The Intelligence of Flowers, The Blue Bird*): Pelleas

Nancy Mitford (writer, *Love in a Cold Climate, The Sun King*): Dolly, Lottie and others

Jason Priestley (actor, *Cold Blooded, Calendar Girl;* TV series *Beverly Hills 90210*): Swifty

Italian Greyhound

Carl Fisher (first land developer of Miami Beach): Pizza

Frederick the Great (king of Prussia): Biche, Amoretto, Diana, Pan, Pax, Madame de Pompadour

Peter the Great (czar of Russia): Lissette

Japanese Chin

Jefferson Davis (president of the Confederacy during the U.S. Civil War)

Lhasa Apso

Burt Bacharach (composer, pianist, "Raindrops Keep Falling on My Head," "What the World Needs Now"): Hoover

Richard Burton (actor, *Becket, Who's Afraid of Virginia Woolf?*): Georgia

Red Buttons (actor, *Sayonara, Pete's Dragon*)

PHYLLIS DILLER (comedian): Phearlss

EVA GABOR (actress, *Gigi;* TV series *Green Acres*): Baby Lion and others

PEGGY GUGGENHEIM (heiress and art patron): Emily

BOB HOPE (comedian/actor, *Road to Morocco, Road to Singapore*): Coco

CAROL LAWRENCE (actress, singer, *West Side Story*): Miss Magoo

MICHAEL LEARNED (actor, TV series *The Waltons*): Doris

LIBERACE (pianist): Chop Suey

BOB MACKIE (clothing designer): Pansy, Amber

ELIZABETH TAYLOR (actress, *Butterfield 8, Cleopatra, Who's Afraid of Virginia Woolf?*): Elsa (see plate 16)

JONATHAN TAYLOR THOMAS (actor, TV series *Home Improvement*): McCormick

MALCOLM-JAMAL WARNER (actor, TV series *The Cosby Show*): Mecca

GRETCHEN WYLER (Broadway musical actress, *Bye Bye Birdie*): Mickey

Maltese

HALLE BERRY (actress, *Strictly Business, The Last Boy Scout*): Bumper

PHIL DONAHUE (TV talk show host): Tida

BOB HOPE (comedian/actor, *Road to Morocco, Road to Singapore*): Gilby

GEORGE KENNEDY (actor, *Airport, The Gunfighters*): Buttons

ELVIS PRESLEY (rock and roll singer): Foxhugh

BROOKE SHIELDS (actress, *Pretty Baby, The Blue Lagoon*)

HARRIET BEECHER STOWE (author, *Uncle Tom's Cabin*): Calvin

ELIZABETH TAYLOR (actress, *Butterfield 8, Cleopatra, Who's Afraid of Virginia Woolf?*): Sugar and others

HENRY DAVID THOREAU (writer, *Walden*): Min

Pekingese

ALEXANDRA (queen consort of England): Xerxes

RICHARD BURTON (actor, *Becket, Who's Afraid of Virginia Woolf?*): E'en So—shared with Liz Taylor (see plate 16)

CIXI [Tzu Hsi] (dowager empress of China): had many

DOROTHY GISH (silent film actress in D. W. Griffith films such as *Orphans in the Storm*): Rover

BEATRICE LILLIE (comedian/actress, *Blythe Spirit, Thoroughly Modern Millie*): Lord Button

BEATRIX POTTER (author, *The Tale of Peter Rabbit*): Tzutsee

ELIZABETH TAYLOR (actress, *Butterfield 8, Cleopatra, Who's Afraid of Virginia Woolf?*): E'en So—shared with Richard Burton (see plate 16)

VICTORIA (queen of England): Looty

EDITH WHARTON (writer, *Ethan Frome, Age of Innocence*): Mitou and others

BETTY WHITE (actress, comedian, TV series *The Golden Girls, The Mary Tyler Moore Show*): Bandy, Bootie, others

Pomeranian

KARL FRIEDRICH ABEL (German symphonic composer and musician)

SHELLEY DUVALL (actress, *Popeye, The Shining*): Zoë

DAVID HASSELHOFF (actor, TV series *Baywatch, Knight Rider*): Jenny, Killer, others

WALTER SAVAGE LANDOR (Romantic poet, *Imaginary Conversations*): Giallo, others

MARTIN LUTHER (reformation religious leader): Belferlein—often mentioned in his writings

MICHELANGELO (artist): The dog sat on a satin pillow while he painted the Sistine Chapel.

ISAAC NEWTON (physicist): Diamond

CONSTANCE TALMADGE (silent movie star, *Intolerance*): Dinkey

VICTORIA (queen of England): Beppo, Fluffy, Gilda, Lulu, Mino, Nino, and others

TAMMY WYNETTE (country singer, "Stand by Your Man"): Killer

EMILE ZOLA (French novelist, *J'accuse*)

Pug

ANN-MARGRET (actress, *Carnal Knowledge, Tommy, Grumpy Old Men*): owns five

MARIE-JOSÈPHE-ROSE DE BEAUHARNAIS (Napoleon's wife, best known as Josephine)

GEORGE BRENT (actor, *Forty-second Street, The Spiral Staircase*): Whisky

CIXI [Tzu Hsi] (dowager empress of China)

GEORGE ELIOT (novelist, *Middlemarch, The Mill on the Floss*)

CHRISTINE ELISE (actress, *A League of Their Own, Body Snatchers;* TV series *Beverly Hills 90210*): Dempsey

WOODY HARRELSON (actor, TV series *Cheers*)

WILLIAM HOGARTH (English painter): Trump

STAN LEE (cartoonist, Marvel comics publisher): Pookie

JASON PRIESTLEY (actor, *Cold Blooded, Calendar Girl;* TV series *Beverly Hills 90210*): Dempsey

SALLY JESSY RAPHAEL (TV talk show host)

SYLVIA SIDNEY (actress, *Summer Wishes, Winter Dreams; I Never Promised You a Rose Garden*): Lady Bug, several others

JAMES THURBER (writer, humorist, *The Secret Life of Walter Mitty, My Life and Hard Times*): Judge

VICTORIA (queen of England): Bully

VOLTAIRE (French author, *Candide*)

DUCHESS OF WINDSOR (the former Mrs. Wallis Simpson): Davy Crockett, several others

PAUL WINFIELD (actor, *Sounder, Go Tell It on the Mountain*)

Sealyham Terrier

TALLULAH BANKHEAD (actress, *Lifeboat*): Him

HUMPHREY BOGART (actor, *Casablanca*): Dorarich, Butch

A. J. CRONIN (author, *The Citadel, Song of Sixpence*): Bunker

GEORGE V (king of England): Jack

REX HARRISON (British actor, *My Fair Lady, Dr. Dolittle*): William

ALFRED HITCHCOCK (director, *Psycho, Vertigo*): Geoffrey, Stanley

MARGARET (princess of England): Johnny

LILLI PALMER (actress, *Body and Soul, The Pleasure of His Company*): William

WILL ROGERS (humorist): Jocko

MAURICE SENDAK (children's author, *Where the Wild Things Are*): Jennie

Skye Terrier

ALEX KATZ (American artist): Sunny

ROBERT LOUIS STEVENSON (author, *Treasure Island, The Strange Case of Dr. Jekyll and Mr. Hyde*): initially named Woggs, then changed to Walter, then Watty, then Woggy, and finally Bogue

Tibetan Terrier

SUZANNE PLESHETTE (actress, *The Birds, Nevada Smith;* TV series *The Bob Newhart Show*): Gypsy

Whippet

CATHERINE THE GREAT (empress of Russia): Sir Tom

JERRY WIGGINS (psychologist, designer of the IAS Personality Test): had several

GROUP 6: STEADY DOGS

Basset Hound

ALEXANDRA (queen consort of England): Bijou

HARRY ANDERSON (actor, TV series *Night Court, Tales from the Darkside*): Floyd

RICHARD DEAN ANDERSON (actor, TV series *MacGyver*)

CLINT EASTWOOD (actor, director, the Dirty Harry series, *The Unforgiven*): Sidney

REX HARRISON (British actor, *My Fair Lady, Dr. Dolittle*): Homer, several others

BOB HOPE (comedian/actor, *Road to Morocco, Road to Singapore*): Recession

JAMES EARL JONES (actor, voice of Darth Vader)

ARTHUR MILLER (playwright, *The Crucible*): Hugo. He got custody of the dog when he divorced Marilyn Monroe.

ANSON WILLIAMS (actor, owner of Basset Productions): Beau

Beagle

GROVER CLEVELAND (U.S. president)

STANLEY COREN (psychologist, author, *The Intelligence of Dogs, Sleep Thieves, What Do Dogs Know?*): Skipper

EVA GABOR (actress, *Gigi;* TV series *Green Acres*): Lady Ashley

SARA GILBERT (actress, TV series *Roseanne*): Ralph

GEORGE HAMILTON (actor, *Love at First Bite, Godfather III*): Delilah

DUANE HANSON (American artist): Petra

LYNDON B. JOHNSON (U.S. president): Beagle, Him, Her, others (see plate 15)

SUE MONK KIDD (author/contributing editor, *Guideposts* magazine): Caeser, Brutus

BARRY MANILOW (singer, "Mandy," "I Write the Songs"): Bagel, Biscuit

CHARLES SCHULZ (cartoonist, comic strip *Peanuts*): Spike—the model for Snoopy

ROGER STAUBACH (quarterback with Dallas Cowboys): Sky

Bernese Mountain Dog

ELIZABETH VON ARNIM (English writer, *All the Dogs of My Life*)

DAVID CARRADINE (actor, *Bound for Glory;* TV series *Kung Fu*)

WILLIAM DEVANE (actor, *Family Plot;* TV mini-series *From Here to Eternity;* TV series *Knots Landing*): Samson

GOLDIE HAWN (actress, *Private Benjamin, Overboard*)

FRANÇOIS MITTERRAND (French statesman and president)

ROBERT REDFORD (actor, *The Sting, Out of Africa, A River Runs Through It*)

WILLIAM SAFIRE (*New York Times* columnist)

AL SHUGART (CEO, Seagate Technologies, Fortune 500 company): Ernest

Bloodhound

ROBERT BRUCE (king of Scotland): His dog was actually a Talbot, the immediate precursor to the Bloodhound.

CHARLES DARWIN (biologist responsible for the theory of evolution): also a Talbot

CHARLES DICKENS (author, *A Tale of Two Cities, Oliver Twist, A Christmas Carol*): Sultan

F. SCOTT FITZGERALD (writer, *Tender Is the Night, The Great Gatsby*): Trouble

ELVIS PRESLEY (singer and rock and roll legend) (see plate 18)

GEORGE WASHINGTON (U.S. president): Vulcan

Bouvier des Flandres

BILL COSBY (comedian, TV series *The Cosby Show*)

MEADOWLARK LEMON (basketball star with the Harlem Globe Trotters)

GEORGE LUCAS (director, producer, *Star Wars*): His dog may have been the model for Chewbacca the Wookie in *Star Wars*.

BARBARA MANDRELL (country singer)

REBA McENTYRE (country and pop singer)

RONALD REAGAN (U.S. president): Lucky

GENE RODDENBERRY (creator of *Star Trek*)

RINGO STARR (drummer for the Beatles)

DEBRA WINGER (actress, *An Officer and a Gentleman, Terms of Endearment, Leap of Faith*): Bear

Bulldog

CALVIN COOLIDGE (U.S. president): King Cole, Boston Beans

GEORGE ARMSTRONG CUSTER (general, Battle of Little Big Horn): Turk

OLIVIA DE HAVILLAND (actress, *The Heiress, Hush Hush Sweet Charlotte*): Bouboule

WARREN G. HARDING (U.S. president): Oh Boy

ICE-T (rap singer/actor, *New Jack City,* "Ricochet"): Chopper

STAN LEE (cartoonist, Marvel comics publisher): Annabelle

HUGH LOFTING (author, *The Voyages of Doctor Doolittle*): Bob

ANNA PAVLOVA (ballerina): Lebbo

VINCENT PRICE (horror actor who played Dr. Phibes etc.): Johnny

TENNESSEE WILLIAMS (playwright, *A Streetcar Named Desire, The Glass Menagerie, Night of the Iguana*): Baby Doll, Buffo, many others

Clumber Spaniel

JAMES I (king of England)

Great Dane

BRAD ANDERSON (author, comic strip *Marmaduke*)

MARIO ANDRETTI (Indianapolis 500–winning race car driver)

OTTO VON BISMARCK (German chancellor): Odin and several others

CLARA BOW (silent screen actress, *It, Wings*): Duke

JAMES BROLIN (actor, *Westworld, May West;* TV series *Marcus Welby M.D.*): Buck

SID CAESAR (TV comedian, *Your Show of Shows*): Julius

ROGER CARAS (author, *Celebration of Dogs* and other animal books)

WILT CHAMBERLAIN (basketball star): had several

CHUBBY CHECKERS (rock and roll singer who popularized the Twist)

EDWARD J. DEBARTOLO (owner of the San Francisco 49ers football team)

MIKE DOUGLAS (TV talk show host): Duke

FAISAL (king of Saudi Arabia)

KELSEY GRAMMER (actor, TV series *Cheers*)

MAXWELL KNIGHT (author, *My Pet Friends*): Lorna

OLIVIA NEWTON-JOHN (singer, "Let Me Be There," "I Honestly Love You"): Zargon

BRUCE LEE (actor, *Enter the Dragon,* other martial arts films): Bobo

RUTA LEE (actress, *Bullet for a Badman;* TV series *Coming of Age*): Kronen

GREG LOUGANIS (Olympic gold medalist in diving): Freeway and several others

MEREDITH MACRAE (actress, TV series *Mary Hartman, Mary Hartman*): Shinka and others

TOM MIX (early cowboy movie star)

VALERIE PERRINE (actress, *W. C. Fields and Me, Lenny*): Ching and others

ALEXANDER POPE (English poet, *Rape of the Lock*): Bounce

MANFRED FREIHER VON RICHTHOFEN (German air ace known as the Red Baron): Moritz

FRANKLIN D. ROOSEVELT (U.S. president): President

WILLIAM SHATNER (actor, Captain Kirk of *Star Trek*)

LESLIE UGGAMS (singer, actress, *Backstairs at the White House;* TV series *Sing Along with Mitch*)

BURT WARD (actor, played Robin on the TV series *Batman*)

BARBARA WOODHOUSE (dog trainer, author, *No Bad Dogs*)

GRETCHEN WYLER (Broadway musical actress, *Bye Bye Birdie*): Khan and others

Great Pyrenees

DEBORAH KERR (actress, *The King and I, From Here to Eternity*): Guapa

BETTY WHITE (actress, comedian, TV series *The Golden Girls, The Mary Tyler Moore Show*): Captain

Irish Wolfhound

HERBERT HOOVER (U.S. president): Patrick

ROMAN POLANSKI (writer/director, *Rosemary's Baby, Chinatown, Tess*)

SALLY JESSY RAPHAEL (TV talk show host)

STING (actor, rock musician, *Dune, Stormy Monday*): Gideon

RUDOLPH VALENTINO (actor, *The Sheik, Blood and Sand*): Captain Pendragon, Haroun and several others

Mastiff

ALEXANDER THE GREAT (Macedonian general who conquered much of the known world): Peritas

KIRSTIE ALLEY (actress, *Look Who's Talking, Village of the Damned;* TV series *Cheers*)

DIRK BOGARDE (actor, *Death in Venice, Darling, Daddy Nostalgia*): Candida

MARLON BRANDO (actor, *The Godfather, On the Waterfront*): Schlubber

GEORGE DICENZO (actor, *Omega Syndrome;* TV series *Dynasty, Equal Justice*): Pookie and several others

DOUGLAS FAIRBANKS (silent movie star, *The Three Musketeers, Robin Hood*)

RUTHERFORD B. HAYES (U.S. president): Duke

GEORGE C. SCOTT (actor, *Patton, The Hospital, Day of the Dolphin*): Max

Newfoundland

BURT BACHARACH (composer, pianist, "Raindrops Keep Falling on My Head," "What the World Needs Now"): Noofy—shared with Carole Bayer Sager

J. M. BARRIE (author, *Peter Pan*)

JAMES BUCHANAN (U.S. president): Lara

LORD BYRON (English poet): Boatswain

ULYSSES S. GRANT (U.S. president, Civil War hero): Faithful

ROBERT KENNEDY (senator, U.S. attorney general)

GEORGE McGOVERN (U.S. senator, presidential candidate): Atticus

CAROLE BAYER SAGER (songwriter): Noofy—shared with Burt Bacharach

SALLY STRUTHERS (actress, TV series *All in the Family*): Hailey

RICHARD WAGNER (classical composer, best known for the operas that make up the Ring Cycle): Russ, King Marke

Saint Bernard

Lucius Beebe (eccentric and author, *The Trains We Rode*): T-bone
Charlton Heston (actor, *Ben Hur, The Ten Commandments*): Portia
Carl Reiner (comedian/director, *Dead Men Don't Wear Plaid, The Man with Two Brains*)
Marge Schott (owner, Cincinnati Reds baseball team): Shottzie
Betty White (actress, comedian, TV series *The Golden Girls, The Mary Tyler Moore Show*): Stormy

Scottish Deerhound

Robert Bruce (king of Scotland): Help and Hand—one dog's name
Isak Dinesen (author, *Out of Africa*): Duck and several others
Francine Racette (French-Canadian actress)
Sir Walter Scott (author, *Ivanhoe*): Maida

GROUP 7: CLEVER DOGS

Australian Cattle Dog

Pam Dawber (actress, TV series *Mork and Mindy*): Red Dog
Mel Gibson (actor, *Braveheart, Lethal Weapon*)
Mark Harmon (actor, *The Presidio, The Deliberate Stranger;* TV series *St. Elsewhere*): Cooper, Paddy, Red, and others
Kelly McGillis (actress, *Witness, Top Gun*): Cheyenne
George Strait (country singer): Buster
Gary Wilkes (writer, animal behaviorist): Tug

Australian Shepherd

Sally Field (actress, *Places in the Heart, Murphy's Romance*)
Steven Jobs (inventor of Apple and NeXT computers)
Demi Moore (actress, *A Few Good Men, Indecent Proposal*): Junior, several others—shared with Bruce Willis
Jack Perkins (TV series *Wild Kingdom, Biography*)
Tim Robbins (actor, *Bull Durham, The Shawshank Redemption;* director, *Dead Man Walking*)
Susan Sarandon (actress, *Dead Man Walking, The Client*)

BRUCE WILLIS (actor, *Die Hard, Last Man Standing*): Junior, several others—shared with Demi Moore

FLIP WILSON (comedian): Natasha

Belgian Sheepdog, Malinois, Tervuren

BEATRICE ARTHUR (actress, TV series *Maude, The Golden Girls*): Ruby

DONNY OSMOND (singer): Lady

BASIL RATHBONE (actor, played Sherlock Holmes): Moriza

RONALD REAGAN (U.S. president): Fuzzy

SHARON KAY RITCHIE (Miss America): Ranu

BRENDA VACCARO (actress, *Midnight Cowboy, Once Is Not Enough*): Brindle

Border Collie

MATTHEW BRODERICK (actor, *Ferris Bueller's Day Off, Glory*)

JANE FONDA (actress, *Klute, Coming Home, The Morning After*)

TOM HAYDEN (political activist, author, co-founder of Students for Democratic Action): Scott

JOHN JAMES (actor, *Haunted by Her Past;* TV series *Dynasty, The Colbys*): Cub

MICHAEL KEATON (actor, *Beetlejuice, Batman*): Dusty

DONALD McCAIG (author, *Nop's Trials*)

DAVID ROSE (TV talk show host)

JERRY SEINFELD (actor, TV series *Seinfeld*)

ANDREW SHUE (actor, TV series *Melrose Place*)

Corgi (Cardigan and Pembroke)

DIRK BOGARDE (actor, *Darling, Death in Venice, Daddy Nostalgia*): Bogie and several others

DICK CLARK (TV personality, TV series *American Bandstand, TV Bloopers and Blunders*)

ELIZABETH II (queen of England): Dookie, Diamond, Spark, Phoenix, Myth, Fable, Pharos, Kelpie, and others (see plate 13)

GEORGE VI (king of England): Carol

DAVID LLOYD GEORGE (British prime minister): Dai

MICKEY ROONEY (actor, *National Velvet, Baby Face Nelson, The Black Stallion*)

BEVERLY SILLS (opera diva): Bumper, Corky

Doberman Pinscher

WILLIE AAMES (actor, TV series *Eight Is Enough*): Shuttz

BEATRICE ARTHUR (actress, TV series *Maude, The Golden Girls*): Jennifer

MARK BRELAND (welterweight boxing champion)

MARIAH CAREY (rock and roll singer, "Vision of Love"): Duke and several others

SHARON DAVIES (Olympic gold medal swimmer, now a media person in the U.K.)

LANCE ITO (judge of the O. J. Simpson murder trial): owns several

JOHN F. KENNEDY (U.S. president): Moe

MARK LINDSAY (rock singer with Paul Revere and the Raiders): Scott and others

BELA LUGOSI (actor, best known as Dracula): Hector

PRISCILLA PRESLEY (actress, *The Naked Gun;* TV series *Dallas*): Willie

VICTORIA PRINCIPAL (actress, *Naked Lie, Sparks: The Price of Passion;* TV series *Dallas*)

TANYA ROBERTS (actress, *Sheena, Body Slam;* TV series *Charlie's Angels*): Catcher

WILLIAM SHATNER (actor, Captain Kirk of *Star Trek*): Kirk and others

RUDOLPH VALENTINO (actor, *The Sheik, Blood and Sand*): Kabar

RAQUEL WELCH (actress, *The Three Musketeers, Kansas City Bomber, Hannie Caulder*)

GRETCHEN WYLER (Broadway musical actress, *Bye Bye Birdie*): Nadia

German Shepherd

DOC AND KATY ABRAHAM (horticultural writers; syndicated column, *Green Thumb*): Geraldine

J. R. ACKERLY (writer, *My Dog Tulip*): Tulip

DWAYNE ANDREAS (CEO, Daniels Midland, Fortune 500 company): Seco

LUCILLE BALL (comic actress, *Mame;* TV series *I Love Lucy*): Junior

RONALD "SCOTTY" BOURNE (TV/movie director, *Three without Fear*):
Bandit

BING CROSBY (singer/actor, *White Christmas, Going My Way*)

GARY DAHL (inventor of the Pet Rock): Buckwheat

YVONNE DECARLO (actress, *Criss Cross, The Mark of Zorro;* TV series
The Munsters): Pepe

BO DEREK (actress, *10, Woman of Desire*): Aiwa and others

PHYLLIS DILLER (comedian): Kelly

SHANNEN DOHERTY (actress, TV series *Beverly Hills 90210*): Elfie

MIKE DOUGLAS (TV talk show host): Love

AL DUNLAP (multi-industry CEO, Scott Paper, Sunbeam, Lily-Tulip;
author, *Mean Business*): Cadet

IRENE DUNNE (actress, *Life with Father, I Remember Mama*): Major

EDWARD VIII (king of England): Ajax

PATRICIA ELLIS (author, *Keeping Up with the Joneses*): Major

JOAN FONTAINE (actress, *Rebecca, Suspicion, Tender Is the Night*): Fang

GEORGE FOREMAN (world champion boxer)

ANNA FREUD (psychologist, psychoanalyst, daughter of Sigmund Freud):
Wolf

EVA GABOR (actress, *Gigi, It Started with a Kiss;* TV series *Green Acres*):
Blackie and others

ZSA ZSA GABOR (actress, author, *Moulin Rouge, Lili, How to Catch a
Man*): Kis, Lany

MELISSA GILBERT (actress, *Penalty Phase, Killer Instinct;* TV series *Little
House on the Pairie*)

ROBERT GOULET (singer, actor, *Camelot, I'd Rather Be Rich*): Lance

STEFFI GRAF (tennis star): Max

LOU GRAMM (rock and roll singer with the group Foreigner): Mr. Bear

LINDA GRAY (actress, *The Wild and Free, Not in Front of the Children;*
TV series *Dallas*): Giorgio

DEVON GUMMERSALL (actor, TV series *My So-Called Life*): Nick

GEORGE HAMILTON (actor, *Love at First Bite, Godfather III*): Loba

RUTHERFORD B. HAYES (U.S. president): owned two

CHARLTON HESTON (actor, *Ben Hur, The Ten Commandments*): Drago

ADOLF HITLER (German Führer): Blondi

EARL HOLLIMAN (actor, *The Biscuit Eater, The Solitary Man;* TV series *Policewoman, T. J. Hooker*)

EVANDER HOLYFIELD (heavyweight boxing champion): Ego

HERBERT HOOVER (U.S. president): King Tut, Pat and others

BOB HOPE (comedian/actor, *Road to Morocco, Road to Singapore*): Snow Job, Shadow

ELTON JOHN (rock singer, songwriter, "Don't Let the Sun Go Down on Me," "Rocket Man"): Bruce

JACQUELINE KENNEDY (wife of U.S. president): Clipper

JOHN F. KENNEDY JR. (celebrity son of U.S. president): Sam

JACK LALANNE (author/physical fitness expert): Walter

CAROL LAWRENCE (singer, actress, *West Side Story*): Odin and others

DAVID LETTERMAN (TV talk show host)

ART LINKLETTER (radio/TV broadcaster, author): Max

KONRAD LORENZ (Nobel Prize–winning animal behaviorist; author, *King Solomon's Ring, Man Meets Dog*): Tito

ROBERT LUDLUM (writer of spy novels, *The Osterman Weekend, The Icarus Agenda*): Rikki Tikki Tavi

BELA LUGOSI (actor, best known as Dracula): Bodri and others

NORMAN MAILER (writer, *The Naked and the Dead, Armies of the Night*): Karl

STANLEY MARCUS (CEO, Neiman Marcus Department Store): Pinon

MATTHE MARGOLIS (author, National Institute of Dog Training founder): Tillie and others

RAYMOND MASSEY (actor, *Abe Lincoln of Illinois, East of Eden;* TV series *Dr. Kildare*): Bunga

MAUREEN MCGOVERN (singer, composer, "The Morning After"): Calaban, McGillicuddy

DIKEMBE MUTOMBO (all-star pro basketball center): Big Fella—white German Shepherd

KEN NORTON (heavyweight boxer): Rama

DONNY OSMOND (singer, part of the Osmond Family): Lady

JACK PAAR (early late-night TV talk show host): Leica

PABLO PICASSO (artist): Sentenelle

TYRONE POWER (actor, *Witness for the Prosecution, The Sun Also Rises*): Lady

STEPHANIE POWERS (actress, *Death in Canaan, The Interns;* TV series *Hart to Hart*)

RONALD REAGAN (U.S. president): Lady

JOAN RIVERS (comedian, TV series *Live with Regis & Kathie Lee*): Wheezy

GENE RODDENBERRY (creator of *Star Trek*): E.T.

ROY ROGERS (western actor, singer): Bullet

FRANKLIN D. ROOSEVELT (U.S. president): Major

WILLIAM SAFIRE (*New York Times* columnist): Henry

HELMUT SCHMIDT (German chancellor): Rocco Van Hammerich

ROBERT SCHULLER (clergyman/author; TV series *Hour of Power*): Ambassador

MAURICE SENDAK (children's author and artist, *Where the Wild Things Are*): Agamemnon, Runge, and several others

SIDNEY SHELDON (writer, *Rage of Angels, Other Side of Midnight*): Jennifer and others

TALIA SHIRE (actress, *The Godfather, Rocky*): several, all white

TARAN NOAH SMITH (actor, TV series *Home Improvement*): Geordie

SAM SNEAD (professional golf star): Adam

GLORIA STEWART (wife of actor Jimmy Stewart): Bello

BLAIR UNDERWOOD (actor, TV series *L.A. Law*): Kinga and others

RUDOLPH VALENTINO (actor, *The Sheik, Blood and Sand*): Prince

REGGIE WILLIAMS (pro football star)

DEBRA WINGER (actress, *An Officer and a Gentleman, Terms of Endearment, Leap of Faith*): Pete

BARBARA WOODHOUSE (dog trainer, author, *No Bad Dogs*): Argus

Maremma Sheepdog

FRANCO ZEFFIRELLI (director, *Hamlet, Last Temptation of Christ*): Boboli

Papillon

JOHN BROWNING (concert pianist): Tyler

LOUIS XIII (king of France)

T. BOONE PICKENS (controversial millionaire businessman, known as a "corporate raider"): Sir Winston

Poodle (Standard, Miniature, and Toy)

DON ADAMS (comic actor, TV series *Get Smart*): Brandy and others

JANE ALEXANDER (actress; head, National Endowment for the Arts): Martini

MARIE ANTOINETTE (ill-fated queen of France)

MARY KAY ASH (cosmetics mogal and franchiser): Gigi, Monet

LUCILLE BALL (comic actress, *Mame;* TV series *I Love Lucy*): Tinkerbell

KAY BALLARD (comic actress, TV series *The Mothers-in-Law*): Pockets and others

TALLULAH BANKHEAD (actress, *Little Foxes, Lifeboat*): Daisy

INGMAR BERGMAN (director, *Through a Glass Darkly, Cries and Whispers*): Teddy

ERMA BOMBECK (humorist, author, *Motherhood: The Second Oldest Profession, The Grass Is Always Greener over the Septic Tank*): Jessanmyn

PAT BOONE (singer, "Love Letters in the Sand," "April Love"; actor, *April Love, State Fair*): Frosty

OMAR BRADLEY (U.S. general in WWII): Beau

CAROL BURNETT (comedian/actress, *Pete 'n Tillie, The Four Seasons;* TV series *The Carol Burnett Show*): Beau Jangles

RED BUTTONS (actor, *Sayonara, Pete's Dragon*): Lucy Brown and others

MARIA CALLAS (opera singer): Djedda, Pixie, and several others

BARBARA CARTLAND (author of over 250 books and 170 romantic novels)

WINSTON CHURCHILL (British prime minister): Rufus I, Rufus II (see plate 5)

MARY HIGGINS CLARK (mystery writer, *While My Pretty One Sleeps, Loves Music*): Porgy

CLAUDETTE COLBERT (actress, *It Happened One Night, The Egg and I*): Missy and others

CATHERINE COOKSON (author)

JOAN CRAWFORD (actress, *Mildred Pierce, What Ever Happened to Baby Jane?*): Cliquot

SAMMY DAVIS JR. (singer/actor, *Sweet Charity, Tap*): Bojangles and several others

DORIS DAY (singer/actress, *The Pajama Game, Midnight Lace*): Bubbles, Columbus, Ivana, Dido, Muffy

WALT DISNEY (animator, film producer, *Snow White, Lady and the Tramp*): Duchess

KIRK DOUGLAS (actor, *20,000 Leagues under the Sea, Spartacus, The Man from Snowy River*): Teddy

BARBARA EDEN (actress, *Chattanooga Choo Choo, Harper Valley P.T.A.;* TV series *I Dream of Jeannie*): Annie

JOAN FONTAINE (actress, *Rebecca, Suspicion*): Hazber

JOHN FORSYTHE (actor, *Topaz, And Justice for All;* TV series *Charlie's Angels, Dynasty*): Fallon and several others

JOE GARAGIOLA (baseball player, TV sportscaster): Wellington, Napoleon

JENNIE GARTH (actress, TV series *Beverly Hills 90210*)

JANE GOODALL (anthropologist known for her studies of monkeys): Gigi

RUTH GORDON (actress, *Rosemary's Baby, Harold and Maude;* writer *Adams Rib*): Sacha

CARY GRANT (actor, *To Catch a Thief, North by Northwest, Charade*): Suzette

MICHAEL GRAY (actor, TV series *The Brian Keith Show*): Butch and others

ROBERT AND RUTH GROSSMAN (authors, *Chinese Kosher Cookbook*): Beauregard

HELEN HAYES (actress, *A Farewell to Arms, Candleshoe, Airport;* TV series *The Snoop Sisters*): Chiquita

KATHARINE HEPBURN (actress, *The African Queen, The Lion in Winter, On Golden Pond*): Button

MARJORIE HOLMES (religious writer, *I've Got to Talk to Somebody, God; Two from Galilee*): Tanjy

BOB HOPE (comedian/actor, *Road to Morocco, Road to Singapore*): Mike

SHIRLEY JONES (actress, *Music Man, Elmer Gantry;* TV series *The Partridge Family*): Skoshie

LAINIE KAZAN (actress, singer): Sheltie

GRACE KELLY (actress turned princess, *High Noon, High Society*): Oliver and others

JACK LaLANNE (author, physical fitness expert): Gnathy

GYPSY ROSE LEE (stripper): Bootsie

JOHN LEHMANN (British writer): Chico

VIVIEN LEIGH (actress, *Gone With the Wind, A Streetcar Named Desire*):
Sebastian

JACK LEMMON (actor, *Mister Roberts, Save the Tiger, Grumpy Old Men*):
Chloe and others

LIBERACE (pianist, entertainer): Coco and many others

WALTER LIPPMANN (journalist, *New Republic, New York Times*)

LOUIS XIV (king of France, known as the Sun King)

LOUIS XVI (king of France, executed during the French Revolution)

ALLEN LUDDEN (TV quiz show host): Emma and others

JERRE MANGIONE (author, *Mount Allegro*): Pushkin

JAYNE MANSFIELD (actress, *Will Success Spoil Rock Hunter?, It Takes a
Thief*)

DEBI MAZAR (actress, *Batman Forever, Money for Nothing*): Dolores

JOHN MITCHELL (U.S. attorney general in Nixon administration):
Buttons

ROBERT MONDAVI (owner, Robert Mondavi Winery): Fume Blanc

MARILYN MONROE (actress, *Some Like It Hot, Bus Stop*): Maf

MARY TYLER MOORE (actress, *Ordinary People, Flirting with Disaster;*
TV series *The Mary Tyler Moore Show*): Diswilliam and others

MIKE NICHOLS (director, *The Graduate, Silkwood, Wolf, Biloxi Blues*)

JULIE NIXON (daughter of U.S. president Richard M. Nixon): Vicky

ORIBE (hairstylist): Pierre

DOROTHY PARKER (humorist, short story writer, wit, and critic): Misty

PABLO PICASSO (artist)

VINCENT PRICE (horror actor who played Dr. Phibes, etc.): Pablo and
many others

SALLY JESSY RAPHAEL (TV talk show host): Fame

DEBBIE REYNOLDS (actress, singer, dancer, *Singin' in the Rain, The Un-
sinkable Molly Brown*): Killer and several others

DON RICKLES (comedian, actor, *Kelly's Heroes, Innocent Blood;* TV series
The Don Rickles Show, Daddy Dearest): Joker

ROBIN RIKER (actor, TV series *Thunder Alley*): Woody

DAN ROWAN (of the Rowan and Martin comedy team, TV series
Laugh-In)

PRINCE RUPERT OF THE RHINE (English royalist general): Boy

GEORGE SAND (author, *Story of My Life, Tales of a Grandmother, Indiana*)

DIANE SAWYER (TV journalist, TV series *Prime Time Live*)

JACLYN SMITH (actress, *The Bourne Identity, Windmills of the Gods;* TV series *Charlie's Angels*): Albert and others

ELKE SOMMER (actress, *Zeppelin, The Double McGuffin*): Hasi

AARON SPELLING (producer, TV series *Dynasty, The Colbys*): Angel

TORI SPELLING (actress, TV series *Beverly Hills 90210*): Greta

GERTRUDE STEIN (writer, *Three Lives*): Basket, Basket II

JOHN STEINBECK (Nobel Prize–winning author, *Of Mice and Men, East of Eden, Travels with Charley*): Charley (see plate 6)

BARBRA STREISAND (singer, actress, *Funny Girl, A Star Is Born, Prince of Tides*): Sadie

JACQUELINE SUSANN (author, *Valley of the Dolls, Every Night, Josephine!*): Joseph, Josephine

PATRICK SWAYZE (actor, *Dirty Dancing, Point Break, Ghost*): Derek

JAMES THURBER (humorist, author, *The Secret Life of Walter Mitty, My Life and Hard Times*): Christabel, Medve, and others

IVANA TRUMP (former wife of Donald Trump)

JANINE TURNER (actress, TV series *Northern Exposure*): Eclair

ROBERT VAUGHN (actor, *Hangar 18, Hour of the Assassin;* TV series *The Man from U.N.C.L.E.*): Beans

ALBERTINA WALKER (gospel singer): Pierre

BARBARA WALTERS (TV news interviewer)

BETTY WHITE (actress, comedian, TV series *The Golden Girls, The Mary Tyler Moore Show*): Dancer

MICHAEL WILDING (actor, *In Which We Serve, The Glass Slipper*): Gee Gee

ANDREW WYETH (artist): Eloise

Shetland Sheepdog

CALVIN COOLIDGE (U.S. president): Calamity Jane, Jolly-Jane

GENE KELLY (actor, dancer, choreographer, *Singin' in the Rain, Brigadoon*): Bambi

WILLIAM HOWARD TAFT (U.S. president)

RICK WALLACE (director, TV series *L.A. Law, Hill Street Blues*)

How the Statistics Were Done for This Book

Most people reading this book are not scientists, hence in the main body of the text I did not include much in the way of details as to how the statistics were actually done and the conclusions reached. For those who want a bit more detail, let me briefly outline the procedures.

THE NEW DOG BREED GROUPINGS

Determination of Dog Behavior Dimensions

Eleven dog experts, in addition to myself, listed all of the dog behavior dimensions that they thought helped to determine whether an individual would be happy with any breed of dog. Items that appeared on seven or more of the lists were retained. The items were then reduced on the basis of redundancy or overlap, ease of rating, etc. to twenty-two dimensions. These dimensions could be roughly categorized as dominance, territoriality, guard dog ability, watchdog ability, friendliness to strangers, congeniality toward family and others who are well known, amicability around children, indoor activity level, outdoor activity level, suitability for city living, adaptability to indoor living, adaptability to weather extremes, exercise needs, learning ability, problem solving ability, suitability for obedience training, willingness to work for people, how vigorous or determined the dog is in general behaviors, the predictability or constancy of the dog's day-to-day behaviors, how emotionally stable or constant the dog is, the average height of the breed, and the average weight of the breed.

Breed Ratings

A computer program was generated to create questionnaires, each of which contained 40 breeds randomly selected from 162 registerable breeds. Each questionnaire asked for a 5-point rating on the 22 dimensions (excluding height and weight) for each of the 40 different breeds. In addition raters could score up to 20 additional breeds that they knew well. This form was sent to 400 dog experts in the United States and Canada, and 96 complete rating forms were returned. To be included, a breed had to have at least 25 ratings, which resulted in a sample size of 133 breeds. For each breed, all of the ratings from all of the raters were then averaged for each dimension separately. These were then normalized, and the resulting standard scores (z scores) were computed, and these served as the raw scores for each of the breeds.

To reduce the number of dimensions to a manageable number, these breed ratings were subjected to a factor analysis using a Quartimax rotation and Kaiser normalization. This resulted in six quite clean factors which met all of the criteria for simplicity of factor structure. These factors could be named *dominance and territoriality, sociability, learning and obedience ability, stability vs. excitability, mass and activity,* and *indoor vs. outdoor suitability.* The factor scores for each individual breed on each of these factors were then computed, and these served as the data for the analysis that determined the new dog groupings.

Dog Groupings

To determine the dog groupings, the six factor scores for each of the 133 breeds were entered into a cluster analysis. The algorithm for entering items into a cluster was based on the weighted pair-group centroid and on the simple Euclidean distance (in multidimensional space). The initial hierarchical or "tree" analysis suggested that there would be seven breed clusters or groups; however, the distance measures suggested that these clusters were "stingy" and would have to be better optimized. To this end a *k*-means cluster analysis, based on the assumption of seven clusters, was then conducted with the goal of finding the optimum partitions such that the within-cluster variance was minimized and the between-cluster variance was maximized. We programmed the computer to use a full 50 iterations, so that the program would continue beyond the usual stopping point and would try moving breeds from cluster to cluster until an optimal solution was found. This turned out to be a bit of an overkill since after 17 iterations there was very little movement between clusters. This extensive analysis resulted in the seven breed groupings:

> Group 1: **Friendly,** affectionate, and genial dogs
> Group 2: **Protective,** territorial, and dominant dogs
> Group 3: **Independent,** personable, and strong-willed dogs
> Group 4: **Self-Assured,** spontaneous, and audacious dogs
> Group 5: **Consistent,** self-contained, and home-loving dogs
> Group 6: **Steady,** good-natured, and tolerant dogs
> Group 7: **Clever,** impulsive, and trainable dogs

The **bold-faced** words in the list are the short labels that I use for the groups in the text. The full group names were based on the profile plots of each of the clusters on each of the six criterion factor scores; thus Group 1 dogs had a profile that was dominated by an extremely high sociability rating, Group 2 had a very high dominance and territoriality score, and so forth.

In situations where a single dimension did not dominate I tried to use descriptive labels that conveyed the essence of the cluster's profile.

THE PERSONALITY INVENTORY

The Interpersonal Adjective Scales

The Interpersonal Adjective Scales or IAS was developed by Jerry S. Wiggins as a measure of those aspects of personality that affect our interactions with other people (and presumably all other living things, such as dogs). Its relationship to other personality scales is fully described in the scientific literature.[1] It is a 64-item scale in which individuals rate how accurately various adjectives describe their own behaviors. It is analyzed as eight dimensions that define a circular space or circumplex. These are PA (ambitious/dominant), NO (gregarious/extroverted), LM (warm/agreeable), JK (unassuming/ingenuous), HI (lazy/submissive), FG (aloof/introverted), DE (cold/quarrelsome), and BC (arrogant/calculating). These scales can be considered as independent personality scales for some analytic purposes; however, several alternative analytic procedures can be used. One involves determination of a single vector in the circumplex space which summarizes the person's personality; another involves computation of the main underlying axes which represent the global personality dimensions of *dominance* and *nurturance*.

In a published study using the IAS, I was able to demonstrate the usefulness of reducing the eight dimensions defining a circumplex to four bipolar dimensions that can be looked at independently.[2] For the purposes of this book I have renamed these dimensions as *extroversion* (scales NO and FG), *dominance* (PA and HI), *trust* (JK and BC), and *warmth* (LM and DE).

Development of the Short Form of the IAS

The short form of the IAS was developed by an item selection procedure involving two separate studies. The first one used a sample of 971 people who took a test including the full 64-item IAS (current version) and also items from former versions of the scale to use as possible alternate items. Each of the eight scales was separately calculated. An item analysis then was undertaken to see how well each item (or alternate adjective) predicted the whole scale, and then an "all sets" procedure was used to see how each pair of items predicted the full scales. On the basis of this a new 16-item form of the scale was prepared. Since several pilot studies had indicated that including the full definitions of the adjectives, instead of the one- or two-word items by themselves, provided more stable data, these were included in the final version for the research participants.

Next a cross-validation sample of 1,454 people were tested with the new shortened version of the IAS and, on a separate day, with the full scale. The four bipolar scales were computed for each version and correlations between full scale and short scales were: extroversion, $r=0.87$; dominance, $r=0.82$; trust, $r=0.81$; warmth, $r=0.86$. Given these extremely high correlations, the validity of the short scale used in this book seems to be confirmed.

A simplified scoring procedure, to guarantee all positive numbers and simple calculation, was next developed. The classification of individuals is based on a relative, internal ranking of scores for each of the four dimensions, considered separately. After separation by sex (there are sex differences in the base values of the personality dimensions), individuals who fall in the highest quartile are ranked as *high* on that dimension, individuals in the lowest quartile are ranked *low,* and the middle quartiles produce a ranking of *medium* on that personality trait. These values are incorporated in the scoring of the test in the present volume.

DETERMINATION OF PERSONALITY TRAIT AND DOG GROUP FIT

The sample consisted of 6,149 people, aged 16 to 94 years. Included were 1,223 cat owners and 1,564 people who had never lived with either a cat or a dog. All were also asked to indicate the breeds of dog that they had lived with and their satisfaction with those breeds. Several other questions were also included.

The initial set of analyses involved normalizing the IAS personality data and then using the resultant z scores as the dependent measures in a series of analyses of variance. Individuals were sorted into categories depending on which of the seven groups of dog breeds they had lived with. Next they were sorted into subgroups based on whether they liked or disliked the dog breeds. Finally they were sorted by sex of the person. The four resulting $7 \times 2 \times 2$ ANOVAs (one for each personality trait) showed statistically significant differences for each of the four personality dimensions. Subsequent analyses showed that the results could be simplified by using a reflection procedure that is common in studies of preferences. In this case it involved an inversion of the personality trait scores around the zero point (z score of zero) of the individual bipolar scales, for the disliked breeds. This gave a similar pattern of results to the original analyses, but the significance levels were higher and interpretation of the patterns was easier with this composite coding procedure since it eliminated one dimension, reducing the ANOVAs to a 7×2 analysis.

The final preference ratings were determined separately for each sex and each personality dimension. These 14 one-way ANOVAs all showed clear differences in breed category preferences, with high levels of statistical significance, and in every case there were significant pairwise differences in the post hoc analyses (using Tukey's HSD procedure) between the two highest and two lowest breed groupings (in fact there was high overall separation among breed preferences). The two breed classes that were then associated with the highest scores on the personality trait were designated as the preferred breeds for individuals who were in the highest quartile on that dimension (those coded as *high*), while the two breed classifications that were associated with the lowest scores on that dimension were designated as appropriate for individuals in the lowest quartile (individuals coded as *low*). The selection of the best breeds for those scoring in the middle two quartiles involved selecting the two breed groupings that had score values closest to a z score of zero on that dimension. When scores were very similar (not different until the second decimal place), decisions were based on the pairwise significance levels representing differences from the highest and lowest ranked breeds.

To ascertain personality factors associated with cat ownership (or not owning a dog at all), the final set of ANOVAs were recomputed, adding *cat* and *no dog* categories to the seven breed groups. This required 14 one-way ANOVAs (separating by sex), each with a 10-category partition. Again, recommendations were based on the quartile ranking of individuals on the four personality traits with separate scoring for males and females. For these groupings the mean ratings are reported rather than simple classification scores as is done with the breed selection recommendations.

The Breed Groups

Throughout this book I have been referring to the seven new groupings of dog breeds based on their behavioral characteristics. When you are trying to see which dog fits best with a particular personality type, you will obviously want to know the list of specific breeds in each dog group. That is what I have provided here. Since I only use the one-word main label of each breed group when I am talking about the needs of various individuals, it may be helpful if you leave a bookmark at this page so that you can look back to find out which breeds are in each group.

GROUP 1. FRIENDLY DOGS
(includes affectionate and genial dogs)

Bearded Collie
Bichon Frise
Border Terrier
Brittany
Cavalier King Charles Spaniel
Cocker Spaniel
Collie
Curly-Coated Retriever
English Cocker Spaniel
English Setter
English Springer Spaniel
Field Spaniel
Flat-Coated Retriever
Golden Retriever
Keeshond
Labrador Retriever
Nova Scotia Duck Toller
Old English Sheepdog
Portuguese Water Dog
Soft Coated Wheaten Terrier
Vizsla
Welsh Springer Spaniel

GROUP 2. PROTECTIVE DOGS
(includes territorial and dominant dogs)

Akita
American Staffordshire Terrier
Boxer
Briard
Bullmastiff
Bull Terrier

Chesapeake Bay Retriever
Chow Chow
German Wirehaired Pointer
Giant Schnauzer
Gordon Setter
Komondor
Kuvasz

Puli
Rhodesian Ridgeback
Rottweiler
Schnauzer
Staffordshire Bull Terrier
Weimaraner

GROUP 3. INDEPENDENT DOGS
(includes personable and strong-willed dogs)

Afghan Hound
Airedale Terrier
Alaskan Malamute
American Foxhound
American Water Spaniel
Black and Tan Coonhound
Borzoi
Chinese Shar-Pei
Dalmatian
English Foxhound
German Shorthaired Pointer

Greyhound
Harrier
Irish Setter
Irish Water Spaniel
Norwegian Elkhound
Otterhound
Pointer
Saluki
Samoyed
Siberian Husky

GROUP 4. SELF-ASSURED DOGS
(includes spontaneous and sometimes audacious dogs)

Affenpinscher
Australian Terrier
Basenji
Brussels Griffon
Cairn Terrier
Irish Terrier
Jack Russell Terrier
Lakeland Terrier
Manchester Terrier
Miniature Pinscher
Miniature Schnauzer
Norfolk Terrier

Norwich Terrier
Schipperke
Scottish Terrier
Shih Tzu
Silky Terrier
Smooth Fox Terrier
Welsh Terrier
West Highland White Terrier
Wire Fox Terrier
Wirehaired Pointing Griffon
Yorkshire Terrier

GROUP 5. CONSISTENT DOGS
(includes self-contained and home-loving dogs)

Bedlington Terrier
Boston Terrier
Chihuahua
Dachshund
Dandie Dinmont Terrier
English Toy Spaniel
   (King Charles Spaniel)
French Bulldog
Italian Greyhound
Japanese Chin

Lhasa Apso
Maltese
Pekingese
Pomeranian
Pug
Sealyham Terrier
Skye Terrier
Tibetan Terrier
Whippet

GROUP 6. STEADY DOGS
(includes solid, good-natured, and tolerant dogs)

Basset Hound
Beagle
Bernese Mountain Dog
Bloodhound
Bouvier des Flandres
Bulldog
Clumber Spaniel

Great Dane
Great Pyrenees
Irish Wolfhound
Mastiff
Newfoundland
Saint Bernard
Scottish Deerhound

GROUP 7. CLEVER DOGS
(includes observant and trainable dogs)

Australian Cattle Dog
Australian Shepherd
Belgian Malinois
Belgian Sheepdog
Belgian Tervuren
Border Collie
Cardigan Welsh Corgi

Doberman Pinscher
German Shepherd
Maremma Sheepdog
Papillon
Pembroke Welsh Corgi
Poodle (Toy, Miniature, and Standard)
Shetland Sheepdog

Notes

Chapter One

1. Most of the material on Rex Harrison is drawn from N. Wapshott, *Rex Harrison: A Biography* (London: Chatto & Windus, 1991), and from R. Moseley, P. Masheter, and M. Masheter, *Rex Harrison: A Biography* (New York: St. Martin's, 1987).
2. W. Proxmire, *Uncle Sam—The Last of the Big Time Spenders* (New York: Simon & Schuster, 1972).
3. Material and quotes are mostly from F. G. Kenyon, ed., *The Letters of Elizabeth Barrett Browning* (New York: Macmillan, 1908).

Chapter Two

1. R. Bergler, *Man and Dog: The Psychology of a Relationship* (Oxford: Blackwell, 1988).
2. N. Endenburg, *Animals as Companions* (Amsterdam: Thesis Publishers, 1991).
3. S. H. Coleman, *Humane Society Leaders in America* (Albany, N.Y.: American Humane Association, 1924).
4. Z. Steele, *Angel in Top Hat* (New York: Harper, 1942).
5. L. Ware, *Jacob A. Riis, Police Reporter, Reformer, Useful Citizen* (New York: Collier, 1938).

Chapter Three

1. The story about Mike Tyson and Mimi Einstein is told in J. Stern and M. Stern, *Dog Eat Dog* (New York: Scribner, 1997).

Chapter Four

1. T. M. Newcomb, *The Acquaintance Process* (New York: Holt, Rinehart & Winston, 1961).
2. R. L. Moreland and S. R. Beach, *Journal of Experimental Social Psychology* 30 (1961): 527–55.
3. R. B. Zajonc, *Journal of Personality and Social Research Monographs* 9 (1968): 1–27.
4. T. H. Mita, M. Dermer, and J. Knight, *Journal of Personality and Social Psychology* 35 (1977): 597.

Chapter Five

1. K. Hirsh-Pasek and R. Treiman, *Journal of Child Language* 9 (1982): 229–37.

Chapter Seven

1. This scale is more fully described in J. S. Wiggins and R. Broughton, *European Journal of Personality* 5 (1991): 342–65, and the history and rationale for interpersonal personality measures is outlined in J. S. Wiggins, *Journal of Personality Assessment* 66 (1996): 217–33.

Chapter Eight

1. Most of this material is drawn from P. Lisca, *John Steinbeck, Nature and Myth* (New York: Crowell, 1978), and the conversational quotes are from J. Steinbeck, *Travels with Charley: In Search of America* (New York: Viking, 1962).
2. Most of the material in this section comes from M. W. Estrin, ed., *Conversations with Eugene O'Neill* (Jackson: University of Mississippi, 1990), and T. Bogar and J. R. Bryer, *Selected Letters of Eugene O'Neill* (New Haven: Yale University Press, 1988), with the exception of *Blemie's Will*, which is reprinted with permission from the Yale Collection of American Literature, The Beineke Rare Book and Manuscript Library, Yale University.

Chapter Nine

1. For a number of insights and quotations about the dogs of U.S. presidents I have drawn on the memoirs of the White House kennel keeper Traphes Bryant, which were published as T. Bryant and F. S. Leighton, *Dog Days at the White House* (New York: Macmillan, 1975).
2. This quote is from a letter that is part of the collection in the Dwight D. Eisenhower Presidential Library.
3. See note 1 above.

Chapter Ten

1. Much of this material is drawn from E. Gaskell, *The Life of Charlotte Brontë* (originally published in 1857; reprint, London: Penguin, 1985), and R. Fraser, *The Brontës: Charlotte Brontë and Her Family* (New York: Fawcett Columbine, 1988).
2. D. K. Simonton, *Journal of Personality and Social Psychology* 51 (1986): 149–60.
3. Material in this section comes mostly from R. Morris, *Richard Milhous Nixon: The Rise of an American Politician* (New York: Holt, 1989), and from the extensive writings of historian Stephen Ambrose, e.g., S. E. Ambrose, *Nixon: The Triumph of a Politician* (New York: Simon & Schuster, 1989). See also Chapter 9, note 1.
4. Much of the biographical information for this section was drawn from the two-volume biography by J. Richardson, *A Life of Picasso* (New York: Random House, 1991), which also contains a full version of the Lagut letter.

Chapter Eleven

1. The poem "Beau" was published in the book *Jimmy Stewart and His Poems* (New York: Crown, 1989).
2. Most of this material was extracted from the twelve-volume collection of Byron's letters and journals: L. A. Marchand, ed., *Byron's Letters and Journals* (Cambridge, Mass.: Harvard, 1973–82), with additional biographical information from E. Longford, *The Life of Byron* (New York: Little Brown, 1976).

Chapter Twelve

1. This section is mostly based on C. Hibbert, ed., *Queen Victoria in Her Letters and Journals: A Selection* (New York: Viking, 1985); S. Weintraub, *Victoria; An Intimate Biography* (London: Truman Talley, 1987); and A. Plowden, *The Young Victoria* (London: Stein & Day, 1981).
2. Most of the early biographical material is drawn from R. Lacey, *Majesty: Elizabeth II and the House of Windsor* (London: Avon, 1978), and E. Longford, *The Queen: The Life of Elizabeth II* (London: Knopf, 1983), with more recent material from newspaper and broadcast sources.

Chapter Thirteen

1. Much of the biographical information is drawn from E. Ludwig, *Napoleon* (London: Liveright, 1927), and N. MacKenzie, *The Escape from Elba: The Fall and Flight of Napoleon 1814–1815* (Oxford: Oxford, 1982), while the

long quote is my translation of the material reported by the Count of Las Cases (Emmanuel) in *Mémorial de Sainte-Hélène,* published in 1815.

2. Material for this section was drawn from the two volumes of J. Durant and A. Durant, *The Presidents of the United States* (Boston: Gaché, 1981); M. Miller, *Plain Speaking: An Oral Biography of Harry S. Truman* (San Francisco: Berkeley, 1974); and from various newspaper accounts.

3. See Chapter 9, note 1.

Chapter Fifteen

1. The quotations here are taken from E. B. White, *The Letters of E. B. White* (New York: Harper & Row, 1976); E. B. White, *One Man's Meat* (New York: Harper & Row, 1944); and from selected articles that appeared in *The New Yorker.*

Chapter Sixteen

1. Material in this section was drawn in part from L. T. More, *Isaac Newton: A Biography* (New York: Scribner, 1934), and from the two volumes by R. S. Westfall, *Never at Rest: A Biography of Isaac Newton* (Cambridge: Cambridge, 1981).

Technical Notes

1. See Chapter 7, note 1.
2. S. Coren, *Journal of Research in Personality* 28 (1994) 214–29.

Index

MIDDLETOWN

MAY 29 1998

2 1982 00625 8127